Inside the American Couple

Inside the American Couple

New Thinking/New Challenges

EDITED BY

Marilyn Yalom and Laura L. Carstensen

Estelle Freedman and Barbara Gelpi
Consulting Editors

UNIVERSITY OF CALIFORNIA PRESS
Berkeley · Los Angeles · London

University of California Press
Berkeley and Los Angeles, California

University of California Press, Ltd.
London, England

© 2002 by
The Regents of the University of California

Library of Congress Cataloging-in-Publication Data

Inside the American couple : new thinking, new challenges / Marilyn Yalom and Laura Carstensen, editors.
      p.   cm.
  Includes bibliographical references and index.
  ISBN 0-520-21975-9 (Cloth : alk. paper).—ISBN
0-520-22957-6 (Paper : alk. paper)
    1. Couples—United States.   2. Interpersonal rela-
tions—United States.   I. Yalom, Marilyn.   II. Carstensen, Laura L.

HQ801 .I67   2002
306.7—dc21   2002000716

Manufactured in the United States of America
10 09 08 07 06 05 04 03 02
10 9 8 7 6 5 4 3 2 1

The paper used in this publication is both acid-free and
totally chlorine-free (TCF). It meets the minimum requirements of ANSI/NISO Z39.48-1992 (R 1997)
(Permanence of Paper). ♾

Contents

Acknowledgments

We would like to acknowledge the support of many people who made this volume possible. Mary Stiles provided exceptional and conscientious technical support. Without exception, the contributing authors were open and responsive to feedback from us and our consulting editors, Professors Estelle Freedman and Barbara Gelpi, both of whom offered gracious assistance. We would also like to acknowledge the Stanford Institute for Research on Women and Gender, which for twenty-five years has housed a community of scholars whose critical analysis of gender from widely varying disciplines and perspectives has helped move the field of feminist scholarship forward.

Introduction

Laura L. Carstensen and Marilyn Yalom

One of the most fundamental urges of human existence is to form a pair. Something in us calls for another—friend, lover, companion, spouse. Or perhaps it is something *not* in us, some lack, some deficit, that hungers for completion. In the *Symposium,* Plato fancifully expressed this craving by having Aristophanes contend that the first humans were unseparated twins who, once they were split apart, pined away for the missing half.

Sociobiologists assume that the search for a mate is propelled by an animal instinct to copulate. Human attachment theorists locate the source of adult pairing in the child-mother bond. Anthropologists look to the central importance of kinship systems in human cultures as an explanation for the universality of marriage. Political scientists understand marriage as an institutional means of assuring societal stability. Existentialists see the desire to merge with another as a way of attenuating a basic sense of isolation. Jews and Christians traditionally believe that marriage is ordained by God. Whether primacy is accorded to sexual, psychological, anthropological, political, existential, or religious factors, there is broad agreement that coupledom provides a viable answer to a basic human longing.

Here we are at the dawn of a new millennium still cherishing the belief that being half of a couple represents some central part of being human. Individuals, despite gender and sexual orientation, continue to search for soul mates, to move in together, to vow to love each other, and, when legally allowed, to enter into marriages. Despite myriad modern tendencies that could render long-term couplehood obsolete (such as casual sex, cohabitation, and increase in divorce and single parenting), more than 90 percent of Americans marry at some time during their lives. However anxious we may be as a society in the face of dissolving marriages and dysfunctional families, individuals continue to place their hopes in the marital bond. They exchange public promises to remain together—for better, for worse, for a lifetime. And among those who do not marry, partnering is still very widespread; few people live through adulthood without at least one lengthy, intimate relationship.

Our aim in this volume is to draw attention to issues that question the unspoken traditional practices underlying coupling in America. To accomplish this aim, we turned to feminist scholars who consider the couple in their work and the dramatic changes couples have experienced during the past fifty years, such as the proliferation of divorce, the increase in ethnically mixed relationships, the preponderance of older couples, and the new visibility of same-sex unions. By focusing on some of these changes, we hope to contribute to scholarly and public dialogue about a fundamental unit in human societies.

Gender has been at the core of the traditional image of the couple in America, an image generalized from an idealized middle-class marriage in which husbands have provided (or were expected to provide) financial support for wives and children, and wives have carried responsibility for housekeeping and child rearing. Even though this image has never been reflected in working-class couples, the image itself has been held up as the (often unmet) standard of the typical marriage. In cases where the wife was employed, her work was often viewed as supplemental to the husband's work, even if she earned more than her husband. Yet, in the second half of the twentieth century a significant sea change took place. Women began to enter the workforce in record numbers, and the separation of domestic and public spheres began to blur. Not only did women work, as many always had, they also developed identities as paid workers outside the home and pursued long-term careers. Although it occurred less frequently, men began to enter the domestic sphere and share more in household and child-care responsibilities. This overlap of professional and personal boundaries, much feared by nineteenth-century Europeans and Americans raised with an ideology of separate spheres for men and women, became reality in the late twentieth century.

By many measures, the age-old education gap between men and

women is rapidly narrowing. Females now receive educations comparable to those of males—women in the United States earn the majority of associate, bachelor's, and master's degrees and an increasingly greater share of advanced degrees.[1] Women expect to be able to support themselves, and most women in America do work outside the home (Folbre and Nelson 2000). Few think in terms of *Marriage as a Trade,* the title of a well-known Edwardian book that exposed the compulsory economic nature of marriage for women. Because many women now earn income independently of their husbands (albeit usually less income) and share similar educational and work histories, they have many more relationship options than their female predecessors. They can choose not to marry or, conversely, to marry in the expectation of an egalitarian union. Although women's increased educational and professional opportunities presumably lead to greater compatibility in marriage, the reality is that the more education a wife has, the more likely she will be to divorce her husband. Not only are women today more easily able to say "no" to a prospective marital partner, they are—like men—able to say "no" later on, if the marriage turns sour.

In the past four decades, divorce has skyrocketed, and marriage rates have shown a decrease. Roughly 40 percent of women aged twenty-five to twenty-nine are today unmarried. The average age of first marriages has moved upward from twenty for women and twenty-three years for men in 1960 to twenty-five and twenty-seven, respectively, in 1998.[2] Delays in marriage are particularly striking among African Americans; indeed, many African American women are delaying marriage so long that "delaying" may prove to be avoiding the institution altogether. It is conceivable that rising divorce rates have weakened the long-term investment both husbands and wives previously put into marriage. When a couple faces statistical odds of divorcing that are as high as the odds that they will stay together, the commitment to a marriage may be undermined from the start. Economically, too, educated women who enter into a marriage contract today recognize that they are unlikely to benefit financially in the way that their mates will if the marriage fails. One year after a divorce, husbands are faring better than wives. Ironically, one might argue that even the thirty-year increase in average life expectancy that occurred during the twentieth century may have put a damper on marriage. With longer life expectancy the urgency to marry has lessened. The prospect of lifelong marriage may have seemed more appealing and more viable when couples expected to live together for twenty or thirty years rather than fifty or sixty.

Similarly, the demographics of children enter into the decrease in marriage rates and the rising incidence of divorce.[3] At the beginning of the century, the average number of children per Caucasian, American-born mother was 3.5, with immigrant and African American women bearing more (this was down from 7 children per mother in 1800). Even in 1960, despite fluctuations during the century, American women were, on average, bearing 3.5 children. Today, the American mother, like her counterparts in other developed nations, bears roughly two children. While women in the nineteenth century spent most of their adult lives raising children, motherhood per se now takes up a relatively shorter part of the life span.[4] If a woman waits until her late twenties to have children, as many do, and lives until she is eighty, she will have spent only a third of her life in the active phase of mothering young children. Such a life pattern may afford new perspectives on the later years. Whereas, in the past, life may have been winding down by the time the children had been raised, women today can anticipate additional decades after middle age. If the marriage has been frankly unhappy or merely unsatisfying, a wife may choose to leave her husband, especially if she has the financial means to survive on her own. Unfortunately, for many older women who had lower (or no) earning capacity earlier in their lives, this decision usually entails serious economic consequences. Importantly, despite the fact that young women today will be more likely to come to old age with incomes and pensions of their own, other societal changes (such as increased likelihood of divorce) ensure that they will face just as great a risk of poverty as older women do today (Smeeding 1999).

Yet these statistics and practices do not suggest that people are giving up on marriage. A different sort of change is in the air. Some scholars believe that we have entered an era of serial marriage, with multiple marriages and remarriages becoming the norm. Most people who divorce do remarry within a few years. Perhaps lifelong commitment will cease to be a common goal. Perhaps procreation will occur increasingly outside of marriage; already more than 40 percent of first births in the United States occur out of wedlock.[5] It is even possible that heterosexual marriage will lose its privileged place among other forms of couples. But it is unlikely that marriage itself will disappear.

As we enter the twenty-first century, the essential ingredients in marriage are love and shared material resources—the primary bases for unions during the last two centuries. Together they contribute to a powerful bond between spouses. However, without the dependence of one (the wife) on the other (the husband) for economic support, love alone bears the burden of holding the couple together, and love is often not enough. A combination of factors—respect, commitment, shared values, and mutual interests, as well as love and money—makes for a considerably more solid marital foundation. In cases where love holds strong, even on the part of only one partner, marriages can and do survive. But if love turns sour for both parties and it is economically feasible to separate, there is little motivation to remain together, especially when there are no children.

Another dramatic change in coupledom concerns the increased visibility of same-sex unions. Today, in many parts of America, lesbian and gay couples not only live together openly but also enjoy commitment ceremonies blessed in churches, and many are claiming the right to legal marriages. Following the pattern of the Netherlands and several other northern European nations, we expect to see legislation in this country that will grant full privileges to same-sex couples sometime in this century. In fact, we believe that someday Americans will look back upon the interdiction on same-sex marriage the same way that we now view antimiscegenation laws forbidding marriage across races.

The authors of the essays in this book focus on the ties between two people who commit to a long-term union, primarily, but not exclusively, within marriage. The authors come from various disciplines (anthropology, economics, education, history, law, literature, psychology, and sociology) and are interested in the couple as an enduring paradigm for human relationships, despite the changes in ideology and practice that couples have experienced over time.

The authors of the first three chapters deal with the historical roots of modern marriage: those found in Judeo-Christian scripture, in early colonial America, and in nineteenth-century capitalism. Yalom compares marital proscriptions and prescriptions in the Hebrew Bible and the New Testament and traces some ongoing effects of these beliefs within Western civilization. Gelles portrays the union of Abigail and John Adams as a larger-than-life example of eighteenth-century companionate marriage. Washington examines the nineteenth-century British public debate that compared marriage for money with prostitution: Each institution was purportedly characterized by an exchange of male financial support for female sexual services.

In the next two chapters, the authors address lesbian and homosexual unions. Rothblum asks how sex, or the lack of it, defines the lesbian couple, while Lewin describes the recent phenomenon of lesbian and gay commitment ceremonies. Both of these essays raise questions that are central not only to gay and lesbian couples but to all couples. Rothblum asks the fundamental question of whether genital sexual activity is the core condition for lesbian couplehood; she suggests that contemporary society has fixated upon sex as the defining characteristic of lesbians, whereas other feelings and behaviors, such as attachment, friendship, love, and companionship, tend to be overlooked. If we define couples by genital sexual activity, many couples—both heterosexual and same-sex—are no longer couples by this standard.

Lewin's essay reminds us that public validation of private unions is at least as important to gay and lesbian couples as it is to heterosexuals. Humans seem to need rituals of public affirmation that involve the community. In a country marked by few mandatory rites of passage, the wedding becomes one rite in which it is now possible for both heterosexual and homosexual couples to proclaim publicly their joint identity and enlist family and friends for ongoing support. Not only do couples need societal affirmation but societies benefit from couples. The economic and emotional stability of couples benefits society at large in innumerable ways (Wald 1999; Waite 1995).

In chapters 6 and 7, Noddings and Felstiner consider the physical realities within and surrounding the couple. Noddings explores the home as a place of refuge and a workplace, with different meanings for men and women. Felstiner focuses on the human body when one partner is chronically sick. Both authors raise questions about caregiving, a traditionally female responsibility, that is now, in the wake of feminist pressure, demanding greater participation from men. In chapter 8, Fuchs Epstein examines marriages when they cross the boundaries of home and work by describing the complex issues that arise when couples who are both lawyers share legal practices.

Skolnick's work in chapter 9 examines psychological and sociological research, including her own, that tries to understand similarities in good marriages as well as the stresses that turn a happy marriage into an unhappy one. She articulates a good/bad marriage model, drawing from Jesse Bernard's notion that every marriage contains two marriages, the husband's and the wife's, and from the work of John Gottman and Robert Levenson, who found that marital success could be predicted by a high ratio of positive to negative emotion expressed to one another within the couple's relationship. Skolnick's most recent work looks at the impact of stress on couple interaction, stress resulting from outside employment rather than conflict generated solely from spousal interaction. In focusing on working-class couples in cases where the husband is a police officer, she illustrates the ways that stress outside the marriage can come inside the marriage in disastrous ways. Her analysis leads into the following two chapters on divorce.

Rhode first explodes the myth that feminists in our time are responsible for divorce and its lamentable sequellae—impoverished families, displaced homemakers, and fatherless children—and then proposes some legal solutions to these problems. Strober, focusing on the divorce case of *Wendt v. Wendt,* in which she was an expert witness, asks what a wife is worth financially after the demise of a long-standing marriage. On the basis of "human capital theory," she argues that such a woman is entitled to half of the family assets plus a declining proportion of future assets.

In chapters 12 and 13, the authors address ethnic issues arising from the cultural diversity of America today. Tsai, Przymus, and Best discuss Asian American interethnic dating and marriage from psychological and cultural perspectives and the role that gender plays in ethnically mixed relationships. Pasupathi raises intriguing questions based on her knowledge of East Indian marriages about the consequences and practices of arranged marriages. Contrasting love matches with arranged ones, she asks whether Western assumptions about the damaging nature of arranged marriages are necessarily warranted and suggests that similarities between the two kinds of marriages may outweigh their differences.

In the last chapter, Charles and Carstensen consider couples in old age. They refute the common stereotype that older couples are emotionally and romantically lifeless and argue instead that they are generally happier than younger couples. They do, however, highlight the difficulties of this period of life, especially for women, who are at greater risk than men for financial, physical, and psychological problems associated with widowhood.

From these essays we get a complex picture of the challenges facing couples in our time. Characteristically, studies of this sort tend to focus on problems, such as internal and external stress, divorce, and the difficulties faced by outsiders to the heterosexual and ethnic norm. Yet here and there, we glimpse some of the joys of living as a couple. Noddings reminds us that the home can be a place of shared aesthetics and mutual care. Felstiner's chapter is a testimony to the triumph of love over the stresses inherent in chronic illness. Lewin speaks of the affirmation experienced by gay and lesbian couples who enact public commitment rituals. Tsai, Przymus, and Best show how some interethnic couples see each other first and foremost as loving partners rather than in terms of the stereotypes foisted upon them. Charles and Carstensen believe that couples in old age can attain a kind of happiness that would be unthinkable in earlier years—one that grows out of shared experiences, those that are painful as well as pleasurable, and a more complete acceptance of one's partner, warts and all.

Surprisingly, perhaps, we do not dwell very much on the subject of sex, except for the interesting question raised by Rothblum concerning lesbian couples: Are they truly "couples" if they are not having sex? Certainly sexual desire provides the impetus for the formation of most couples, but we suspect that sex—even good sex—does not in and of itself keep partners together, at least not for a lifetime. Charles and Carstensen point out, for example, that heterosexual couples reduce genital sexual activity over the years, but this does not mean that eros has died, only that it has taken on different, nongenital forms.

Similarly, we do not explicitly take up the issue of children, although the advent of children alters the parents' relationship in innumerable ways, both bad and good. Children introduce stressors to a marriage that for many lead ultimately to divorce. For countless other couples, children cause partners to remain together in the face of formidable reasons to separate and, as Charles and Carstensen point out, in the later years of a marriage, children often come to represent a great source of shared pleasure. Even when older couples experience heartaches due to problems of adult children, these heartaches less frequently become a source of conflict within the couple.

In the United States today, the desire for children is no longer the primary impetus to marriage. During the past hundred years, Americans have moved away from the widespread religious belief that sex was ordained for procreation and that it should occur only within marriage. Fewer wait for marriage to experience sex, and many do not consider marriage a prerequisite for bearing children. In the early 1990s, 41 percent of first births occurred out of wedlock. This contrasts with only 8 percent in the early 1930s (Bachu 1998). Clearly, many of these mothers marry the fathers during pregnancy or after the birth of the child, yet the phenomenon does suggest that procreation and marriage are becoming less closely linked. The large number of women, both heterosexual and lesbian, who bear children without the benefits of holy matrimony can be viewed as a threat, or an alternative, to traditional marriage.

Couples now take many visible forms: legal spouses, heterosexual and same-sex lovers, married and out-of-wedlock parents. Perhaps the most striking change during the last thirty years is not so much the very real increase in extramarital sexual activity, out-of-wedlock births, divorce, and serial marriages but the way our society has accommodated such previously condemned practices. Of course, there is great variation in practice and acceptance along religious and ethnic and regional and socioeconomic lines. To give a few examples, Fundamentalist Christians still vehemently oppose premarital sexual activity of any kind. Sexually active white women who become pregnant are more likely to marry before giving birth than either African American or Hispanic American women. Japanese Americans intermarry more frequently than Filipino or Chinese Americans. African American women and men are less likely to marry than European Americans. Divorced men and women, commonplace in the Western world, are still frowned upon by the Catholic church. Same-sex couples may "come out" less fearfully in cities like San Francisco and New York than in many Midwestern and Southern towns.

The weakening of taboos once attached to love, sex, and marriage makes it possible for individuals to choose each other across religious, ethnic, regional, and class boundaries. But, like most things American, this freedom of choice has created a new set of problems. Without the limits set in the past by one's family, religion, and community, couples today have to negotiate not only the adjustments required by any intimate partnership but also those that derive from vast cultural differences, many of which are not apparent at the onset of a relationship. For example, some potential conflicts may not surface until well into a relationship, say, when a child is of the age to receive religious instruction or when one partner faces a life-threatening illness. Disturbed by the problems associated with free love and free marriage, young people today sometimes look back with nostalgia at the lives of their parents and grandparents, who had no choice but to marry within their religion and ethnic clan. The current popularity of singles groups in churches and synagogues indicates a continuing desire to find a mate from one's own religious background. At the least, they provide a more familiar context than dating services or Internet matches. Some East Indian Americans are willing to have their marriages arranged by their families, and as Pasupathi demonstrates, these "arranged" marriages now allow the prospective bride and groom freedom to "choose" each other from a selected group of candidates.

Many of these diverse challenges to couplehood will undoubtedly be with us in the coming century. It is our opinion that gender issues will continue to constitute core problems within the legal institution of marriage. The old quid pro quo, whereby women offered men sexual, reproductive, and housekeeping services in return for financial support and social protection, is no longer viable for most Americans. In its place, a new, more egalitarian model has come kicking and screaming into the world. Women are willing (or obliged) to earn income for their families and expect men to participate in housekeeping and child care. Many men expect women to contribute to the family income, and while some are learning to play more significant roles in the household, others still cling to an outdated vision of the archetypal, self-sacrificing, all-nourishing wife. So far, the balance is not equal in either case. Women do not, on average, earn as much as men (about 74 percent of what men earn), and men do not participate equally in domestic duties.[6] Much of the malaise within heterosexual couples today centers around gendered differences in expectations. A plethora of books on this subject, ranging from the conservative author Danielle Crittenden's *What Our Mothers Didn't Tell Us,* which enjoins women to get married young and promptly have babies, to Susan Faludi's groundbreaking *Stiffed,* which sympathetically examines the sense of betrayal experienced by working-class males, attest to the fractious situation between the sexes.

It will probably take another generation or two before these problems are sorted out, and by then new ones will undoubtedly have arisen. The only certainty—and of this we are sure—is that couples will continue to form and reform throughout the next millennium. Partners will continue to say to each other some version of Matthew Arnold's poetic pledge: "Ah, love, let us be true to one another!"

NOTES

1. National Center for Education Statistics, "Projections of Education Statistics to 2009" (1999).

2. U.S. Bureau of the Census, "Estimated Median Age at First Marriage" (Internet release date: January 7, 1999).

3. R. Lee, "Long-Term Projections and the U.S. Social Security System," *Population and Development Review* 26 (2000): 137–43.

4. Life-expectancy increases have also led to a dramatic increase in grandmothers raising grandchildren, but the absolute number of such households remains relatively small. See E. LeShan, *Grandparenting in a Changing World* (New York: Newmarket Press, 1997).

5. Amara Bachu, "Trends in Marital Status of U.S. Women at First Birth: 1930 to 1994," U.S. Census Bureau, Population Division Working Paper No. 20, 1998.

6. U.S. Department of Labor Statistics, *Employment and Earnings* (January 1999).

REFERENCES

Bachu, Amara. 1998. "Trends in Marital Status of U.S. Women at First Birth: 1930 to 1994." U.S. Bureau of the Census, Population Division Working Paper No. 20. March.

Bernard, Jesse. 1972. *The Future of Marriage*. New York: World Publishing.

Crittenden, Danielle. 1999. *What Our Mothers Didn't Tell Us: Why Happiness Eludes the Modern Woman*. New York: Simon and Schuster.

Faludi, Susan. 1999. *Stiffed: The Betrayal of the American Man*. New York: Morrow.

Folbre, N., and J. Nelson. 2000. "For Love or Money—Or Both?" *Journal of Economic Perspectives* 14, no. 4:123–40.

Graffe, E. J. 1999. *What Is Marriage For? The Strange Social History of Our Most Intimate Institution*. Boston: Beacon Press.

Johnson, Miriam M. 1988. *Strong Mothers, Weak Wives: The Search for Gender Equality*. Berkeley and Los Angeles: University of California Press.

Lee, R. 2000. "Long-Term Projections and the U.S. Social Security System." *Population and Development Review* 26:137–43.

LeShan, E. 1997. *Grandparenting in a Changing World*. New York: Newmarket Press.

Maccoby, Eleanor E. 1998. *The Two Sexes: Growing Apart, Coming Together*. Cambridge, Mass.: Harvard University Press.

Matthews, G. 1987. *"Just a Housewife": The Rise and Fall of Domesticity in America*. New York and Oxford: Oxford University Press.

National Center for Education Statistics. 1999. "Projections of Education Statistics to 2009."

Schwartz, Pepper. 1994. *Peer Marriage: How Love between Equals Really Works*. New York: The Free Press.

Skolnick, Arlene. 1991. *Embattled Paradise: The American Family in an Age of Uncertainty*. New York: Basic Books.

Smeeding, T. 1999. *Social Security Reform: Improving Benefit Adequacy and Economic Security for Women*. Syracuse, N.Y.: Syracuse University Policy Brief, no. 16. Center for Policy Research.

U.S. Bureau of the Census. 1999. "Estimated Median Age at First Marriage." Internet release date: January 7, 1999.

U.S. Department of Labor Statistics. 1999. *Employment and Earnings* (January).

Waite, L. J. 1995. "Does Marriage Matter?" Presidential address to the Population Association of America, University of Chicago.

Wald, M. 1999. "Same-Sex Couples: Marriage, Families, and Children: An

Analysis of Proposition 22, The Knight Initiative." Stanford, Calif.: Institute for Research on Women and Gender, Stanford University.

Wallerstein, Judith S., and Sandra Blakeslee. 1995. *The Good Marriage: How and Why Love Lasts*. New York: Houghton Mifflin.

Whitehead, Barbara Dafoe. 1998. *The Divorce Culture: Rethinking Our Commitments to Marriage and Family*. New York: Vintage Books.

Yalom, Marilyn. 2001. *A History of the Wife*. New York: HarperCollins.

CHAPTER I

Biblical Models

From Adam and Eve to the Bride of Christ

Marilyn Yalom

"It is not good for a person to be alone." With these words the God of the Hebrew Bible created the first human couple.[1] What if God had decided to leave Adam alone in the Garden of Eden? After all, God did not have a wife. Unlike his Greek counterpart, Zeus, the Hebrew God was sufficient unto himself. Why did Adam need a companion? He might have reigned over the plants and animals in splendid isolation—a loner, an existential hero, God's duplicate on earth. But no, God said it was not good for man to be alone. It was better to live with a mate.

I have always liked this part of the creation story. It suggests that Adam and Eve were initially united for the sheer sake of companionship. It does not privilege sexuality or the creation of children. It even gives the conjugal relationship priority over all other forms of human attachment, as stated in these memorable words: "Therefore does a man leave his father and his mother and cling to his wife and they become as one flesh."

The exalted status of the heterosexual couple is a special feature of the Judeo-Christian tradition. Other religions and civilizations tend to be less enthusiastic. In most Asian countries, for example, the family or clan is still the privileged unit. Until very recently, a Japanese or Chinese son owed more to his parents than to his wife. (Indeed, the word *love*

A different version of this paper appears in *A History of the Wife* (New York: Harper-Collins, 2001).

between spouses did not even exist in the Chinese language until a group of Chinese intellectuals invented it in 1920.) In Islamic countries, where polygamy is not uncommon, the "couple" is often a cluster of couples, with several co-wives sharing one husband. Once the monogamous couple begins to rise in the kinship hierarchy, as it has recently in parts of Africa and Asia, that change is recognized as a form of "Westernization."

This is not to suggest that either Judaism or Christianity has a moral superiority over Islam or Buddhism or Hinduism but merely that it honors the couple above all other family ties. And it is certainly not meant to suggest that males and females have shared equal rights in Jewish and Christian marriages. The biblical story of the creation of Eve from Adam's rib and the subsequent catastrophe attributed primarily to Eve reflect age-old gender biases.[2] Favoring the male is a fact of human history. Whether we look east or west, to biblical Israel or imperial China, patriarchy has been the rule. As God tells Eve after she persuaded Adam to eat from the tree of good and evil: "Your urge shall be for your husband and he shall rule over you." Like most myths, this one sought to explain a cultural phenomenon that had been entrenched for so long it seemed to be the will of God.

As a late-twentieth-century Western woman, I shudder at the thought of life with a biblical husband. I would have been his property, his chattel, a grade above his livestock. Doesn't the Tenth Commandment order a man not to covet his neighbor's wife or his neighbor's ox, practically in the same breath? And because polygamy existed among the ancient Jews, I might have been one of several co-wives.[3] Abraham, Sarah, and Hagar; Jacob, Rachel, and Leah; King Solomon and his seven hundred wives were all inhabitants of cultures that entitled a man to more than one woman . . . if he could afford them. For the "principal" wife, he had to give his father-in-law a sum of money, the *mohar* of fifty silver shekels (Ex. 22:15–16, Deut. 22:28–29) and provide for her sustenance. Under certain conditions, most notably if his wife were barren or insane, he was also entitled to take one or more concubines (wives of lesser social and legal status), captive wives, and slave-wives, all of whom required upkeep. This probably meant that only the affluent could afford more than one wife and that the ordinary biblical Hebrew practiced monogamy.

Before marriage, I would have been able to circulate with relative freedom. Like Rebekah tending the sheep, I would have gone by myself into the fields or to the well. But I would have been warned to be wary of males, for if someone had raped me, I would have been considered damaged goods and lost my chance of finding a husband—unless the rapist himself wanted to marry me (as in the story of Dinah and Schechem, Gen. 34).

Given the more normal course of events, my parents would have found a husband for me, to whom I would have become engaged very young and married soon after puberty. As the daughter of a wealthy father (had I been so lucky), I would have been provided with a substantial *chiluhim,* or dowry. The dowry might have consisted of silver, gold, or material goods to be used in the future household, such as furnishings, servants, livestock, and even land. The specific sum of the dowry, as well as the sum from the husband's side that would be settled on me in case of divorce or his death, would have been written down in the marriage contract, or *ketubah.*[4]

On my wedding day, I would have been decked out in finery, veiled, and led to my husband under the marriage canopy, the *chupah* still used in many Jewish weddings, before being taken to his home. There the marriage had to be consummated in order to make it valid. The bloody sheet that we slept on during the first night would have been displayed to the community as a sign of my defloration. (This practice remained in certain Near Eastern Jewish communities into the twentieth century.) But if my husband found that I was no longer a virgin, he could have killed me according to the words of the Torah: "Then they shall bring out the damsel to the door of her father's house, and the men of the city shall stone her with stones that she die" (Deut. 22:20–21). Assuming that this was not my lot, I would have settled into my husband's household as an obedient wife, at least in public. Obedience was so fundamental to the biblical idea of a wife that it remained in Jewish and Christian wedding vows until the late twentieth century. And above all, I would have been consumed by the need to produce a son. For only as the mother of a son, would I have had some clout in the family.

And even then, if my husband had wanted to get rid of me, he had only to write out a bill of divorce, hand it to me in the presence of two witnesses, and send me away. The Hebrew law allowed that "a husband can cast off his wife if she doesn't win his favor because he finds something shameful in her" (Deut. 24:1). What was shameful in those days? Adultery and even the suspicion of adultery, immodesty, disregard for the ritual law, insults addressed to one's husband or his father, refusal to have sex with one's husband, refusal to follow him to another domicile, and such chronic illnesses as epilepsy. But under no circumstance could the wife initiate divorce or any other legal action on her own. Except in one peculiar case.

If a woman were widowed and childless, her dead husband's brother was expected to marry her, whether he was already married or not. His obligation was to "raise seed for the deceased brother" and perpetuate his brother's name. This custom known as "levirate" marriage was also a means of retaining a widow within the family that had originally paid for her and of providing her with protection and sustenance. But if the dead husband's brother refused to marry her or to have sex with her after their enforced marriage, the wife was permitted to go to the elders at the town gate and lay her claim against him in a formal ceremony known as *chalitza*. There, in front of the whole populace, she was allowed to humiliate him for not fulfilling his obligations: "She shall pull his sandal off his foot and spit in his face and declare: 'Thus we requite the man who will not build up his brother's family'" (Deut. 25:9–10). The overriding Hebrew concern with progeny, especially in the case of a husband who had died without children, allowed for this one rare display of female revenge. The brother who had submitted to the stigmatizing ceremony of *chalitza* was henceforth absolved from his obligation to his brother's widow, and she became free to wed another.

It is true that this wifely scenario is based upon prescriptive texts, which were probably modified in everyday life. We do find many indications in the Bible that suggest behaviors different from the prescribed norm. For example, despite the great pressure on wives to produce children, a husband might continue to love his barren wife and even to favor her over a first or second wife who had given him a son. This was the case of Jacob and Rachel, and that of Elkanah, who preferred his childless wife, Hannah, to his other wife, Peninnah, the mother of his children. Once, finding Hannah weeping over her childless state, Elkanah tried to soothe her by saying: "Hannah, why are you crying and eating nothing? Why are you so miserable? Am I not more to you than ten sons?" (I Sam. 8–10). Even with all the societal honor heaped upon a mother and the humiliation incurred by a childless wife, there was then, as now, no way to legislate individual inclination.

Married couples were held in high esteem among the ancient Hebrews, as evidenced by the many stories about them. This contrasts with the New Testament, in which couples do not play significant roles. In time, Jews and Christians alike looked to the older Hebrew examples for positive (and negative) conjugal models.

Among the positive examples of what one might hope for in a wife,

Sarah, the wife of Abraham, comes first to mind. Hers was a careful balancing act of wifely strength and submission. As a good Israelite spouse, she was obliged to follow even the most morally questionable of her husband's commands. Twice at his behest she passed herself off as his sister, rather than his wife, so that he could gain favor first with the Egyptian pharaoh, then with the king Abimelech. Though this entailed sleeping with a foreign monarch, Sarah followed her husband's orders; in the end, this strategy proved beneficial, since they came away from each incident with increased riches. For centuries, biblical exegetes have tried to justify Abraham's actions, though, of late, some have seen this strategy as an unethical, self-serving ploy.

The domestic models held up for men were more ambiguous. For Abraham, Moses, Kings David and Solomon, and all the other married Hebrew heroes, the role of husband was always second to the role of religious leader. What was good for the preservation of the Israelite people took precedence over everything else. Thus Sarah not only slept with two foreign monarchs in the interest of furthering her husband's lot, but she also encouraged him to take her Egyptian servant, Hagar, as a concubine so as to produce an heir. Later, when Sarah felt humiliated by Hagar's pregnancy, Abraham found himself in the awkward situation of having to decide between the two women. As a good Israelite husband, he decided in favor of the first wife and sent Hagar into exile. But God Himself intervened, sending the servant back to her former mistress and assuring Hagar that she would bear a son to Abraham and become the ancestor of a great people. Thus Abraham once again had two wives in residence and a firstborn son, named Ishmael. (Centuries later he would be claimed by Muslims as the forefather of the Arab people.) In their old age, Abraham and Sarah miraculously produced a son of their own, Isaac, who would ultimately beget the chieftains of the twelve tribes of Israel.

Abraham, the father of the Hebrew people, is the quintessential patriarch. Through his wit, wile, and unswerving loyalty to God, he overshadows all the other players in the first act of Jewish history. Even when God asks him to sacrifice his beloved son Isaac, he is willing to take that step. I cannot believe Sarah would have agreed, had he consulted her. But fortunately, the command to sacrifice Isaac was only a test of Abraham's faith and did not have to be enacted.

The story of Abraham and Sarah, like many of the stories in the Hebrew Bible, cannot be proven historically. Nevertheless, as one follows their narrative, one gets the feel of a real couple living together in biblical times: They wander as nomads to villages and cities, moving with their kinsmen, animals, servants, slaves, and goods; they set up their tent among peoples who cannot be counted on for kindness; they show hospitality to strangers in the form of curds and milk and freshly made loaves of bread; they exchange opinions, complaints, laughter. And when Sarah dies before her husband, we are not surprised to read that "Abraham came to mourn Sarah and to keen for her" (Gen. 23:2). However mythical its origins, theirs is a believable union that gives meaning to the idea of a lifelong partnership.

For narratives concerning younger couples, the marriages of Sarah and Abraham's son, Isaac, to Rebekah and that of their grandson, Jacob, to Rachel (and Leah) are replete with elements of love, longing, and jealousy. In the case of Rebekah, a servant is sent to the land of Abraham's birth to contract a marriage for Isaac, without the bride or groom ever seeing one another. Note that the servant makes the marriage agreement not with Rebekah herself, but with Rebekah's brother Laban. Still, Rebekah has some say in the matter. After Laban has given his acquiescence, he says: " 'Let us call the young woman and ask for her answer.' And they called Rebekah and said to her, 'Will you go with this man?' And she said, 'I will' " (Gen. 24:58–59). This is one of the few indications that a nubile woman in the ancient world may have been able to refuse a prospective groom.

The actual meeting of Rebekah and Isaac does not take place until she had journeyed with his servant back to Canaan. The story ends with a cameo picture of Isaac's favorable reaction to his bride. "And Isaac brought her into the tent of Sarah his mother and took Rebekah as wife. And he loved her, and Isaac was consoled after his mother's death" (Gen. 24:67). The last sentence is particularly moving, for Isaac not only loves the wife who had been chosen for him but finds an emotional replacement for his mother. We can imagine Freud nodding in agreement.

The later story of the marriage of Isaac and Rebekah's son, Jacob, to Rachel has many more complications, though it parallels the earlier story in several ways. When the time comes for Jacob to marry, Rebekah sends him (rather than a servant) back to her brother Laban in the land of her birth. Laban receives his nephew Jacob hospitably but not without making him work for his keep. After a month, they reach an agreement on the wages Jacob will receive if he remains in Laban's service. The wages are in effect a bride-price for Rachel. As the story is told: "Laban had two daughters. The name of the elder was Leah and the name of the younger Rachel. And Leah's eyes were tender, but Rachel was comely

in features and comely to look at, and Jacob loved Rachel" (Gen. 29:
16–18). Jacob contracts to serve seven years for Rachel. In the eloquent
words of the biblical narrator: "And Jacob served seven years for Rachel, and they seemed in his eyes but a few days in his love for her"
(Gen. 29:21).

But when the time comes for Jacob to reap the fruits of his labors, he
is cruelly deceived by his uncle. In the dark of night, he is given Leah
rather than Rachel and beds the wrong woman. In the morning, seeing
that it was Leah, Jacob said to Laban: "What is this you have done to
me? Was it not for Rachel that I served you?" Laban replied that it was
not the custom in his land "to give the younger girl before the firstborn,"
and proposed that Jacob serve another seven years to acquire Rachel as
well.

All in all, Jacob spent twenty years serving his crafty uncle Laban,
acquiring two wives and their slave girls and quite a number of children.
Since sons represented the ultimate good in biblical households, the
wives competed with each other in producing male offspring. First Leah,
the least loved, was compensated by the birth of three sons, and Rachel,
who remained barren, became jealous of her sister. So she said to Jacob:
"Here is my slave girl Bilhah. Come to bed with her, that she may give
birth on my knees, so that I, too, shall be built up through her"(Gen.
30:3). Placing the baby on her knees after its birth was the gesture that
indicated adoption, a practice that allowed a childless wife to maintain
her position as the head of the household. Then Rachel claimed that she
had won out over her sister. But Leah, too, had a slave girl, and she,
too, was drawn into the birthing contest. The competition between
wives was intensified by the use of mandrakes, plants thought to have
magical aphrodisiac and fertility-promoting properties. With the help of
these plants, Leah continued to produce more sons and a daughter, and
Rachel, finally, gave birth to a son. Jacob was now the father of a min-
iature tribe. This story reveals the fierce rivalries between wives living
in a society that honored married women primarily as the mothers of
sons. It also suggests the ordeals a polygamous husband went through
in trying to fulfill his conjugal obligations.

And finally, like the story of Sarah, Abraham, and Hagar, it offers
information about the role of female "outsiders" within Hebrew households—Egyptian slaves, for example, who occasionally shared some of
the social benefits of wives, if few of their legal rights. A slave-wife
always remained "property." She was initially purchased, either by the
husband or his wife, and was never legally married to her master. But

she did have the right to "meat, clothes, and conjugal relations" (Ex. 21:10), just like a first wife or a concubine. If her master-husband denied her any of these rights, she could leave him. Otherwise, she would be freed in her seventh year, as the Hebrew law stipulated for all slaves.

The Hebrew Bible has a rich cast of characters with many marital scenes. One of my favorites is the terse interchange between Job and his wife, after Job had been laid low by God. Having lost all his sons and daughters, his servants and animals, then afflicted with boils from head to toe, Job sat down among the ashes and accepted the will of God. But not his wife, as is evident from the following verses.

> Then said his wife unto him. "Dost thou still retain thine integrity? Curse God, and die."
> But he said unto her, "Thou speakest as one of the foolish women speaketh. What? shall we receive good at the hand of God, and shall we not receive evil?" In all this did not Job sin with his lips.
>
> (Job 2:9–10)

We hear the bitter voice of the wife and mother, overwhelmed by sorrow and unforgiving of a God responsible for the death of her children. She is presented as "one of the foolish women" who cannot bear up to suffering. Job, on the other hand, resists despair—at least initially. Their interchange draws from an antique Mediterranean tradition in which women were often seen as foolish: Caught up in the grief of their losses, insolent to indifferent gods, they were presumably unable to see the "larger picture," be it political or metaphysical. Like the Greek queen Clytemnestra, who never stopped blaming Agamemnon for the sacrifice of their daughter, Iphigenia, Job's wife had no compunctions about cursing the God who had taken away her children. Whatever the prescriptions about wifely obedience, wives obviously opposed their husbands in the privacy of their homes and even opposed the supreme patriarch—God Himself.

Men are supposed to be more steadfast. Though Job experiences grave psychological anguish and questions God's justice, he never succumbs to blasphemy. In the end God rewards him with "twice as much as he had before" (Job 42:10). At this point the narrator does not deign to mention Job's wife.

If the Hebrew Bible has an overriding prejudice in favor of the male half of the couple—think only of Adam and Eve, Samson and Delilah, Job and Job's wife—a few notable exceptions come easily to mind. The love poems in the Song of Songs, traditionally attributed to King Solomon but probably written by more than one author including some women, present an unparalleled picture of egalitarian lovers. The man calls out to his "sister," his "bride," his "dove," his "perfect one." The woman calls out to her "lover," her "love," her "man of pleasure." In contrast to the rest of the Hebrew Bible, the lovers in the Song offer a rhapsody of erotic joy, with the sensual delights of both men and women equally praised.

A more conventional picture of the ideal female is found in the final section of Proverbs. It is clearly written from the male point of view, beginning misogynistically with the notion that a good woman is hard to find and rising to an encomium of the wife unique in all the Bible.

> Who can find a virtuous woman? for her price is far above rubies.
> The heart of her husband doth safely trust in her . . .
> She will do him good and not evil all the days of her life.
> She seeketh wool, and flax, and worketh willingly with her hands.
> She is like the merchants' ships; she bringeth her food from afar.
> She riseth also while it is yet night, and giveth meat to her household, and a portion to her maidens. . . .
> She stretcheth out her hand to the poor . . .
> Her children arise up, and call her blessed; her husband also, and he praiseth her.

Such is the dutiful, hardworking, charitable woman who brings honor to her husband and children. Any man in any age might dream of such a wife. And what of the male counterpart to this image? The Hebrew husband had obligations more pressing than domestic duties. His first loyalty was to the Hebrew God and to the continuity of his people, as her first loyalty was to her husband. This model of the couple, with domestic responsibilities borne solely by the wife and religious responsibilities borne solely by the man, endured among Jews into the late twentieth century. Only recently has this model begun to change. Today, throughout the Western world and in Israel, there is a greater interpenetration of conventionally "masculine" and "feminine" spheres. Some Jewish women have been ordained as rabbis, and some Jewish men change their babies' diapers. Still, this is by no means common practice, especially among ultraorthodox Jews, who cling to the idea of the traditional patriarchal couple and resist upstart models that defy three millennia of Jewish history.

Married couples are notably absent from the Gospels. Aside from the miraculous story of Mary and Joseph, briefly told in Matthew and Luke, there is no New Testament couple of any significance.

The emphasis in the Gospels is on the individual and his or her per-

sonal salvation. How we behave on earth, as individuals responsible for
our actions, will determine whether we inherit the Kingdom of Heaven
or whether we shall spend eternity in Gehenna, the Hebrew equivalent
of Hell. In any event, in the afterlife, there is no marriage, as Jesus makes
explicit. "When they rise from the dead, they neither marry, nor are
given in marriage, but are as the angels" (Mark 12:25). The strong apoc-
alyptic bent in Jesus's message seems to have made marriage "irrele-
vant."

It can be argued that the teachings of Jesus focus on the individual
and the nascent Christian community at the expense of family connections. This is implied in the story of the visit of Jesus's family—his siblings and mother—to the synagogue where he was teaching. When they
asked him to meet them outside the temple, Jesus answered: "Who is
my mother, or my brethren?" and pointing to the multitude around him,
added: "Behold my mother and my brethren! For whosoever shall do
the will of God, the same is my brother, and my sister, and mother"
(Mark 3:33–35). His words point to a broad vision of human family
beyond the clan mentality of his Mediterranean contemporaries. He
conceived a new, primary "family" born from the community of his
followers.

Another of Jesus's sayings pushes this line of thought to the extreme
by envisioning the terrible family conflicts that would ensue from an-
tagonistic religious loyalties:

> Think not that I am come to send peace on earth: I came not to send
> peace, but a sword.
> For I am come to set a man at variance against his father, and the daughter
> against her mother, and the daughter-in-law against her mother-in-law.
> And a man's foes shall be they of his own household.
> He that loveth father or mother more than me is not worthy of me; and he
> that loveth son or daughter more than me is not worthy of me.
>
> (Matt. 10:34–37)

This is no longer the gentle Jesus, the friend of children and the down-
trodden; here Jesus echoes the jealous God of the Hebrew Bible, a fire-
and-brimstone deity who brooks no rivals. It is noteworthy that husbands and wives do not appear on Jesus's list of family members to be
riven apart. Spouses are perhaps granted immunity because they have
become "one flesh." Nonetheless, the implication here and elsewhere in
the New Testament is that everyone's primary commitment must be to
Jesus, a commitment likened to a marriage with Jesus assuming the role
of the bridegroom. Such is the imagery found on his tongue when he and

his disciples are rebuked for not fasting like the Pharisees. Jesus is quoted as answering: "Can the children of the bridechamber mourn, as long as the bridegroom is with them? but the days will come, when the bridegroom shall be taken from them, and then they shall fast" (Matt. 9:15; also Mark 2:19–20). Jesus as bridegroom is a metaphor that was taken up by subsequent Christian thinkers and effectively used in countless sermons and ceremonies until our own time. For centuries, Catholic nuns have taken their final vows as the bride of Christ, in a ritual reminiscent of the marriage ceremony down to the veil and the wedding ring.

What did Jesus himself think about marriage between an ordinary wife and an ordinary husband? His thoughts on marriage were expressed in the synoptic Gospels around the subject of divorce, a practice he explicitly condemned. Citing the creation story when God made both male and female and they became one flesh, Jesus declared: "What God hath joined together, let not man put asunder" (Mark 10:9). The first human couple was treated as the norm for all subsequent marriages. Then Jesus went on to specify that "whosoever shall put away his wife . . . and shall marry another, committeth adultery" (Mark 10:11–12; Matt. 5:31–32). It is important to remember that the ancient Hebrew law proscribing adultery applied exclusively to women, requiring them to limit their sexual activity to only one man. There was no such requirement for married men, who were allowed to have sex with unattached women, such as widows, concubines, servants, and slaves, as well as their wives. A convicted adulteress could be put to death by stoning, along with her illicit sexual partner. His crime was to have invaded another man's space. Jesus challenged this tradition by equating divorce and remarriage—which had been legal and religious rights for men—with adultery, thus putting men on a par with women. Whoever wanted to be a Christian and married, regardless of one's sex, would have to be permanently monogamous.

Jesus also challenged the excessive punishment meted out to the adulteress. In a by-now famous incident, he was asked whether a woman "taken in adultery, in the very act," should be stoned, according to Mosaic law. His response has become proverbial: "He that is without sin among you, let him first cast a stone at her"(John 8:7). Jesus's emphasis upon compassion rather than revenge and upon the equality of all men and women in sin, opened a new chapter in religious history. Nonetheless, Christian society continued to treat adulterers harshly for centuries to come. In the third century, the Church was already excommunicating those convicted of adultery and even supported the death sentence in certain times and places (Reynolds 1994, xviii). For example, both parties to adultery were subject to impalement in fourteenth-century Germany according to the laws of Saxony and to execution in Puritan New England, though public whipping was the usual form of punishment

So far, all the couples we have considered have been heterosexual. Given the biblical view of sexuality as a procreative function, this should come as no surprise. In the Hebrew Bible, homosexuality was expressly forbidden. The command reads: "Thou shalt not lie with mankind, as with womankind: it is abomination" (Lev. 18:22). Both parties contributing to an "abomination," such as homosexuality, bestiality, or adultery, were "put to death." In the case of bestiality, this also included the animal.

It took me a long time to realize that this injunction against lying "with mankind, as with womankind" is to be taken literally. That is, the prohibition is directed exclusively toward male homosexuality. There is no similar prohibition against female homosexuality in the Hebrew Bible. A number of explanations have been offered for this distinction. One of the most convincing argues that lesbians were passed over because they are not party to the "spilling of seed" resulting from male homosexual practices (Eilberg-Schwarz 1990, 183). Or perhaps female homosexuality was disregarded because the male writers of the Bible were interested only in the behavior of other males and ignored or trivialized lesbian sexual activity (Brooten 1996, 62).

So abhorrent was male homosexuality to the authors of the Bible that it inspired one of the most vengeful acts attributed to God—the destruction of Sodom and Gomorrah. The story reads as follows. Lot, the nephew of Abraham, was living in the Canaanite city of Sodom. When two messengers arrived at the gate of the city at nightfall, he offered them hospitality. But no sooner had he taken them into his home and given them bread than the men of Sodom, "every last man of them," went to the house and demanded that the two messengers be turned over to them. " 'Where are the men who came to you tonight?' they shouted. 'Bring them out to us so that we may know them!' " (Gen. 19: 4–6). The word "know" is generally interpreted in the sense of carnal knowledge.

Lot, a good host, refused to consent to this proposed gang rape. He even offered the Sodomites his two virgin daughters instead, which says a great deal about the relative worth of a man's daughter as opposed to that of a male guest. But the men of Sodom would not be pacified. At this point, the messengers, who were in reality angels sent by God, held off their would-be rapists and urged Lot to flee with his family, because God was about to destroy Sodom with all its inhabitants. Lot, his wife, and two daughters managed to get away, though the ill-fated wife who looked behind her was turned into a pillar of salt. When the sun came up the next day, "the Lord rained upon Sodom and Gomorrah brimstone and fire. . . . And He overthrew all those cities and all the plain and all the inhabitants of the cities and what grew in the soil" (Gen. 19: 24–25). As in the story of the Flood, God wiped out an entire population because of its sins—in this case, the specific sins of homosexuality and lack of hospitality—and spared only one family.

Why homosexual acts were so reviled by the biblical Hebrews has been the subject of endless debate. One answer has to do with the ancient focus on procreation: Any sexual act that did not contribute to progeny—for example, masturbation, coitus interuptus, and bestiality—was vehemently condemned. Another interpretation, advanced by Harvard preacher Peter J. Gomes, is that the ban on homosexuality was established to differentiate the Jews from the surrounding Canaanites; it was a matter of what Gomes calls self-identification and "nation building" in a "frontier community" (1996, 153). Other inhabitants of the ancient Mediterranean world, most notably the Greeks but also the Romans, tolerated same-sex couples (Boswell 1995), but Judaism was fiercely antihomosexual.

As for Christianity, Jesus said nothing on the subject of homosexuality—and this in contrast to numerous condemnations of adultery. Saint Paul, however, explicitly condemns homosexuality in three places, and he specifically mentions both female and male homosexuals. In Romans 1:26–27, he writes of "men committing shameless acts with men" and of women "who exchanged natural relations for unnatural" ones. In I Corinthians 6:9, he states that "neither fornicators, nor idolators, nor adulterers, nor effeminate, nor abusers of themselves with mankind" will inherit the kingdom of God, and in Timothy 1:9–10, he condemns "them that defile themselves with mankind," along with murderers, whoremongers, menstealers, liars, and perjured persons.

Paul's negative view of same-sex eroticism was rooted in a system of thought that took heterosexual relations as "natural" and all other forms of sexuality as "unnatural." God had established the "natural" order of things in Genesis, and any deviation from heterosexual coupling was seen as a rejection of God's design.

Nonetheless, the early Christian church did not concern itself significantly with homosexual practices; it focused on sins of the flesh in general and concupiscence (sexual desire) between men and women in particular. It was not until the late Middle Ages that the Christianized Western world became increasingly vocal in expressing its horror of homosexuality (Boswell 1980).

When I think about ancient Judaism and early Christianity, I am struck by certain basic differences in their conceptions of marriage—differences that have persisted in some form to this very day. Judaism taught that marriage was connected to the *mitzvah* of procreation—a divine commandment and a blessing. Because marriage was seen as the only sanctioned way Jews could fulfill their obligation to reproduce, men and women were obliged to marry. Numerous rabbinical sayings found in the Torah and Talmud reaffirm this sentiment; for example, "Whoso findeth a wife findeth a good thing, and obtaineth favor of the Lord" (Prov. 18:22), and "He who liveth without a wife is no perfect man" (Yebamoth 62).

Early Christianity, on the other hand, developed a different hierarchy of values. Following the models of Jesus and Saint Paul, it valued celibacy above marriage. In the words of Saint Paul, "The unmarried man cares for the Lord's business; his aim is to please the Lord. But the married man cares for worldly things; his aim is to please his wife; and he has a divided mind" (I Cor. 7:32–34). Forming an earthly couple was seen as interfering with the primary business of forming a union with the Lord. If, for the Jew, the only way to obey God's commandment was to marry and produce offspring, for the Pauline Christian, the best way to fulfill God's commandment was to abstain from sex altogether. Marriage was only second best, as explicitly stated in another famous passage in which Paul refers to his own exemplary single status: "To the unmarried and to widows I say this: it is a good thing if they stay as I am myself; but if they cannot control themselves, they should marry. Better to be married than to burn with vain desire" (I Cor. 7:8–9).

All the major patristic thinkers, most notably Tertullian, Saint Jerome, and Saint Augustine, placed a higher value on virginal "gold" than on marital "brass." They argued that the Fall, confounded with the sexual act, had conferred a moral taint on all carnal union, even that within marriage. This position became increasingly entrenched within the Catholic church and was related to the rise of monasticism, which, by the sixth century, offered an alternative to marriage for both men and women. (No such option was available to Jews or Muslims.) By the Middle Ages, a Christian man or woman might have felt a real tension between the impulse to pair with another human being and the desire to remain chaste so as to lead a more exemplary life. At the same time, Jewish spouses would have felt compelled to copulate to fulfill the biblical commandment to procreate.

Although the dominant position of the Church from the fourth century onward promoted asceticism and coated physical intimacy with the taint of sin, there were always some theologians who praised marriage. They pointed to the words of Jesus when he defended it as a God-given, indissoluble bond and to the wedding at Cana, where he miraculously provided wine for the wedding guests (Mark 10:6–9; John 2). They could even point to Saint Paul, who, having begrudgingly conceded that marriage provided a solution to the problem of sexual desire, endeavored to endow it with deep Christian meaning by comparing it to the union between Christ and the Church.[5] In that union, the man was seen as the head of his wife, just as Christ was the head of the Church. It was an allegorical model that assumed men had a "natural" right to rule women, in keeping with the gender hierarchy of the ancient world.

And the defenders of marriage could also cite Paul's insistence on the need for mutual love between husband and wife. Paul enjoined both men and women to love their spouses, with specific focus on the marital bed: "The husband must give the wife what is due to her, and the wife equally must give the husband his due" (I Cor. 7:3). Paul may have derived this concept from the Hebrew Bible, which orders a husband to provide his wife—even a slave-wife, as we noted earlier—with food, clothing, and sexual relations. It was this part of Paul's thinking that would lead Luther, fifteen hundred years later, to take a stand on marriage quite different from that of Catholicism.

Luther began by questioning the tenet that priests could not marry. He pointed out that there was no word from Jesus in the New Testament condemning the marriage of the apostles—indeed, the Apostle Peter had been married, and it is possible (according to Luther) that Paul and Jesus himself may have been married as very young men. Choosing the words of Paul that make his case, Luther writes that a bishop should be "the husband of but one wedded wife." In Luther's time, numerous clergymen lived with women, many of whom had borne them children, although these unions were not sanctioned by the Church. At the age of forty-two, Luther married a runaway nun and set about to establish the model of the married pastor's home that was to become influential in Protestant circles.

The idea of the couple that has evolved in the West since biblical times is still rooted, to a large extent, in religious precepts. Most people still marry with the expectation of monogamy and lifelong commitment, even in an age when half of all first marriages in the United States end in divorce. The model couple is heterosexual, even in an age when from 5 to 10 percent of the population is estimated to be homosexual, and same-sex couples are increasingly visible. There is still a strong bias toward the creation of offspring and the joint raising of children, even in an age when four out of ten children are born out of wedlock and one out of three spends some part of his or her life living with a single parent. And despite all the attacks upon marriage, there is still the hope of enduring mutual love.

The idea of love, central to our twentieth-century sensibility, has taken very different forms over the ages. The erotic love of the Song of Songs and the conjugal love urged upon husbands and wives by Saint Paul were in time supplemented by medieval notions of courtly love, Enlightenment models of companionate love, and nineteenth-century expressions of romantic love. If we today consider romantic love as the sine qua non of couplehood, we do well to remember the relative newness of this view. Most marriages before the modern era (the past two hundred years) probably did not originate in love, especially among those coming from families with means above the subsistence level. They began in family and financial arrangements and developed, at best, into affection and harmony. Love as the first condition for marriage was rare. Companionship, yes. Progeny, yes. Economic concerns, for sure. But what we today consider the primary ingredient for a conjugal couple took a long time to assume top priority.

Our biblical ancestors looked to other measures of suitability. Did the prospective spouses have the same religion? Did the two families have comparable property and social status? Was the prospective bride a virgin whose worth had not been reduced by any form of heterosexual activity, including rape? Would the prospective groom have the means to support a wife and children? Was he likely to honor his first wife's primary position, even if he took a second wife? Or, when monogamy became current among Christians and Jews, was the husband, as well as the wife, likely to be faithful? Most of these questions are still with us today, though they have presumably taken a back seat to the one big question: Do they love each other? "Love conquers all" became the Western watchword in marital matters long after the phrase was coined by the Latin writer Virgil. It was not a phrase that would have weighed very heavily in marriage considerations among Virgil's Roman contemporaries in the first century B. C. E. or among his Hebrew counterparts on the other side of the Mediterranean.

NOTES

I am indebted to Barbara Gelpi, Emeritus Professor of English, Stanford University, and Shulamith Magnus, Associate Professor of History, Oberlin University, for helpful suggestions.

1. The first sentence of this article presents the kind of linguistic problems that are inherent to biblical studies. The King James Version of Genesis 2:18 reads: "It is not good that the man should be alone: I will make him an help meet for him." Robert Alter's Genesis (1996), closer to the Hebrew original, reads: "It is not good for the human to be alone, I shall make him a sustainer beside him." I have compromised between the two, opting for "a person." Throughout this chapter, I cite from the King James Version of the Bible, except for the citations from Genesis taken from Alter's translation.

2. Not surprisingly, it is the second biblical version of the creation of womankind that has dominated the Western imagination. In Genesis 2, God creates Adam first and then Eve from Adam's rib, almost as an afterthought. But in Genesis 1:27, there is a prior, if less dramatic, version: "Let us make a human in his image, in the image of God He created him, male and female He created them."

3. Not until the eleventh century did Jews formally outlaw polygamy. The ban issued by Rabbi Gershom ben Judah of Worms in 1030 at first affected only German and French Jews. Italy and Spain were slower to accept the ban on polygamy, and the Jews of the Orient and North Africa never felt themselves bound by it. Indeed, polygamy continued to be practiced by Jews in these lands until the mid-twentieth century when the Chief Rabbinate of the State of Israel issued an all-inclusive ban.

4. The earliest form of the *ketubah* written in Aramaic would have contained the following, as translated in M. Mielziner, *The Jewish Law of Marriage and Divorce in Ancient and Modern Times* (Cincinnati: Bloch, 1884, 87–88):

On _____(day and month) in the year of _____, according to the Jewish reckoning, here in the city of _____, Mr. _____, son of _____, said to the virgin _____, daughter of : _____, "Be thou my wife in accordance with the laws of Moses and Israel, and I will work for thee, and I will hold thee in honor and will support and maintain thee, in accordance with the customs of Jewish husbands. . . . I will furthermore set aside the sum of two hundred silver denarii to be thy dowry, according to the law, and provide for thy food, clothing and necessaries, and cohabit with thee according to the universal custom." Miss _____, on her part, consented to become his wife. The marriage portion, which she brought from her father's house, in silver, gold, valuables, clothes, etc. amounts to the value of

_____.

In order to render the above declarations and assurances of the said bridegroom, _____, to the said bride, _____, perfectly valid and binding, we have applied the legal formality of symbolical delivery. Signature of the Groom. Signature of the two witnesses.

5. The theme of the marriage between God and His people had appeared on the tongues of the prophets of the Hebrew Bible (Hosea, Isaiah, Jeremiah, and Ezekiel) before Paul applied it to Jesus and the Church. "The author of Ephesians, on the contrary, uses the union between Christ and the Church to illumine marriage." Philip Lyndon Reynolds, *Marriage in the Western Church* (Leiden, New York, Köln: E. J. Brill, 1994, xxv.)

REFERENCES

Alter, Robert. 1996. *Genesis: Translation and Commentary*. New York and London: W. W. Norton.

Alvarez-Pereyre, Frank, and Florence Heymann. 1996. "The Desire for Transcendence: The Hebrew Family Model and Jewish Family Practices." In *A History of the Family*, edited by André Burguière, Christiane Klapisch-Zuber, Martine Segalen, and Françoise Zonaben, translated by Sarah Hanbury Tenison, Rosemary Morris, and Andrew Wilson. Oxford: Polity Press.

Biale, David. 1992. *Eros and the Jews: From Biblical Israel to Contemporary America*. New York: Basic Books.

Boswell, John. 1980. *Christianity, Social Tolerance, and Homosexuality: Gay People in Western Europe from the Beginning of the Christian Era to the Fourteenth Century*. Chicago: University of Chicago Press.

———. 1995. *The Marriage of Likeness: Same-Sex Unions in Pre-Modern Europe*. London: HarperCollins.

Brooke, Christopher. 1978. *Marriage in Christian History*. Cambridge: Cambridge University Press.

Brooten, Bernadette J. 1996. *Love between Women: Early Christian Responses to Female Homoeroticism*. Chicago and London: University of Chicago Press.

Büchmann, Christina, and Celina Spiegel, eds. 1995. *Out of the Garden: Women Writers on the Bible*. London: HarperCollins.

Eilberg-Schwarz, Howard. 1990. *The Savage in Judaism: An Anthropology of Israelite Religion and Ancient Judaism*. Bloomington: Indiana University Press.

Eisenberg, Josy. 1993. *La Femme au temps de la Bible*. Paris: Stock-L. Pernoud.

Epstein, Louis M. 1942. *Marriage Laws in the Bible and the Talmud*. Cambridge, Mass.: Harvard University Press.

Gafni, Isaiah M. 1989. "The Institution of Marriage in Rabbinic Times." In *The Jewish Family*, edited by David Kraemer. New York and Oxford: Oxford University Press.

Gomes, Peter J. 1996. *The Good Book: Reading the Bible with Mind and Heart*. New York: William Morrow.

Lawrence, Raymond J., Jr. 1989. *The Poisoning of Eros: Sexual Values in Conflict*. New York: Augustine Moore Press.

Luther, Martin. 1970. *Three Treatises*. Philadelphia: Fortress Press.

Mielziner, M. 1884. *The Jewish Law of Marriage and Divorce in Ancient and Modern Times*. Cincinnati: Bloch.

Reynolds, Philip Lyndon. 1994. *Marriage in the Western Church: The Christianization of Marriage during the Patristic and Early Medieval Periods*. Leiden, New York, Köln: E. J. Brill.

CHAPTER 2

Dearest Friend

The Marriage of Abigail and John Adams

Edith B. Gelles

According to Adams family lore, when Abigail Smith married John Adams on October 25, 1764, her father, the Reverend William Smith, preached the sermon "For John came neither eating bread nor drinking wine, and Ye say, '*He hath a devil.*'" Charles Francis Adams recorded this story in his memoir of his grandmother, explaining that Reverend Smith chose this Biblical text as a response to his Weymouth congregation. The profession of law, as practiced by John Adams, had only recently emerged in colonial Massachusetts, and a deep prejudice existed against it. Moreover, Adams was the son of a modest farmer. Charles Francis justified the reverend's text in terms of community and social class. It was intended to admonish a "portion of the parishioners" who thought that "the son of a small farmer of the middle class in Braintree, was . . . scarcely good enough to match with the minister's daughter, descended from so many of the shining lights of the Colony."[1]

The Reverend Smith's cryptic message may have included his more personal reflections, which Charles Francis, in a typical Victorian manner, attributed to the community. For many reasons, the Reverend Smith and his wife, Elizabeth Quincy Smith, may have disapproved of the marriage of their middle daughter. Abigail was not yet twenty years old when she married, younger than average for the mid-eighteenth century,

Parts of this chapter appeared in Edith B. Gelles, *Portia: A Life of Abigail Adams* (Bloomington: Indiana University Press, 1992).

and she appears not to have had suitors previous to John Adams, whom she met when she was sixteen.[2] That Adams was a full ten years her senior might have weighed as an advantage, had he been other than a lawyer.[3] But Abigail's roots went deep into the colonial elite. Her mother's family were Quincys, Nortons, and Sheppards, "the solid bedrock of Massachusetts society."[4] The Smiths, while more recently arrived, represented the other respectable strain of New England society, the merchant class. By these standards, Adams's family were commoners.

Given either parental or social disapproval of the match, it is clear that Abigail Smith acted upon her own will when it came to marriage. She chose to marry John Adams because she loved him and because she believed that they were compatible in spirit, intelligence, values, and energy. During their more than three years of courtship, she had measured his character and tested her own intuition, as he had in return, and in the end Abigail believed that she could live her lifetime in this partnership from which there was no escape.

The Adams marriage has become legendary in American history. Just the mention of "Abigail and John" calls forth an image of an ideal marriage, one founded upon love, loyalty, friendship, and courage, which in many respects it was. However, as is often the case with ideals, reality was more complex and gives credibility to the reservations Reverend Smith had expressed. The Adamses lived together as a married couple for only ten years before the events of the rebellion against Great Britain took John away from home. Then, for a full quarter of a century, he served his nation at distant posts. Sometimes Abigail joined him— for four years of the more than ten that he lived in Europe and for a few of the years that he served as vice president and then president at the nation's capital. For much of their married life before John's defeat for the presidency in 1800, the Adamses lived apart from one another. This separation accounts, after all, for their vast correspondence from which generations of historians have constructed the story of their ideal marriage. The ideal, as read into the letters of Abigail and John, overlooks that the letters survive as a testimony to an ideal correspondence if not an ideal marriage.

The Adams marriage is mythologized for other reasons.[5] It appears modern; in fact, it possessed many of the attributes of modern marriage. It was a love match that endured. It produced at least one famous son and established a dynasty of great citizens. It overcame adversity intact. It was a match of equals; Abigail's intelligence, wit, wisdom, and

strength flourished alongside that of her husband, lending legitimacy to
the claim of woman's more equal status. Above all, the Adams marriage
is idealized because Abigail is visible, probably the most visible first lady
until the mid-twentieth century. That makes the Adams marriage appear
more modern than it was.[6]

In fact, recent scholarship in history and anthropology makes it clear
that all human institutions are functions of their culture, marriage as
much as any other, if not more.[7] Eighteenth-century New England was
no exception from the prevailing patriarchy of Western culture. The
Adams marriage was predicated upon its existence within this patriarchy. If Abigail chose to marry John, it was the most spectacular act of
will available to her for the remainder of her life.[8] Never again would
she make a decision of that magnitude to control the direction of her
life. There existed no easy-exit clause from her decision once her vows
were taken. She had little control over the kind of work she performed,
over her reproductive life, or probably over her sex life, although that
is not an area that can be discerned with the historian's skills.[9] Marriage
with its obligations became her destiny in that world that also prescribed
very clear separation of male and female spheres that, certainly, were
not equal but hierarchically organized. The lens through which Abigail
viewed her world revealed a divinely prescribed patriarchy in which it
was her destiny to live in the domestic sphere under the terms that John
Adams's work and choices about place, manner, and style governed.
Abigail accepted that world. "I believe nature has assigned to each sex
its particular duties and sphere of action," she once wrote, "and to act
well your part, 'there all the honor lies.' "[10]

At the same time, Abigail was neither slave nor servant, and she knew
that as well. She had leverage within the marriage bond, both because
of her character and John's and because the patriarchy that existed in
New England was flexible.[11] The physical magnetism that charged their
early companionship remained alive, mellowed into tender familiarity,
and endured as a deep loving commitment. Moreover, both of them
required intellectual parity in a mate, and Abigail's real education—her
own recollections to the contrary—began with marriage to John, with
access to his mind, his library, and his dependence upon dialogue with
her.[12] Rather than contracting under the weight of domestic drudgery,
the scope of her knowledge developed over her lifetime, so that she
became wise and erudite. Both the emotional and the intellectual aspects
of the Adamses' companionship overflowed from life into letters once
they were separated during the Revolutionary War.

In the best sense, then, the Adamses represented what historians call the "companionate marriage," meaning a love match in which there exists enduring friendship and respect.[13] It is for that reason that the Adams marriage is, in the long run, idealized. At its best it presents an ideal accommodation of woman to man in Western culture. We know this because they wrote all of this to each other, and we can read quite intimate letters that provide insights into their private lives. The reason is that Abigail, whose eighteenth-century companionate marriage in fact was one of deep friendship and commitment, actually did project her marriage into letters when John was away. The letters were her way of continuing the companionship she had with him when he was at home.

Abigail Smith had grown up in the parsonage at Weymouth as the second of three daughters. Mary, three years older, was her closest childhood friend, and one brother, William, born in 1746, separated them from the youngest sister, Elizabeth. Abigail described a pleasant childhood—"wild and giddy days"—that she recalled to her own granddaughter. Among her reminiscences, not many of which were recorded in letters, her greatest regret was lack of a formal education, not unusual for young women in pre-Revolutionary America. Abigail and her sisters were taught at home by their mother, whose own intelligence and taste was reflected in her daughters' upbringing. They learned to read, write, and cipher, and they studied rudimentary French literature, which was considered appropriate for young women of their station. They also were given free access to their father's library, which included popular eighteenth-century literature such as volumes of *Spectator.* Primarily, they learned to cook, sew, spin, nurse, and manage a household, for that would be their occupation. They did not consider their immersion in religion, both biblical and ritual, as education in the sense of its being a discipline or a belief system that could be mastered and possibly examined, questioned, or discarded. Religion informed their apprehension of the world they lived in; it was reality, as much as nature and human existence represented reality, and it existed prior to nature and human existence.

Abigail and John became acquainted as result of Mary's courtship with Richard Cranch, a good friend of John's, and characteristic of two exceptionally literate and verbal people, some of their courting took place in letters. At first playful and flirtatious, they used the metaphor of magnetism to describe the immediate dynamic between them. "Miss Adoreable," he addressed her, "By the same token that the bearer hereof

sat up with you last night I hereby order you to give him as many Kisses
and as many hours of your company after 9 O'clock as he shall please
to demand . . . I have good right to draw upon you for the kisses as I
have given two or three million at least when one has been received."[14]
Six months later, John wrote to apologize because weather had prevented his visit the previous day: "Cruel for detaining me from so much
friendly, social company, and perhaps blessed to you, or me, or both
for keeping me at my distance. For every experimental phylosopher
knows," he continued, "that the steel and the magnet and the glass and
the feather will not fly together with more celerity, than somebody and
somebody, when brought within striking distance" (vol. 1, 3, Feb. 14,
1763).

Over time, their exchanges became more tender: "There is a tye more
binding than Humanity and stronger than friendship, which makes us
anxious for the happiness and welfare of those to whom it binds us. It
makes their misfortunes, sorrows and afflictions our own. . . . By this
cord I am not ashamed to own myself bound, nor do I believe that you
are wholly free from it," wrote Abigail, signing herself "Diana" (6, Aug.
11, 1763).[15] He admitted, "Last night I dreamed I saw a lady . . . on the
Weymouth shores, spreading light and beauty and glory all round her.
At first I thought it was Aurora with her fair Complexion. . . . But soon
I found it was Diana, a lady infinitely dearer to me" (8, Aug. 1763). If
Abigail's parents objected to this match, they also recognized the deter-
mination of the young couple to marry.

After their marriage, Abigail and John moved to the Braintree house
that John had inherited from his father, there to begin a lifelong expe-
dition, they believed, along the same route of rural family life that both
of their parents had journeyed. For ten years Abigail and John's family
life did roughly follow a similar pattern, although in retrospect it is
possible to see in their frequent moves and separations—the twin origins
of later disruptions—the escalating pattern of the breach between the
American colonies and Great Britain and John Adams's restlessness,
born of his deep internal dissatisfaction with himself and his ambition
for action on a more global scene than local law and politics.[16]

"Your Diana become a Mamma—can you credit it?" wrote Abigail to
a friend in July 1765, still using her youthful pen name. "Indeed, it is a
sober truth. Bless'd with a charming Girl whose pretty Smiles already
delight my Heart, who is the Dear Image of her still Dearer Pappa" (51,
July 1765). Several months later, John Adams, after first berating himself

for neglecting to maintain his diary, recorded that "The Year 1765 has been the most remarkable Year of my Life," continuing then to account for his extravagant assertion: "That enormous Engine, fabricated by the British Parliament, for battering down all the Rights and Liberties of America, I mean the Stamp Act, has raised and spread thro the whole Continent, a Spirit that will be recorded to our Honour, with all future Generations. . . . Our Presses have groaned, our Pulpits have thundered, our Legislatures have resolved, our Towns have voted, The Crown Officers have every where trembled, and all their little Tools and Creatures, been afraid to Speak and ashamed to be seen."[17] So it was that each of the Adamses recorded the salient events that initiated the only uninterrupted decade of marriage that they would live in together until their old age.

On both fronts, at home and in the political arena, circumstances developed at a similar pace. Abigail gave birth five times in seven years. Her first child, a daughter also called Abigail, was born in 1765. John Quincy, named for his maternal grandfather who had just died, was born in July 1767, followed by Suzanna in 1769, who died after one year. Charles was born in 1770 and Thomas in 1772. Abigail did not become pregnant again until John visited briefly in 1777, and their infant daughter was stillborn. Her family of four children, one daughter and three sons who lived to become adults, was completed.

Meanwhile, Parliament repealed the Stamp Act in 1766. Abigail, who was "very ill of an hooping cough" was unable to attend the celebrations in Boston, where "Bells rung, Cannons were fired, Drums beaten"; the whole province, John exclaimed, "was in a Rapture for the Repeal of the Stamp Act."[18] John Quincy was born the year that Parliament passed the hated Townsend Acts that levied more taxes on the colonies, resulting in immediate acts of resistance. By the time Suzanna was born, the Townsend Acts had been repealed, except for one that was retained on tea.

The year 1770 marked a crescendo in both domestic and public affairs. The infant Suzanna died just months before Abigail gave birth to Charles. The Adamses, who had moved to Boston from Braintree two years previous, were forced to move to a new house on Cold Lane because of the sale of their rented house on Brattle Square. And it was the year of the Boston Massacre, when British soldiers fired into a mob, killing several patriots. This event, if it did not raise popular hostility to Great Britain to its highest pitch, marked a turning point in the career of John Adams by catapulting him into a wholly visible public role.

John recalled that his first consideration upon hearing news that evening of the "massacre" was for his wife, at home alone with servants.
She was "in circumstances and I was apprehensive of the effect of the
Surprise on her. . . . I went directly home to Cold Lane. My Wife having
heard that the Town was still and likely to continue so, had recovered
from her first Apprehensions, and We had nothing but our Reflections
to interrupt our Repose." He added: "These Reflections were to me,
disquieting enough."[19] In that momentous and terrifying evening, the
effects of the impending political rupture reverberated along many dimensions of their private lives, forecasting the intrusion of great public
affairs upon the privacy of their home life. It signified as well the inter-
woven texture of John and Abigail's marriage, his concern for her well-
being, and her sharing of his reflections.

The next day, John was asked to defend Captain Preston and the
British soldiers, a call that he accepted, because, "Council ought to be
the very last thing that an accused Person should want in a free Country."[20] After the three long trials in which John successfully defended
Preston and the British soldiers—"the most exhausting and fatiguing
Causes I ever tried," he recalled—he suffered from a physical and emotional collapse that resulted in the Adamses' return to Braintree.[21] For
Abigail, who preferred rural life to the city and whose health flourished
when she lived in the country, her "humble Cottage" represented freedom:

> Where Contemplation P[l]umes her rufled Wings
> And the free Soul look's down to pitty Kings.

She did choose an apt political metaphor to describe the pleasure that
she experienced at home in the country (76, Apr. 20, 1771).[22]

The Adamses returned to Boston after eighteen months in Braintree,
where Thomas had been born. In another few months, the crisis over
tea developed. "The tea that bainful weed is arrived," Abigail wrote to
her friend Mercy Otis Warren. "The flame is kindled and like Lightening
it catches from Soul to Soul. Great will be the devastation if not timely
quenched or allayed by some more Lenient Measures." Abigail understood the temper of Boston. To John it meant the disruption of his business, for in the wake of the Tea Party, Boston's courts were closed, and
he, who had risen to have "more Business at the Bar, than any Man in
the Province," had no business to conduct.[23] Clearly, it would be a matter of time. "Altho the mind is shocked at the Thought of sheding Hu-

mane Blood, more Especially the Blood of our countrymen, and a civil War is of all Wars, the most dreadfull," Abigail continued to Mercy, "Such is the present State that prevails, that if once they are made desperate Many, very Many of our Heroes will spend their lives in the cause, With the Speach of Cato in their Mouths, 'What a pitty it is, that we can dye but once to save our Country' " (88, Dec. 5, 1773).

In late 1773, Abigail's eldest child was eight, and her youngest just one year. She had moved from Braintree to Boston and back again, changing houses three times on her first sojourn and twice this time before John purchased a house on Brattle Square. She did not write frequently; she did not have the time. But when she did, her letters resonated with the impact of her reading and her conversation with John and their friends. Her world had not yet separated from his.

In fact, Abigail and John had experienced many short separations during this period, due to the structure of the legal system. Whether John maintained his primary offices at home in Braintree or in Boston, he needed to travel the court circuit to obtain a sufficient living. During the second half of 1767, for instance, he attended the Plymouth Inferior Court in July and the Suffolk Superior Court in August; in September he tried cases in Worcester and Bristol, in October in Plymouth, Bristol, and Cambridge, and in December at Barnstable and Plymouth. He traveled as far north as Maine and as far south as Martha's Vineyard. His journeys ranged in length from a few days to some weeks.[24]

During those periods Abigail remained at home or visited her parents in Weymouth, but she was always lonely. In late 1766, she had written to Mary, "He is such an itenerant . . . that I have but little of his company. He is now at Plymouth, and next week goes to Taunton" (56, Oct. 6, 1766). To John she wrote: "Sunday seems a more Lonesome Day to me than any other when you are absent" (62, Sept. 13, 1767). After eight years of marriage, she still wrote: "Alass! How many snow banks divide thee and me and my warmest wishes to see thee will not melt one of them. My daily thoughts and nightly Slumbers visit thee" (90, Dec. 30, 1773).

John's law practice thrived as he traveled the circuit; Abigail tended their home, and their children grew; and meanwhile the events that would lead to revolution escalated. "Such is the present Situation of affairs that I tremble when I think what may be the direfull concequences—and in this Town must the Scene of action lay," Abigail wrote to Mercy from Boston. "My Heart beats at every Whistle I hear, and I dare not openly express half my fears.—Eternal Reproach and Ignominy be the portion of all those who have been instrumental in bringing these fears upon me" (89, Dec. 5, 1763).

She expressed fear once more when John was elected by the Massachusetts General Court to be one of three representatives to the Continental Congress that gathered in Philadelphia in 1774, but she did not prevent him from going. "You cannot be, I know, nor do I wish to see you an Inactive Spectator, but if the sword be drawn, I bid adieu to all domestick felicity and look forward to that Country where there is neither wars nor rumors of War in a firm belief that thro the Mercy of its Kind we shall both rejoice there together" (172–73, Oct. 16, 1774). John departed on August 10 in the company of fellow delegates Samuel Adams, Thomas Cushing, and Robert Treat Paine. Five days later, Abigail wrote to him, and with that letter initiated the correspondence that would become a torrent in the years to follow. Inspired by loneliness, her writing became a substitute for speaking with him. She, of course, did not realize that war was imminent or that her separation from John would be so lengthy, any more than she understood the roles they would play in the course of the developing revolution. She only recognized that events impelled action and that John had been called to be an actor.

For some time both Abigail and John were sustained by the spirit of the growing rebellion. "There is in the Congress a collection of the greatest Men upon this continent," John wrote with enthusiasm from Philadelphia (150, Sept. 8, 1774). "I think I enjoy better Health than I have done these 2 years," Abigail responded from Braintree (151–54, Sept. 14–16, 1774). Time passed and John wrote: "The business of the Congress is tedious, beyond Expression. This assembly is like no other that ever existed. Every man in it is a great Man—an orator, a Critick, a statesman, and therefore every Man in every Question must show his oratory, his Criticism, and his political Abilities" (166, Oct. 9, 1774). At home Abigail became impatient: "I dare not express to you at 300 miles distance how ardently I long for your return. I have some very miserly Wishes; and cannot consent to your spending one hour in Town till at least I have had you 12. The idea plays about my Heart, unnerves my hand whilst I write, awakens all the tender sentiments that years have encreased and matured. . . . The whole collected stock of ten weeks absence knows not how to brook any longer restraint, but will break forth and flow thro my pen" (172, Oct. 16, 1774).[25] Separated for two months, the practice of expressing their private conversations on paper had begun. John wrote about what affected him most—frustration or boredom; Abigail wrote about her loneliness. Of course, they wrote much more, but their moods, as well as the cast of the future were partly expressed by these intimate confessions to each other.

John returned by the end of October, but the forces that led to Lexington were set on course. Abigail wrote to Mercy in January 1775, "Is it not better to die the last of British freemen than live the first of British slaves?" (183, Feb. 3, 1775). Mercy, who was mother to five grown sons, wrote: "Which of us should have the Courage of an Aria or a Portia in a Day of trial like theirs" (182, Jan. 28, 1775). She referred to Portia, wife of Brutus, the Roman statesman. Abigail found the image appealing.

By the end of April 1775, John Adams traveled to Philadelphia, but no longer to mediate. The Battle of Lexington had occurred; the Revolution had begun. John returned to wage war, and so ended the first decade of the Adamses' marriage. "What a scene has opened upon us," Abigail wrote Mercy. "Such a scene as we never before experienced, and could scarcely form an Idea of. If we look back we are amazed at what is past, if we look forward we must shudder at the view. Our only comfort lies in the justice of our cause." She signed herself Portia (190, May 2, 1775; 193, May 4, 1775).

One historian of marriage points out that social groups tend to legitimate their practices by considering them "natural."[26] Abigail Adams entered into marriage with many expectations that she considered structurally "normal," only to discover the corruption of her expectations over time both because of the—to her—unanticipated transformations caused by war, as well as the shift of her husband's career. Ideologically, Abigail described her accommodation to circumstances as a patriotic sacrifice. "'Tis almost 14 years since we were united, but not more than half that time have we had the happiness of living together," she complained in the summer of 1777. "The unfealing world may consider it in what light they please, I consider it as a sacrifice to my Country and one of my greatest misfortunes" (AFC, vol. 2, 301, Aug. 5, 1777). As a practical consideration, she began to replace John's presence by writing him letters that substituted for their conversations. This is illustrated by two episodes that developed during the early years of the Revolutionary War.

In the fall of 1775, soon after John's departure to serve as one of the three Massachusetts delegates to the Continental Congress in Philadelphia, an epidemic of dysentery swept through the Boston area. Abigail's entire household, herself included, was afflicted. Despite the weakening

effects of her own illness, Abigail, assisted by her mother, functioned as
the primary nurse and physician in the hospital that her household became. In that time of widespread sickness, when no outside help was
available and her own servants were sick and dying of the disease, the
major responsibility fell to Abigail.

"Since you left me I have passed thro great distress both Body and
mind," she wrote to John in early September, indicating that her hardships were emotional as well as physical. Isaac, her servant boy had been
taken with a "voilent [sic] Dysentery" and "there was no resting place
in the House for his terible Groans." Abigail's descriptions to John
would invoke sound and odor as well as image. After a week, Isaac
recovered, but "two days after he was sick, I was seaz'd with the same
disorder in a voilent [sic] manner." Abigail recovered, but next her servant Susy was ill. "Our Little Tommy was the next, and he lies very ill
now. . . . I hope he is not dangerous. Yesterday Patty (a servant girl) was
seazd. . . . Our House is an hospital in every part and what with my
own weakness and distress of mind for my family I have been unhappy
enough" (vol. 1, 276, Sept. 8, 1775). Abigail wrote not just to keep John
informed of conditions at home but to dispel her feelings.

One week later she described her mounting misery: "I set myself
down to write with a Heart depressed with the Melancholy Scenes ar-
round me . . . we live in daily Expectation that Patty will not continue
many hours. A general putrefaction seems to have taken place, and we
can not bear the House only as we are constantly clensing it with hot
vinegar." Abigail continued to cite the number of deaths among her
neighbors and friends (vol. 1, 278–79, Sept. 17, 1775).[27] Another week
passed, and she wrote, "I set down with a heavy Heart to write to you.
I have had no other since you left me. Woe follows Woe and one affliction treads upon the heal of an other" (284, Sept. 25, 1775).

One week later, grief overflowed into her letter to John: "Have pitty
upon me, have pitty upon me o! thou my beloved for the hand of God
presseth me soar," she pleaded. Her mother had died. "How can I tell
you (o my bursting Heart) that my Dear Mother has Left me, this day
about 5 'clock she left this world for an infinitely better." Abigail wrote
this grief as she would have spoken it: "At times I almost am ready to
faint under this sever and heavy Stroke, seperated from *thee* who used
to be a comfortar towards me in affliction" (288, Oct. 1, 1775). Her
grief was compounded, Abigail informed John. She grieved for her
mother but also for her separation from John whose role it had been to
comfort her. She did not reprimand him, but rather she emphasized the

unnatural condition of their separation; he was supposed to be with her during this crisis. Her writing had become the substitute for his presence. She comforted herself by this means.

Another week passed, and Patty still lingered, "the most shocking object my Eyes ever beheld, and so loathsome that it was with the utmost difficulty we could bear the House . . . a most pityable object." Then Patty died, and the epidemic had run its course (296, Oct. 9, 1775).

Throughout this time, while she wrote about her woes, Abigail worried as well about the effect of her letters on John. "I know I wound your heart," she wrote. "Ought I give relief to my own by paining yours?" (310, Sept. 22, 1775). Another time she wrote, "Forgive me, then, for thus dwelling upon a subject . . . I fear painful. O how I have long'd for your Bosom to pour forth my sorrows there, and find a healing Balm" (296, Oct. 9, 1775). With these words she described her continued expectations of the relationship between a wife and husband, to describe what their relationship had been when they were together.

John's responses were as consistent as they were immediate. "I feel—I tremble for you," he admitted when her troubles began. "Surely if I were with you, it would be my Study to allay your griefs, to mitigate your Pains and to divert your melancholly thoughts" (303, Oct. 19, 1775). Later he wrote to relieve her concern about troubling him: "If I could write as well as you, my sorrows would be as eloquent as yours. but upon my Word I cannot" (312, Oct. 23, 1775). John consoled Abigail, but also by letter—he did not return. If there was an undercurrent of requesting his presence in her letters, if John felt great tension between his country and his family, his greater loyalty was expressed by his behavior. He wrote comforting letters to her from Philadelphia.

A different episode developed less than two years later. John finally had returned from Philadelphia for a visit in the winter of 1776, and Abigail became pregnant. They knew about the pregnancy before John's return to Congress, and he wrote shortly after his departure: "I am anxious to hear how you do. I have in my Mind a Source of Anxiety, which I never had before." Because of eighteenth-century reticence about pregnancy and also because mail was often intercepted by the British, John continued cryptically: "You know what it is. Cant you convey to me, in Hieroplyphicks, which no other Person can comprehend, Information which will relieve me. Tell me you are as well as can be expected," he wrote, demanding good news as a means of relieving his conscience for leaving her (vol. 2, 159, Feb. 10, 1777).

"I had it in my heart to disswade him from going and I know I could

have prevaild," Abigail admitted to Mercy Otis Warren, "but our pub-
lick affairs at that time wore so gloomy an aspect that I thought if ever
his assistance was wanted it must be at such a time. I therefore resignd
my self to suffer much anxiety and many Melancholy hours for this year
to come" (150, Jan. 1777). Abigail had not abandoned her expectations
for marriage, but she certainly had suspended them. To Mercy she cited
patriotism, probably even as she rationalized John's departure to herself.
Once more she used reason to suppress her desire to dissuade John from
leaving her. Partly that reason may have incorporated her understanding
of John's now driven need to participate, which was reshaped in her
own mind to a vision of patriotic service by her uniquely qualified husband. Her representations included as well a transformation of a spiritual into a secular calling, and she resigned herself to carrying on her
marriage in letters.

Using "hieroplyphicks," she wrote to John in March, "I think upon
the whole I have enjoyed as much Health as I ever did in the like situation—a situation I do not repine at, tis a constant remembrancer of an
absent Friend, and excites sensations of tenderness which are better felt
than expressd" (173, Mar. 9, 1777). Writing in code, Abigail expressed
the intimacy that pregnancy represented to her, a different dimension of
the "companionate marriage" in which children were the consequence
of a loving relationship rather than the purpose of marriage.[28]

One month later, Abigail wrote in a different vein as a friend of hers
had died in childbirth: "Everything of this kind naturally shocks a person in similar circumstances," she admitted. "How great the mind that
can overcome the fear of Death!" (212, May 17, 1777).[29] Eighteenth-
century women were vividly aware of the risks of childbirth under normal circumstances. During a war, the fears multiplied. By May she was
reporting, "I cannot say that I am so well as I have been" (232, May 6,
1777).[30] And within weeks she wrote explicitly about fear. Troops were
passing her house day and night, and she believed more fighting might
take place. "I should not dare to tarry here in my present situation, nor
yet know where to flee for safety," she wrote John with mounting concern over the rumors she was hearing: "The recital of the inhumane and
Brutal Treatment of those poor creatures who have fallen into their
Hands Freazes me with Horrour. My apprehensions are greatly in-
creasd; should they come this way again I know not what course I should
take" (241, May 18, 1777). Pregnancy had weakened Abigail's resolve,
made her vulnerable, indecisive, and afraid. Soon her fear turned to
anger.

She complained: "I loose my rest a nights . . . I look forward to the midle of july with more anxiety than I can describe." Rising to an emotional crescendo, she exclaimed, "I am cut of from the privilidge which some of the Brute creation enjoy, that of having their mate sit by them with anxious care during all the Solitary confinement" (250, June 1, 1777). In late-eighteenth-century terms, hers was a bold wifely indictment, perhaps a transference into letters of a confrontation that could have occurred between them. Or perhaps, the letter form allowed her more distance to complain, to express her autonomous feelings of indignation at a world that was violating her expectations—a world that appeared brutal and uncivilized to her.

Further signs of physical complications developed on the eve of childbirth: "I sit down to write you this post, and from my present feelings tis the last I shall be able to write for some time if I should do well," she wrote mildly, this time understating her anxiety. "I was last night taken with a shaking fit, and am very apprehensive that a life was lost. As I have no reason to day to think otherways; what may be the consequences to me, Heaven only knows" (277, July 9, 1777).

Abigail did not describe her household during this crisis. It is not clear which children were present, whether her sisters were with her, or even a midwife. Her entire concentration in her letters of this period was upon John, upon telling him what was happening to her, of recording the events and her feelings. She brought him into her chamber during childbirth by writing her ordeal, and she closed out the rest of the world.

"I received a Letter from my Friend," she wrote, "begining in his manner 'my dearest Friend.' That one single expression dwelt upon my mind and playd about my Heart." This time she allowed both her mind and her heart to experience her affections. "It was because my heart was softened and my mind enervated by my sufferings, and I wanted the personal and tender soothings of my dearest Friend," she wrote explicitly. Then she shifted to her topic: "Tis now 48 Hours since I can say I really enjoyed any Ease . . . Slow, lingering and troublesome is the present situation." She was in labor. "The Dr. encourages me to Hope that my apprehensions are groundless . . . tho I cannot say I have had any reason to allter my mind . . . I pray Heaven that it may be soon or it seems to me I shall be worn out." By "it" she meant the birth of her child. Then she wrote the most astonishing statement: "I must lay my pen down this moment, to bear what I cannot fly from—and now I have endured it I reassume my pen." Abigail wrote to John through her labor (278–79, July 10, 1777).

The child, a girl, was stillborn, but Abigail survived the birth. Within a week she was writing to John: "Join with me my dearest Friend in Gratitude to Heaven, that a life I know you value, has been spaired . . . although the dear Infant is numberd with its ancestors" (282, July 16, 1777). Abigail revived physically and in spirit, and her life continued. As in the earlier episode of the dysentery epidemic, Abigail had written to John during her pregnancy and childbirth in order to re-create in her fantasy the conditions of marriage that fulfilled her expectations for wife and husband. During the time that she wrote she was able to retreat from the reality of their interrupted companionship and sense that they were together.

Because of these experiences, and others, Abigail learned about letter writing as a means of dispelling her emotions, and in time her writing became abstracted from John, serving its own end. She began to write with the intensity of one who enjoyed the process itself. She discovered that writing allowed her the satisfactions of re-creating her world in letters as well as the therapy that came from this method of confession. Abigail also began to redefine her vision of her marriage from that of normal companionship to separate living. She accepted John's participation as their patriotic sacrifice in wartime and further justified his repeated choice to serve as mandated by conditions that required his unique genius.

In 1777 the Revolutionary War was not yet at mid-point, nor had John departed yet for Europe, and while a few of her worst experiences had passed, many were yet to come. In time circumstances like the dysentery epidemic and pregnancy compounded her self-confidence, and she began to trust her ability to function alone. She even learned how to survive economically as the major source of support for her household during wartime. However, her experience and accomplishments to the contrary, she never considered herself an independent unit, but always as the subordinate partner in marriage. To do otherwise would deviate from the socially prescribed form of marriage in the late eighteenth century. Abigail never considered such an option.

NOTES

1. Charles Francis Adams, ed., *Letters of Mrs. Adams, The Wife of John Adams, with an Introductory Memoir by her Grandson, Charles Francis Adams* (Boston: C. C. Little and J. Brown, 1840), xxxii–xxxiii.

2. Historians have variously calculated the average age at marriage for

women in mid-eighteenth-century America as between twenty-one and twenty-three; see Philip J. Greven Jr., *Four Generations: Population, Land and Family in Colonial Andover, Massachusetts* (Ithaca, N.Y.: Cornell University Press, 1970), 208–9; James A. Henretta, *The Evolution of American Society, 1700–1815* (Lexington, Mass.: Heath, 1973), 12; Daniel Scott Smith, "Parental Control and Marriage Patterns: An Analysis of Historical Trends in Hingham, Massachusetts," in *The American Family in Social-Historical Perspective,* ed. Michael Gordon, 2d ed. (New York: St. Martin's Press, 1978), 95–96.

3. For the emergence of the legal profession, see Richard D. Brown, *Knowledge Is Power: The Diffusion of Information in Early America, 1700–1765* (New York: Oxford University Press, 1989), 82–84; Gerard W. Gawalt, *The Promise of Power: The Emergence of the Legal Profession in Massachusetts, 1760–1840* (Westport, Conn.: Greenwood Press, 1979); and John M. Murrin, "The Legal Transformation: The Bench and Bar of Eighteenth-Century Massachusetts," in *Colonial America: Essays in Politics and Social Development,* ed. Stanley N. Katz and John M. Murrin, 3d ed. (New York: Knopf, 1983), 540–72.

4. Adams, *Letters,* xxxii–xxxiii.

5. Myths stabilize and integrate social organizations. They express or codify beliefs. They resolve contradictions, even prophesy. See Clifford Geertz, *Myth, Symbol, and Culture* (New York: W. W. Norton, 1971); Peter Novick, *That Noble Dream* (Cambridge: Cambridge University Press, 1988), 4–5.

6. For changing marriage patterns, see Alan Macfarlane, *Marriage and Love in England 1300–1840* (New York: B. Blackwell, 1986); Lawrence Stone, *The Family, Sex and Marriage in England 1500–1800* (New York: Harper & Row, 1977).

7. For cultural relativity, see Michel Foucault, *History of Sexuality,* 3 vols. (New York: Pantheon Books, 1978–1986); Clifford Geertz, *The Interpretation of Cultures* (New York: Basic Books, 1973); Richard Handler, "Boasian Anthropology and the Critique of American Culture," *American Quarterly* 42 (1990): 252–73.

8. Macfarlane makes this point. *Marriage,* 35–41.

9. For general remarks about sexuality in eighteenth-century New England, see John D'Emilio and Estelle B. Freedman, *Intimate Matters: A History of Sexuality in America* (New York: Harper & Row, 1988), 39–54.

10. Letter to Francis Vanderkemp, Feb. 3, 1814, cited in Adams, *Letters* (Boston: Wilkins, Carter, 1848), 416.

11. See John Demos, *A Little Commonwealth: Family Life in Plymouth Colony* (New York: Oxford University Press, 1970); Greven, *Four Generations;* Edmund S. Morgan, *The Puritan Family: Essays on Religion and Domestic Relations in Seventeenth-Century New England* (New York: Harper & Row, 1966); Laurel Thatcher Ulrich, *Good Wives: Image and Reality in the Lives of Women in Northern New England, 1650–1750* (Oxford: 1983).

12. As an older woman, Abigail attributed her early education to her brother-in-law Richard Cranch, claiming that he first introduced the Smith sisters to literature. Library of Congress, *Papers of the Shaw Family* (L.C.), microfilm version, 4 Reels, AA-Elizabeth Shaw, Reel 1, Feb. 28, 1811. (Hereafter cited

as Shaw.) In 1811, Abigail reminisced to her sister Elizabeth that their brother-in-law Richard Cranch, who was then dying, had first introduced them to literature. It is, furthermore, clear that after her marriage to John Adams, Abigail read books in her husband's vast library: literature, religion, philosophy, science, and more.

During John Adams's long periods of absence, Abigail took charge of her children's education, reading history with John Quincy and Latin with her daughter. *Adams Family Correspondence I*, March 16, 1776; AFC IV, Feb. 3, 1781-.

13. The definition of the companionate marriage is, in fact, more complex. It may involve: choice of mate; the centrality of a couple in family life; the separation of household from either family of origin; the focus on children as economical drain on family resources rather than contributors; focus on family rather than lineage; equation of love, sex, and reproduction; monogamy and, until recently, durability. See Macfarlane, *Marriage*, 154–58, 174–90, and Stone, *Family*, 378–90.

14. L. H. Butterfield et al., eds., *The Adams Family Correspondence*, 6 vols., vol. 1, *December 1761–May 1776* (Cambridge: Belknap Press of Harvard University Press, 1963–1993), p. 2, entry Oct. 4, 1762. Hereafter cited in parentheses in the text.

15. Historians, philosophers, psychologists, theologians, and lovers attempt to define love; in this passage Abigail has done well. Following the convention for young women to use pen names in their correspondence, Abigail, until after her marriage, signed herself Diana.

16. For John Adams, see John Ferling, *The Atlas of Independence* (forthcoming); Peter Shaw, *The Character of John Adams* (Chapel Hill: University of North Carolina Press, 1976).

17. L. H. Butterfield et al., eds., *Diary and Autobiography of John Adams*, 4 vols., vol. 1, *Diary, 1755–1770* (Cambridge: 1961), 263, entry Dec. 18, 1765. Hereafter cited as DA.

18. Ibid., 312, May 26, 1766.

19. L. H. Butterfield et al., eds. *Diary and Autobiography of John Adams*, 4 vols., vol. 3 (Cambridge: Harvard University Press, 1991), 291.

20. Ibid., vol. 3, 291–93. (References to the autobiography are not dated as are diary references.)

21. For John's "collapse," see John Ferling, *John Adams: A Life* (Knoxville: University of Tennessee Press, 1992), 71; Shaw, *Character*, 64–65.

22. The source of the quotation is not identified.

23. DA, vol. 1, 294. For events leading to the Revolution, see Edmund S. Morgan, *The Birth of the Republic, 1763–1789* (Chicago: University of Chicago Press, 1956).

24. DA, vol. 1, 338, n. 1.

25. The Battle of Lexington was the opening skirmish of the Revolutionary War. See Morgan, *Birth*, 1–3.

26. Macfarlane, *Marriage*, 35–40.

27. She also notes that she had sent Charles and Nabby to stay with relatives.

28. Macfarlane, *Marriage*, 148.

29. For childbirth, see Catherine M. Scholten, *Childbearing in American Society: 1650–1850* (New York: New York University Press, 1985), chap. 1; Laurel Thatcher Ulrich, *A Midwife's Tale: The Life of Martha Ballard, Based on Her Diary, 1785–1812* (New York: Knopf, 1990).

30. During the spring of 1777, there were rumors in New England of an invasion by Admiral Howe. Howe, commander of the British Royal Navy, "played cat and mouse," with George Washington. His position was ambiguous for several months and during that time rumors circulated that his fleet would attack in New England. In the end, Howe's ships landed in New York. Don Higginbotham, *The War of American Independence* (New York: Macmillan, 1971), 182–83.

CHAPTER 3

"The Thing Bartered"

Love, Economics, and the Victorian Couple

Kate Washington

For one [prostitute] who . . . sells herself to a lover, ten sell
themselves to a husband. . . . The barter is as naked and
as cold in the one case as in the other; the thing bartered is
the same; the difference between the two transactions lies
in the price that is paid down.

—W. R. Greg

W. R. Greg's article "Prostitution," published in the *Westminster Review* in 1850, draws an explicit parallel between prostitutes and women who marry for money, using the terminology of economics to compare marriage to prostitution. Greg urges his middle-class British readers not to be "shocked by the juxtaposition," and in so doing tacitly acknowledges the incongruity of an association between marriage and prostitution. Arguably, Greg compares the most hallowed institution of the Victorian age with the most reviled. The purpose of this essay is to explore the significance within Victorian British culture of the analogy that Greg draws and so to examine the crucial and controversial intersection of love and economics in the cultural construction of marriage among the Victorian middle class.

This comparison of prostitution to marriage would undoubtedly have been edited out of most British periodicals in 1850. Indeed, although rescue homes and reformist (usually evangelical) tracts about prostitution were becoming increasingly common in the 1840s, references to prostitution per se were rare in British periodicals before the 1860s.[1] In that decade, however, the control of prostitution, which came to be known as "the great social evil," became something of a cause célèbre, as Parliament, the British medical community, and the nascent feminist movement engaged in a public controversy surrounding the passage and eventual repeal of the Contagious Diseases Acts in the 1860s.[2] The question of what to do about prostitution interested a vast cross-section of Victorians, from evangelical reformers to liberal doctors to radical journalists, and not surprisingly, there was little accord among these groups about the best legal and social measures to combat what was referred to as "magdalenism." There were, however, two constants in the anti-prostitution literature: The majority of the reform-minded Victorian middle class seems to have agreed that prostitution was a major social problem that threatened to infect the nation, both morally and physically, and for the most part, they agreed that prostitution was an illicit sale of sexual services by women. Although this definition may seem to be self-evident, nearly all Victorian tracts on prostitution included some version of it. Indeed, the question of defining prostitution became a matter of some legal urgency in the 1860s, when parliamentary debate over the framing of the Contagious Diseases Acts focused in part on the question of the legal definition of a "common prostitute."[3]

Some hard-line religious reformers contended that any woman who had sex outside of wedlock was a prostitute, but most discussions of prostitution centered on the crucial exchange of money for sex. For instance, Ralph Wardlaw, an evangelical minister whose *Lectures on Magdalenism* were published in 1843, writes that "A *harlot* is generally understood of one who makes her livelihood by whoredom. . . . Among the varieties there are, first of all, your kept mistresses;—and these are of very various grades, from the first-rate style of keeping down to the lowest."[4] Wardlaw, then, draws no essential distinction between street prostitutes and kept mistresses, and neither does Greg, who argues that the most morally objectionable cases of prostitution are those in which the women "deliberately sell themselves to shame, and barter, in a cold spirit of bargain, chastity and reputation for carriages, jewels, and a luxurious table."[5] As we have seen, Greg goes on to compare these prostitutes directly to women who marry for money. William Acton, the medical reformer whose 1857 tract *Prostitution Considered in Its Moral, Social, and Sanitary Aspects* was a crucial catalyst for the passage of the Contagious Diseases Acts, argues "that the fact of 'hiring,' whether openly or secretly, whether by an individual or a plurality in succession, constitutes prostitution."[6] For all of these major Victorian

writers on prostitution (and for many others as well), the crucial factor in defining prostitution was "hiring"—the exchange of money for
women's sexual services.

Just as Greg took this definition one step further and included certain
wives in his criticisms of women who used their sexuality for monetary
gain, many Victorian social critics saw marriage and prostitution as similar because of their traditionally parallel economic underpinnings: Each
institution was characterized by an exchange of the man's money or
financial support for the woman's body or sexual availability. Before the
Victorian period, Mary Wollstonecraft had expressed much the same
view Greg was later to adopt. In the 1830s, Harriet Taylor (the future
wife of John Stuart Mill) criticized the social roles of women: "Women
are educated for one single object, to gain their living by marrying—
(some poor souls get it without the churchgoing in the same way—they
do not seem to me a bit worse than their honoured sisters). . . . One
observes very few marriages where there is any real sympathy or enjoy-
ment of companionship between the parties. . . . [Women's] minds are
degenerated by habits of dependance [sic]."[7] Taylor implicitly connects
the lack of "sympathy" between married partners with the dependency
to which women were consigned by their lack of education and opportunities, and their consequent need to sell themselves, within the confines
of marriage or, as she says, "without the churchgoing," to gain financial
security.

Even if it was primarily radical thinkers or reformers like Greg who
were willing to state flatly that Victorian marriage was all too often a
form of prostitution, some canonical Victorian novelists criticized mercenary marriages by drawing direct comparisons between such marriages and prostitution: For instance, Dickens's *Dombey and Son* (1846)
and Charlotte Brontë's *Jane Eyre* (1847) both use allusions to prostitution and references to the economic exchange of sexuality to construct
a sharp critique of Victorian marriage as it was frequently practiced. In
the 1860s and 1870s, legal reforms of marriage led to an explosion of
writing on marriage in the Victorian periodical press. These articles
range from learned legal treatises to frothy humor pieces, but they nearly
all exhibit uneasiness about the economics of marriage.

Despite this obvious anxiety over the nature and purpose of marriage,
contemporary images of the Victorian age have frequently assumed that
at the time romantic love was unproblematically ascendant: After all, it
was the age of the sentimental valentine, of "the angel in the house,"

and of innumerable novels ending in a loving marriage. Yet these man-
ifestations of a culture obsessed with love and marriage were reflective
of complex social attitudes that were shifting to produce a new form of
couplehood; such representations showed an ideal that the culture aspired to, rather than a mirror image of the culture as it was. Examining
a range of representations of Victorian couples and couplehood makes
clear that marriage was at the center of the Victorians' conception of
their own culture, but such an investigation also reveals that the Victorians were not always happy with the ways in which marriage was
practiced. During the Victorian period, the middle classes in particular
were sorting out, often contentiously, what it meant to be a part of a
married couple. Was marriage a social contract, an economic partnership, a personal relationship founded on love, a religious sacrament, or
some combination of all four?

It is no wonder that the system of marriage in Victorian Britain often
seems to have been at odds with itself in all its legal, social, economic,
and ideological complexity. On the one hand, the Victorian period was
a time of great sentimentality about the romantic and companionate
nature of marriage and the family; on the other hand, marriage was an
economic and social contract that was often seen as a crucial building
block of the Victorian polity. Mary Poovey's *Uneven Developments*
demonstrates how these two apparently disparate ideological functions
of marriage were actually inextricably linked; she contends that "the
idealized image of domestic woman . . . constituted the basis both for
the oppositional economy that seemed to (but did not) rest on a binary
opposition and for the fundamental model of male identity in a capitalist
society. . . . [T]his image of woman was also critical to the image of the
English national character."[8] Thus domestic happiness (presumably
founded on conjugal love) and capitalist society (founded on male enterprise and economic power, and a socioeconomically sound marriage)
buttress each other. Although Poovey's arguments about the varying and
interlocking functions of marriage are convincing, I also believe that
many Victorians experienced these different ideals of marriage, which
we might term the "romantic" and the "socioeconomic" views, not as
complementary elements in a larger system but as radically and even
necessarily opposed tensions that were harmful not only to the system
of marriage in the abstract but also to married individuals, women especially. Charlotte Brontë, for instance, saw the "socioeconomic" or
contractual side of marriage as interfering with and damaging to the

concept, which she endorsed, of marriage as a romantic union of two essentially equal persons, and this opposition between two conceptions of marriage becomes a driving force behind the plot of *Jane Eyre*.

The economic and contractual character of marriage, however, reflected the legal and the social development of the institution up to Victorian times. The question of when companionate marriage emerged as the norm for British families has been the subject of critical debate; although several influential scholars have placed this development in the eighteenth century, their views have been persuasively challenged. Susan M. Okin demonstrates that changes in women's property law in the seventeenth century (e.g., provisions for the establishment of trusts under equity for married women), which scholars have taken as evidence of changing attitudes toward women and ownership, stem instead from an increase in movable property (known as personalty) in relation to real estate, and the desire of landed or wealthy families to consolidate their wealth through female lines, rather than from changed views of the rights of women to hold property. That the practice of establishing trusts under equity survived may perhaps be attributable to the desire of families to protect their daughters from unreliable or dishonest husbands rather than a desire for egalitarian marriages.

Mary Lyndon Shanley's study *Feminism, Marriage, and the Law in Victorian England, 1850–1895* also challenges, though on different grounds, the view that companionate marriages had become the norm in less sentimentalized views of society. She discusses the attitude of Victorian feminist reformers at midcentury:

> When Victorian feminists began their crusade to change the laws regulating marriage, they explicitly and forcefully challenged what they regarded as society's sentimentalization of family life. They would have looked askance at the interpretations of many modern historians that "companionate marriage"—characterized by "affective individualism, " "romantic love," and "a conscious ideological egalitarianism"—was the norm in both England and the United States by the mid-nineteenth century.[9]

It seems clear that although there was some ideological movement toward companionate marriages before midcentury in Britain, there was still also significant pressure to make "good" matches based on socioeconomic factors, particularly in the upper bourgeois and aristocratic classes, well into (and in many cases, particularly the very upper strata, beyond) the nineteenth century.

British law and legal opinion governing marriage further indicated the contractual and economic nature of this Victorian institution. Carole

Pateman provides a useful description of the sort of contract that underwrote Victorian marriage in *The Sexual Contract:* "The story of the sexual contract tells how contract is the medium through which patriarchal right is created and upheld. For marriage to become merely a contract of sexual use—or, more accurately, for sexual relations to take the form of universal prostitution—would mark the political defeat of women *as women.*"[10] Victorian legal commentator James Hammick, who in 1873 published what he called a "practical guide" to Victorian marriage, unwittingly prefigures Pateman's point that marriage is a contract that helps to establish certain (patriarchal) systems of rights and privileges, though Hammick concentrates on property and also adds a new element to the definition: "From its consequences as regards property and the rights of husbands and wives, children, &c., matrimony may be correctly designated a civil contract; but as an institution deriving its origin from God, and not from any human legislation, it must also be deemed a divine or religious contract."[11] In Hammick's discussion, love is not mentioned as a primary or even as a secondary foundation for marriage. Although Hammick mentions the "conjugal" and consensual nature of the contract at other points in his discussion, he sums up the nature of marriage as being first "a civil contract" (because of its consequences for property and rights) and second as a "divine or religious contract." This discussion was based on English law in 1873, which, apart from the possibilities of divorce raised by the Matrimonial Causes Act of 1857, had not changed substantively since the middle of the eighteenth century (see Hammick 15–20), when Lord Hardwicke's Act (1753) "enacted that thenceforward all marriages should be celebrated in a church and by banns or licence."[12]

English marriage law has a rather convoluted history and derives from both earlier English common law and Catholic canonical law. To complicate the matter further, various parts of Great Britain had different marriage laws for much of the Victorian period. For instance, the substance of Lord Hardwicke's Act contrasted sharply with Scottish law, which derived from medieval canonical law and under which either an unwitnessed verbal exchange of vows or a promise of marriage followed by consummation constituted a valid and legally binding marriage contract. Furthermore, even "regular" Scottish marriages—that is, those celebrated by a clergyman and witnessed—did not have to be performed in a church, and the religion of the participants did not matter. This requirement in its turn stood in contrast to Irish law, under which only parties of the same religion could be married.[13]

The discrepancies among these laws came under fire in the 1860s because of their diverse effects on property and inheritance rights. The public debate about the rationalization of the marriage laws across Great Britain and in parts of the empire was prompted by the Yelverton case, which turned on the differing religions of the parties in an invalidated Irish marriage; the debate demonstrates that during the Victorian period marriage was regarded in law as a social and economic contract that underlay the system of property—and, by extension, the social order. W. Harris Faloon, for instance, claimed: "Marriage is a contract of natural law,—the parent, not the child of civil society" (Faloon 436).

Faloon's article "The Marriage Laws of the Three Kingdoms" appeared in the *Cornhill Magazine* in 1867 and was one of a rash of essays on marriage laws that appeared in the 1860s. Although they had as their primary purpose the discussion of the discrepancy in marriage laws between different parts of Great Britain, to my mind the essays are most interesting for their assumptions about the social and economic importance of marriage. William O'Connor Morris, an Irish judge writing in the *British Quarterly Review,* for instance, called marriage "the most important of social engagements" and, in arguing for rationalizing and simplifying the laws governing marriage, contended that "it is obvious how necessary it is to fix and preserve the evidence of a tie which determines numberless present rights, the prospects and fortunes of future generations, and the devolution and transmission of property in almost every civilized community" (Morris 124, 127). The *Westminster Review,* in a similar vein but with a less overt focus on the socioeconomic elements of marriage, asserted: "The institution of marriage has an influence so obvious, direct, and important upon the welfare and happiness of mankind, whether as individual personas or as collected into communities, that it is right and politic that society should establish certain constituted modes of entering into and retiring from the engagements which it implies."[14] Despite Hammick's concession that marriage is a contract ordained by God, none of these articles discuss the religious or sacramental nature of marriage. Instead, these writers consider it a purely social and economic relationship (though some touch upon its "devolution" from the status of sacrament to that of a "purely civil" relationship), which is particularly striking in that all the articles cite the derivation of marriage law from religious laws of the medieval period.

The position of women within marriage was also becoming a point of public debate in the 1860s. Married women could not own property, and the legal principle of coverture provided that man and wife were legally one person before the law and that the husband was the legal representative of this person.[15] Because this legal fiction made wives non-persons politically and economically, their dependence on their husbands' goodwill for their own economic and personal well-being became a major flashpoint of protofeminist anger and organization in the 1850s. The well-known case of Caroline Norton, who was denied access to her children and to her earnings as a writer by her estranged husband, highlights this inequity in the law.[16]

Charlotte Brontë's depiction of the economics surrounding marriage in *Jane Eyre* is particularly revealing about how a self-aware (but not necessarily politicized) Victorian woman might have viewed the traps awaiting her when she attempted to become part of a couple as an independent partner. Feminist literary criticism of *Jane Eyre* has frequently focused on Jane's anger and her attempts to gain emotional or psychological independence; it has too often overlooked how important her quest for economic independence is and how deeply her economic status affects her. For most of the novel, Brontë presents marriage as a relationship built on the dependence of women by playing on the various meanings of the word "mistress," with its connotations of both licit and illicit sexual partnerships. The tale of Jane's entrance into Rochester's house as a governess, the planned marriage that goes awry when Rochester is shown to be married already, and their eventual reunion is well known. Although Rochester's revelations of his sordid past life (which included a collection of continental mistresses) are perhaps less well remembered, Jane is more than once compared, and compares herself, to the European women who were formerly Rochester's kept mistresses. Even when planning the wedding and fantasizing about the marriage, Jane worries about the possibility that she will be like them—economically dependent on Rochester, exchanging her sexual availability for Rochester's financial support—and that others (including Rochester himself) will conclude that she has married for money, sold herself to become Rochester's mistress.

The conviction that financial independence is an important marker of women's personal and subjective autonomy is evident when Rochester takes Jane shopping for wedding clothes before the failed wedding. Jane is disturbed both by Rochester's choices of clothes for her (she sees his choices as gaudy) and by his proprietary attitude toward her: "With anxiety I watched his eye rove over the gay stores: he fixed on a rich silk of the most brilliant amethyst dye, and a superb pink satin. I told him . . . that he might as well buy me a gold gown and a silver bonnet at once: I should certainly never venture to wear his choice."[17] Jane's refusal of fine new clothes is particularly significant in that "fancy dress" was one of the primary social markers of the Victorian prostitute, as Mariana Valverde demonstrates, contending that "medical and political discourses . . . constructed the love of finery as a chief cause of women's descent into prostitution."[18] What constituted "finery" was class-determined, in that the term denoted clothing that was inappropriate to a woman's class or station in life: "Finery in [the] pejorative sense meant clothes that were too showy . . . what was or was not finery depended on the socioeconomic and moral status of the wearer" (Valverde 170–71). Jane's fear of being brightly dressed, then, stems from the contrast between the significance of these new clothes and that of the accustomed and expected plainness of her dress as a governess. On Jane, the bright silks and satins would be inappropriate because of her class position (though not, as Valverde's argument makes clear, to her new station after her marriage) and would therefore indicate a lack of economic and sexual integrity. Brontë suggests this anxiety still further by choosing the adjective "gay" for Jane's half-censure of the shops, since "gay woman" was a common term for a prostitute at the time.[19]

As another means of asserting independence, Jane insists on keeping her salary and her work schedule down to the very last minute and frames this insistence explicitly in the terms of a refusal to be one of Rochester's mistresses: "Do you remember what you said of Céline Varens?—of the diamonds, the cashmeres you gave her? I will not be your English Céline Varens. I shall continue to act as Adèle's governess: by that I shall earn my board and lodging, and thirty pounds a year besides. I'll furnish my own wardrobe out of that money" (Brontë 283). Here, Jane tries to negotiate two separate relationships between herself and Rochester: one as employee and employer, and another as wife and husband. In other words, she is trying to do what was legally impossible for early Victorian women: to separate the financial and emotional sides of marriage in order to avoid a dependent position. Jane is very clear that what she is rejecting is not Rochester's love—not even his sexual attentions—but the exchange of his money for the loss of her autonomy. Jane's suggestion is deeply ironic. She could not be paid by Rochester if she were his wife, because he would, by law, be paying himself. Still, she seems to think that the symbolic act of working for her keep would protect her from dependency and mistresshood in marriage. At the end of the discussion, she returns, finally, to the question of wardrobe: Mr. Rochester will not dress her, not even for her wedding. She will buy her own clothes, plain as they are, and thus signal that she is neither a mistress nor a prostitute, but a loving fiancée who is not motivated by financial desires.

In the end, Jane marries Rochester not only because she loves him, but also because she has received a large inheritance from her uncle in Madeira, which enables her to live wherever and however she wants to. As Maurianne Adams maintains: "Jane reaches the threshold of marriage three times in the novel. She cannot cross it until she can meet her 'master' as his partner and equal, his equal by virtue of her inheritance and family solidarity, his partner by virtue of their interdependence."[20] Although Jane's marriage to Rochester may not seem terribly equal to us (particularly given Jane's willingness to serve Rochester), to a woman accustomed to a lifetime of dependency and ill-paid employment, the financial autonomy she insists on having before the marriage would be extremely important and unusual. It also shows that she has rejected the trap of losing her moral agency, which Amanda Anderson contends is the main marker of the sexually fallen woman in Victorian discourses of gender and sexuality.[21] Jane firmly declares her hard-won autonomy to Rochester: "I told you I am independent, sir, as well as rich: I am my own mistress" (Brontë 458). Her choice of words signals to Rochester (after his long search for a good mistress, in either sense of the word) the idea that he cannot have her as an inferior. Jane's statement redefines the word "mistress" at the novel's end. If she is her "own mistress," then she must be economically dependent on herself alone: She keeps herself. The word, then, ceases to mean surrender of economic and sexual power over oneself and comes to signify (within *Jane Eyre* if not within Victorian culture) the independence and power of the novel's heroine.

Brontë thus offers a solution to the seemingly insoluble problem of female dependence, and the resultant parallel between prostitution and marriage, by depicting a heroine who is able to claim for herself a measure of autonomy. Jane's legacy from her uncle ensures for herself, and signals to readers, that the marriage is wholly a romantic union, with no hint of prostitution and dependency: The economic exchange that Brontë criticizes sharply throughout the novel drops out of the marriage plot.[22] The only way that this equality within marriage can be achieved, within the fictional world of *Jane Eyre*, is to base marriage on love rather than on socioeconomic factors and thus to avoid producing marriages of convenience that could lead only to dependency (and hence a sort of quasi prostitution) for the female partner.

That marriages of convenience—of finance rather than romance—
were common is evinced by many Victorian texts. Seven years after
Brontë's novel was published, G. R. Drysdale wrote: "A great proportion of the marriages we see around us, did not take place from love at
all, but from some interested motive, such as wealth, social position, or
other advantages; and in fact it is rare to see a marriage in which true
love has been the predominating feeling on both sides."[23] Marriages of
convenience come under direct attack in Dickens's *Dombey and Son,* a
novel that was published serially in the years immediately before the
publication of *Jane Eyre.* Dickens, like Brontë, lambastes economically
based marriages, but from a different point of view. Dickens's novel is
a wide-ranging indictment of the overvaluing of wealth and commerce
in Victorian society, and the sections of the novel that deal with marriage
undertaken for financial reasons form a large part of this critique. A
particularly direct attack on mercenary marriage centers on the character of Edith, the second Mrs. Dombey, who marries Mr. Dombey
solely for his wealth. Edith is herself ashamed of her actions; her mother
asks, "What are you?" and Edith replies, " 'I have put the question to
myself,' said Edith, ashy pale, and pointing to the window, 'more than
once when I have been sitting there, and something in the faded likeness
of my sex has wandered past outside; and God knows I have met with
my reply' " (Dickens 514).

Edith here compares herself directly to a prostitute—that is, the
"faded likeness" of a woman "wandering" the streets. This language,
though it might seem rather evasive to us, would to a Victorian reader
have denoted a prostitute all too clearly. Victorian prostitutes tend to
be shadowy figures in the literary and historical records of this period,
not least because of the periphrastic language that, for propriety's sake,
was used to describe them. Moreover, Edith is frequently paired with
her long-lost cousin Alice Marwood, a onetime prostitute described as
a "fallen sister" (Dickens 563), and the parallel between the two
strengthens the critique of economic marriage throughout the novel.

The theme of marriage, romantic and economic, is one that Dickens
was to work out continually in his novels after *Dombey and Son;* in
different ways, *Little Dorrit* (1857), *Great Expectations* (1860), and
Our Mutual Friend (1864) all explore the economic trials of would-be
couples through both major characters and subplots. One darkly hu-
morous example in *Our Mutual Friend* is the story of the Lammles, a
pair of adventurers who marry because each is convinced the other is
rich and realize their error, to their shared disgust, on their wedding

night. The couple are among the most sordid and dishonest characters in a novel brimming over with dishonest schemers, and their desire to marry for money is at the heart of their portrayal. Dickens consistently rejects the idea that marriages should be contracted for monetary gain— as indeed do most of the novelists who were his contemporaries. A broad sampling of canonical mid-Victorian fiction—novels by Brontë, Dickens, Anthony Trollope, Elizabeth Gaskell, Wilkie Collins, and others— would seem to reveal a more or less straightforward cultural attitude that love is essential as the only foundation of marriage, and that marriages for financial or class reasons are doomed to failure.

The periodical press—which began to look at the institution of marriage more critically in the 1860s—presented a more ideologically complex picture. The 1860s were the major decade of debate over the reform of marriage laws. At issue were the economic effects of both the inconsistencies in marriage laws across the empire and the inequities between husbands and wives. Furthermore, the liberalization of the law of divorce that took place with the Matrimonial Causes Act in 1857 provoked widespread (and often slightly panicked) reevaluation of the meaning and stability of marriage. It has become a critical commonplace, for instance, to say that the rash of novels in the early 1860s focusing on bigamy—notably Mary Elizabeth Braddon's *Lady Audley's Secret* and Amelia Edwards's *Barbara's History*—sprang from questions about the institution of marriage that arose with the new divorce law. Such novels also tend to comment on the economic ramifications of marriage—Lady Audley, for instance, marries and commits bigamy in a bid for money and high social station. Bigamy is nearly always seen in such novels and in other Victorian discussions as a crime of property: It disrupts orderly inheritances and thus undermines the economic base and security of the upper classes. Anxious discussions of the economics of marriage also began to proliferate in the periodical press, particularly in the more popular journals; these avoided the legalistic approach taken by the serious reviews that debated the legal niceties of the Yelverton case and the Royal Commission on Marriage, and instead took a lighter approach to the marriage market that nevertheless examined critically the very bases of that most basic Victorian institution.

Verses published in 1860 by the little-known Ralph A. Benson in the magazine *Once a Week* (one of the few nineteenth-century journals in which articles were signed) obliquely present a similar view of the pressure that could be exerted on young women to marry "well." The poem begins by depicting an apparently happy wedding, but it soon becomes

apparent that all is not well between the groom, a "high lord," and his
bride, who has "no tender glance of love" for him. The point of view
shifts from that of the omniscient narrator, observing the wedding rather
impassively, to that of a spurned lover—rejected, it becomes clear, because he is poor. In the final stanzas, he links his pain directly to the
bride's decision to marry for money:

> [Not] kneeling beside the dear one dead,
> Were half the agony
> That sears the soul, and burns the brow,
> At consciousness of this,
> That lips once his are shrinking now,
> Beneath a barter'd kiss![24]

The violence of the young man's emotions is striking: The "agony" that
"sears the soul, and burns the brow" seems almost a description of his
own sin, reminding us of the tenor of descriptions of repentance common in the same period. Coupled with the reference to a "barter'd kiss,"
the young man's sickness could remind readers that prostitution of any
sort was considered contagious and dangerous within Victorian culture.
The bride's clear unhappiness, with her "shrinking" lips, effectively demonstrates the social and personal harm that the author of this piece associates with mercenary marriages.

Not all of the writers in the periodical press, of course, took Benson's
view. In "Keeping Up Appearances," an unsigned 1861 article in the
Cornhill Magazine, for instance, Fitzjames Stephen argues that the increasingly popular idea of love in a cottage was overrated, and that the
young—as well as their parents—should select a partner with financial
security in view.[25] Stephen's argument seems to be directed against
claims that those who wished to marry despite poverty should do so
without worry about the desire to "keep up appearances." He writes:

> Whatever may be said to the contrary, it does cost a great deal of money to
> be a gentleman, and a great deal more to be a lady. . . . Unless a woman
> has extraordinary health and vigour, her husband will enjoy very little
> of her society if she is always looking after the children or the dinner; and
> if both he and she are forced to spend a great deal of time and thought
> in contriving ways to make their income cover their expenses, their minds
> will . . . be fixed for the most part on small and somewhat sordid though
> important objects. . . . It follows from all this, that the desire to keep
> up appearances is neither an empty nor a vulgar one, for the appearances
> so kept up cover substantial realities.[26]

This passage demonstrates the two key elements of Stephen's argument. First, he stipulates that the demands of living up to one's class position should forestall the desire to marry without money. Second, he argues that far from preventing or tainting a solidly loving marriage, the existence of plenty of money within marriage will solidify the partnership and indeed lead to increased love (because the wife need not become a drudge) and presumably produce a more economically and emotionally stable union.

Unlike Dickens, Brontë, and Ralph Benson—whose polemics against mercenary marriages are all-or-nothing propositions—Stephen conveys some of the difficult gray areas of the issue. The author claims that it is the duty of young men who do not have enough money to marry to wait and speaks of this decision as nobler than rushing into marriage: "It is surely unwise to weight the scale of feeling and inclination, and to stigmatize the discharge of one of the most painful of all duties as an act of cowardly deference to a vulgar admiration of wealth" (318). Indeed, the writer to some extent blames novelists who have exalted love above all else for unhappy and imprudent marriages: "The discussion of the objects for which people ought to live has been almost entirely abandoned by serious inquirers to novelists and sentimental writers; and in our own time and country they hold up to admiration with one consent domestic happiness as the ideal towards which men's efforts should be directed" (312). The writer, instead, believes that young men without money should devote themselves to work and enterprise and that marriage can only hinder such men's work in life: "The proverb that it is hard for an empty sack to stand upright, goes far toward exhausting what is to be said as to the bearing upon professional success of marriages in which appearances and the realities they cover are set aside" (311).

In "Keeping Up Appearances," the reader sees one Victorian ideal—the work ethic of enterprise and industry—placed in conflict with another—love-based marriages. Stephen recommends the former, commenting: "Many an enterprise of real pith and moment has been gently smothered by a happy marriage, and a large family of fine children" (318). The article shows that the debate over the mixing of love and economics was indeed a debate (that is, that there was disagreement over the nature and meaning of marriage). Moreover, it demonstrates that despite this disagreement, companionate marriage was becoming both more widespread and more widely accepted. In protesting the quixotic and impractical romance of those who wish young people to marry without a sound financial footing, Stephen displays his concern that too many young people are doing just that.

A slightly later article, "Marriage *Not* À-la-Mode," published by Alfred Austin in *Temple Bar* in 1863, similarly claims that a certain amount of money is necessary to marriage.[27] This writer, however, is far from being an advocate of mercenary marriages, though he concedes that it is common to marry with some pecuniary concerns in mind: "Indeed, it must be pretty evident that in all ages of the world, even before money transactions had superseded those of simpler barter, some preference must have been extended, in the choice of husbands, to those who possessed, or were likely to possess, substance, as against those who had neither possessions nor prospects" (Austin 506). He goes on to say that women (and their parents) should not prefer those with more money to those with less as they choose a husband, contending that if a man has the "certain amount" necessary to maintain a wife and children in reasonable middle-class comfort (which the author fixes at a modest three hundred pounds a year), that man should not be discriminated against in the marriage market: "A father has as much right to prevent his daughter from marrying a pauper as from cutting her carotid artery. But he has no more right to insist that she shall prefer a man with twice the 'certain amount of money' to one with only exactly the 'certain amount of money,' than he has to force her to wear buttoned boots instead of laced ones, or to use Truefitt's Colombian dye rather than Douglas's Mexican balm" (508). The author's use of commodity culture as a parallel to the culture of romance is a slightly curious one, revealing how completely Victorian notions of love were underwritten by notions of economics. The metaphor nevertheless underscores the growing sense that marriage should be governed by the free choice of the parties involved, provided that certain basic conditions are met.

Austin goes on to contend that marriages made for monetary gain are not merely personally unfulfilling, but also detrimental to society. He contends that the social good requires that couples marry when they are less well off, always provided that the man has "the certain amount":

> Can it be doubted that a girl will make a better wife to the man whom she prefers, than to the man whom she . . . obediently accepts? Does it smack too much of the "Republic" . . . to believe that she will bear nobler children to the former than to the latter? Is it extravagant to believe that she will put up with the little, but frequently-recurring and unavoidable, annoyances of married life with better heart and sweeter temper when

she shares them with, or is burdened with them by, the man whom of all
men she worshipped, than when she can unfortunately aggravate her
troubles by saying to herself, "Ah, if I had married HIM!" . . . And this
additional endurance and urbanity of patience—have they no influence on
the young mimic brood at their knee? . . . I am using only the small
swords of the armoury of argument. I am marshaling the trifles, and showing
that the sum and result of them is no small national matter.

(Austin 510–11)

These arguments against mercenary marriages are in some ways like
Victorian arguments against prostitution: that it undermines the home,
spreading vice and misery first through the domestic sphere and then
through it to the nation that rests on the domestic sphere. The author,
however, draws a more direct link between mercenary marriages and
sexual irregularities, including prostitution; he argues that as young rich
couples form, they will inevitably spend money on luxuries, and in so
doing will make it seem as though a great deal of money is needed to
marry at all. He contends that excess money in any given marriage

will be spent in adding fuel to the fire for domestic display. . . . It will feed
nobody's mouth, instruct nobody's mind, improve nobody's morals,
spiritualise nobody's soul. . . . It will, you say, then, be utterly wasted?
Would to Heaven it were! Alack! It will fructify most dolefully. It will help
to raise the standard of living. It will so prevent many from marrying
who ought to be married, and beggar many others who, having married on
smaller means, cannot resist the awful temptation to compete with their
richer neighbours. Preventing marriage, it will increase the number of men
who tempt, and of women who are tempted.

(Austin 511–12)

Although the chain of causality here seems a bit tenuous, the link between marriages with an excess of money and a society with an excess
of vice reveals much about the Victorian mind-set. This article arguably
represents a point of view that was deeply fearful of *any* excess (believing
that such would lead to sin), but it also seems that there is something
particular and specific about this aversion to an excess of money within
marriage. What the writer here objects to is the likelihood of "vain-
glory," of showy spending (not unlike the spending often attributed to
prostitutes) that is based on an indecent sort of economic exchange: that
of the woman's sexuality for the man's money and financial support.

A more comic turn on the exchange economy of marriage is presented
in *Fraser's Magazine* in an 1867 article titled "On Some of the Impediments to Marriage, by a Bachelor." The unknown author of this piece

draws a more straightforward parallel between marriage and prostitution than most, depicting the London season as a market economy in which mothers are the main traders: "The angels themselves might regard the spectacle of one who is a good woman at bottom (though over fertile, perhaps), stuck up like a scare-crow against the wall of a crowded ball-room from 10 P.M. till 4 A.M., with compassionate pity. She sits there like a Turkey merchant with her merchandise about her."[28] Here, the comparison of the mother to a "Turkey merchant" may evoke Orientalist thoughts of the harem (particularly associated with Turkey; in *Jane Eyre* Brontë uses a similar image). The passage continues to strengthen the association between the mother and a merchant, " 'O, public dear, will you not come and buy? This is Milly, my eldest born; she is not bright, but she is good, which is far better.' And so till dawn the weary auction goes on. . . . She is a good woman, I say, and yet sore necessity has driven her to this. She is fain to dress her daughters like ballet-dancers, . . . to offer them without remorse or shame in the public market" ("On Some of the Impediments," 774). The language of the passage constantly presents the ballroom as an economy unto itself, but as an economy that ought to entail "shame" and "remorse" in its participants; the author employs metaphors for the girls who are "for sale" that would be humiliating to any bourgeois (and presumably virtuous) Victorian girl. The comparison to ballet dancers in particular implies that the women available for sale have, by their very salability, become something less than respectable.

Another lament by the author plays on the same words and images of prostitution that *Jane Eyre* had done some twenty years before:

> Even the man who meets a pleasant comely girl in a ball-room every night of the season, may well pause before he commits himself irretrievably.
> He sees that she wears a preposterously long dress which costs ever so much a yard, that she carries a bouquet of rare exotics, that her jewels are worth a ransom. Prudence inevitably suggests—"How can a plain man afford to *keep* such a brilliant creature? I might contrive to maintain a chimpanzee or a boa-constrictor; but a bird of paradise who spends 1,000*l.* a year on feathers would very speedily drive me in the Gazette."
>
> ("On Some of the Impediments," 775; emphasis added)

Here the references to the woman as a "bird of paradise" and the description of the potential wife's extravagance are reminiscent of Brontë's description of Jane's objection to fancy dress and of Valverde's argument in "The Love of Finery" that overdressing was considered a marker of fallenness. Moreover, the choice of the word "keep" to denote "support" or "maintain" adds a sexual overtone that the more neutral and solely economic words do not have: Mistresses are "kept," and the word implies that they are both sexually available and financially supported.

Despite this author's criticisms of the Victorian marriage market, he closes on a wistful note: "And yet when my poetical friend Apollo Titmouse paints in his graphic way the charms of married life—'the lively wife, the rosy baby, the snug evening beside the domestic hearth . . . '—I sometimes wish that the impediments to marriage were not so insurmountable as we have made them, and that before the grey had coloured my hair, and the chill crept into my heart, I had ceased to sign myself, A BACHELOR" ("On Some of the Impediments," 782).This passage—at the end of the article—captures many of the ideological contradictions that the Victorians perceived in their system of marriage. The author feels that domesticity and love ought to be the foundation of happiness for him—without them, he writes, "the chill" has "crept into [his] heart"—but he finds that his culture has made this an unattainable goal. His wish that the "impediments to marriage were not so insurmountable as we have made them" implies, by the use of the first-person plural, that he himself—a participant in the London season that he deplores, though never a buyer in the marriage market—has helped to create the obstacles.

The contradictory impulses we see in this rueful bachelor are echoed in the facetiously titled "How to Get Married," published in *Belgravia* in 1868. This article—which is mainly about matrimonial advertisements (the nineteenth-century equivalent of the personal ads)—echoes the complaints *Fraser's* makes about mothers selling their daughters and criticizes girls who wish to marry for money:

> There are always managing mammas who are ready to part with their daughters to the highest bidder. . . . A good many of the young ladies of the present day, too, are singularly skilled in husband-hunting, and . . . are ready to marry anybody who promises them a comfortable home. . . . Finally, and unfortunately, there are a great many girls who have no particular vocation for matrimony, but who regard it as a means of getting a living, a little more respectable than some other recognised modes, and good deal less laborious than that domestic service or pursuit of the millinery art for which by nature and education they appear to be fitted. To all such persons the matrimonial market is open.[29]

The "other recognised modes" of getting a living would here seem ostensibly to refer to millinery or domestic service, but the very vagueness of the phrase leaves us free to suppose that the writer is alluding to the

most obvious parallel to marriage for money: prostitution. The outset
of the article addresses more directly the ideological contradictions
within marriage:

> When Mr. Gamaliel Pickle had determined to commit matrimony, he made
> his proposals after a very mercantile fashion. "Madam," he wrote, "having
> a parcel of heart to dispose of, warranted sound, shall be glad to treat with
> you for same." . . . We who live in the nineteenth century are accustomed
> to pride ourselves on having got rid of this sort of thing, and on making
> love after a much more chivalrous fashion than our ancestors. Some of us
> even say—and, what is still more remarkable, even think—that we approach
> the old knightly reverence for women. Every novel that the season produces
> has some of this knightly love-making in it. The modern essayists . . .
> hold by the same faith, and paint ecstatic pictures of the joys of true love,
> the romance of marriage, and the happiness of modern lovers. And their
> example is followed by the gushing leader-writers who expatiate in the
> daily press, and who gravely discuss in the dull season the propriety of
> marrying upon all sorts of fabulously-small incomes. Yet . . . there are
> innumerable proof that by large numbers of persons marriage is regarded
> as the most commonplace and matter-of-fact business transaction in the
> world.

("How to Get Married," 531)

The writer here seems to criticize the assumptions made in "Marriage
Not À-la-Mode" and some of the other articles discussed above. Moreover, he provides a useful reminder that despite all the shifts taking place
in how couples were depicted in Victorian culture (that is, as pairs choosing each other for romantic rather than pecuniary reasons), these depic-
tions were perhaps a bit ahead of their time—or were, more accurately,
wishful thinking that "knightly love-making" and "the joys of true love"
ought to be the order of the day.

It is difficult in the end to gauge the effect of this sort of cultural
wishful thinking. Did the sort of representations I have described here
lead to the ascendancy of love as a factor in choosing marriage partners?
Ultimately, the question of whether positive representations of companionate marriage led to a changing reality, or whether the changing realities of nineteenth-century marriage evoked new and different representations of marriage, becomes a bit like the question of the chicken
and the egg. It is evident that a broad shift in the conception of marriage
was under way in the nineteenth century and that this shift became more
urgent and still broader as the Victorian period went on, erupting in the
1860s with the debates and legal reforms I have discussed.

Clearly, the Victorian writers who grappled with the shifting nature of marriage were participating in a cultural ferment of which many of them were not even fully aware. The changes begun in the period under consideration here did not end, of course, with the 1860s. On the contrary, changes in the social and economic position of women were only beginning. The Married Women's Property Act of 1880 allowed married women to keep and earn their own money, and not surprisingly, in the decades that followed, the educational and economic opportunities available to women expanded quickly. These changes in the position of women contributed to the ever-changing nature of middle-class marriage, as it shifted from being an economic relationship of dependency to a meeting of equals, undertaken by choice and for companionship and love. Though this shift did not happen smoothly or flow chronologically—on the contrary, the story of the development of companionate marriage is one of fits and starts, advances offset by retrogression—it has, on the whole, continued through the twentieth century to produce the forms of marriage we know today.

NOTES

1. The best known discussion of prostitution in the periodical press of mid-century is probably Charles Dickens's 1853 essay "Homes for Homeless Women," printed in *Household Words*, which he himself owned and published. Greg was able to publish his controversial views in the *Westminster* because its owner, W. E. Hickson, was, like Greg, a prominent radical; the magazine, which was founded by Jeremy Bentham and James Mill, had long had a reputation as the preeminent radical-philosophical journal of its era.

2. This controversy is thoroughly documented in Judith Walkowitz's groundbreaking study, *Prostitution and Victorian Society* (Cambridge: Cambridge University Press, 1980). The *Westminster Review*'s major articles on prostitution are reprinted in Keith Nield, ed., *Prostitution in the Victorian Age* (Westmead, Eng: Gregg International Publishers, 1973), which reprints the article from which I draw my opening quotation as well as four other articles, the remainder all from 1869 and 1870.

3. See Walkowitz, *Prostitution*, chap. one.

4. Ralph Wardlaw, *Lectures on Magdalenism* (New York: J. S. Redfield, 1843), 33.

5. W. R. Greg, "Prostitution," *Westminster Review* 53 (1850): 458.

6. William Acton, *Prostitution Considered in its Moral, Social, and Sanitary Aspects*, reprint of second edition (London: Frank Cass, 1972), 2.

7. This excerpt is taken from the essay on women and marriage that Harriet Taylor gave to her future husband, John Stuart Mill. The essay is written

on paper watermarked 1832 but is of uncertain date. Harriet Taylor Mill, *The Complete Works of Harriet Taylor Mill*, ed. Jo Ellen Jacobs and Paula Harms Payne (Bloomington and Indianapolis: Indiana University Press, 1998), 22.

8. Mary Poovey, *Uneven Developments: The Ideological Work of Gender in Mid-Victorian England* (Chicago: University of Chicago Press, 1988), 9.

9. Mary Lyndon Shanley, *Feminism, Marriage, and the Law in Victorian England, 1850–1895* (Princeton, N.J.: Princeton University Press, 1989), 7.

10. Carole Pateman, *The Sexual Contract* (Cambridge, Mass.: Polity Press, 1988), 187.

11. James T. Hammick, *The Marriage Law of England: A Practical Guide to the Legal Requirements Connected with the Preliminary Formalities, Solemnization, and Registration of the Matrimonial Contract* (London: Shaw and Sons, 1873), 2.

12. W. Harris Faloon, "The Marriage Law of the Three Kingdoms," *Cornhill Magazine* 16, 94 (October 1867): 433.

13. The best summaries that I have seen of marriage law in nineteenth-century Great Britain have been in the 1860s periodical press. See especially William Morris O'Connor, "Article V: The Marriage Law of Great Britain," *British Quarterly Review* 24 (July 1861): 124–54.

14. "Article V: The Marriage Laws of the United Kingdom," *Westminster Review* 90 (July 1, 1868): 114.

15. Joan Perkin is particularly clear on the ins and outs of coverture and provides a useful comparison of the legal niceties of common law and equity, which provided differently for married women. (The basic difference between them is that trusts may be established for married women under equity, while under common law all property passed automatically to the husband.) See Perkin, *Women and Marriage in Nineteenth-Century England* (Chicago: Lyceum Books, 1989), 16–17, for a thumbnail sketch and chapters three and six for a more sustained discussion. On coverture and reactions to it by Victorian feminists, see Shanley, particularly the introduction and chapter one. A nineteenth-century feminist perspective can be found in Barbara Leigh Smith (later Bodichon)'s "Brief Summary, in Plain Language, of the Most Important Laws Concerning Women" (1854; reprinted in *The Disempowered: Women and the Law*, ed. Marie Mulvey Roberts and Tamae Mizuta [London: Routledge/Thoemmes Press, 1993]). For a more theoretical discussion of coverture, based in contract theory, see Pateman, 90–100 and chapter six.

16. Perhaps the best concentrated recent discussion of Norton's case is the third chapter of Poovey, but readings of the controversy surrounding the Norton marriage can also be found in Shanley, 22–27 and 136–37. Two of Norton's own discussions of her case, "English Laws for Women in the Nineteenth Century" and "The 'Non-Existence' of Women," are reprinted in Roberts and Mizuta, *The Disempowered*.

17. Charlotte Brontë, *Jane Eyre* (Oxford: Oxford University Press, 1975), 281.

18. Mariana Valverde, "The Love of Finery: Fashion and the Fallen Woman

in Nineteenth-Century Social Discourse," *Victorian Studies* 32, 2 (winter 1989): 170.

19. The *Oxford English Dictionary* gives the first example of this term's use to mean "prostitute" in 1825 and provides examples from texts throughout the nineteenth century.

20. Maurianne Adams, "*Jane Eyre:* Woman's Estate," in *The Authority of Experience,* ed. Arlyn Diamond and Lee R. Edwards (Amherst: University of Massachusetts Press, 1977), 152.

21. Amanda Anderson, *Tainted Souls and Painted Faces: The Rhetoric of Fallenness in Victorian Culture* (Ithaca and London: Cornell University Press, 1993), 5–9.

22. Brontë's solution is hardly a revolutionary one and, because it depends on the deus ex machina of a sudden inheritance, could hardly be applied to Victorian women generally. (For two differing opinions on the political significance of the novel's ending, see Jina Politi ["*Jane Eyre* Class-ified," *Literature and History* 8, 1 (spring 1982), reprinted in *New Casebooks: Jane Eyre,* ed. Heather Glen (Basingstoke and London: Macmillan Press, 1997)], 90, and Poovey 142.) Furthermore, Brontë's solution addresses the symptom (women's lack of money) rather than the cause (a patriarchal system of government and property law) of female economic dependency. Despite the relatively conservative implications of the inheritance plot, however, which catapults Jane to economic and social power, the novel retains a progressive stance toward sexual economics by ending with an equal marriage.

23. Quoted in Walter E. Houghton, *The Victorian Frame of Mind, 1830–1870* (New Haven: Yale University Press, 1957), 381.

24. Ralph A. Benson, "Her Bridal," *Once a Week* 2, 50 (June 9, 1860): 550.

25. The only signed periodical press publication discussed in this essay is "Her Bridal," by Ralph A. Benson. All other attributions have been made by reference to *The Wellesley Index to Victorian Periodicals.*

26. Sir James Fitzjames Stephen, "Keeping Up Appearances," *Cornhill Magazine* 4 (September 1861): 305–18.

27. Alfred Austin, "Marriage Not À-la-Mode," *Temple Bar* 9 (November 1863): 506–21. (The *Wellesley Index* notes that this attribution of the article is probable but not definite.)

28. "On Some of the Impediments to Marriage. By a Bachelor," *Fraser's Magazine* (December 1867): 772–82.

29. "How to Get Married," *Belgravia* 6 (October 1868): 532.

REFERENCES

Acton, William. *Prostitution Considered in Its Moral, Social, and Sanitary Aspects.* Reprint of second edition. London: Frank Cass, 1972.

Adams, Maurianne. "*Jane Eyre:* Woman's Estate." In *The Authority of Experience,* edited by Arlyn Diamond and Lee R. Edwards, 137–59. Amherst: University of Massachusetts Press, 1977.

Anderson, Amanda. *Tainted Souls and Painted Faces: The Rhetoric of Fallen-ness in Victorian Culture.* Ithaca and London: Cornell University Press, 1993.

"Article V: The Marriage Laws of the United Kingdom." *Westminster Review* 90 (July 1, 1868): 104–17.

Austin, Alfred. "Marriage Not À-la-Mode." *Temple Bar* 9 (November 1863): 506–21.

Benson, Ralph A. "Her Bridal." *Once a Week* 2, 50 (June 9, 1860): 550.

Brontë, Charlotte. *Jane Eyre.* Oxford: Oxford University Press, 1975.

Dickens, Charles. *Dombey and Son.* London: Penguin Classics, 1985.

———. "Homes for Homeless Women." *Household Words* n.s. 1, 33 (April 23, 1853): 169–75.

Faloon, W. Harris. "The Marriage Law of the Three Kingdoms." *Cornhill Magazine* 16, 94 (October 1867): 432–39.

Greg, W. R. "Prostitution." *Westminster Review* 53 (1850): 448–506.

Hammick, James T. *The Marriage Law of England: A Practical Guide to the Legal Requirements Connected with the Preliminary Formalities, Solemnization, and Registration of the Matrimonial Contract.* London: Shaw and Sons, 1873.

Houghton, Walter E. *The Victorian Frame of Mind, 1830–1870.* New Haven: Yale University Press, 1957.

"How to Get Married." *Belgravia* 6 (October 1868): 531–37.

Mill, Harriet Taylor. *The Complete Works of Harriet Taylor Mill.* Ed. Jo Ellen Jacobs and Paula Harms Payne. Bloomington and Indianapolis: Indiana University Press, 1998.

Morris, William O'Connor. "Article V: The Marriage Law of Great Britain." *British Quarterly Review* 24 (July 1861): 124–54.

Nield, Keith, ed. *Prostitution in the Victorian Age.* Westmead, Eng.: Gregg International Publishers, 1973.

Okin, Susan M. "Patriarchy and Married Women's Property in England: Questions on Some Current Views." *Eighteenth-Century Studies* 17, 2 (winter 1983–84): 121–38.

"On Some of the Impediments to Marriage. By a Bachelor." *Fraser's Magazine* (December 1867): 772–82.

Pateman, Carole. *The Sexual Contract.* Cambridge, Mass.: Polity Press, 1988.

Perkin, Joan. *Women and Marriage in Nineteenth-Century England.* Chicago: Lyceum Books, 1989.

Politi, Jina. "*Jane Eyre* Class-ified." *Literature and History* 8, 1 (spring 1982). Reprinted in *New Casebooks: Jane Eyre,* ed. Heather Glen. Basingstoke and London: Macmillan Press, 1997, 78–91.

Poovey, Mary. *Uneven Developments: The Ideological Work of Gender in Mid-Victorian England.* Chicago: University of Chicago Press, 1988.

Roberts, Marie Mulvey, and Tamae Mizuta, eds. *The Disempowered: Women and the Law.* London: Routledge/Thoemmes Press, 1993.

Shanley, Mary Lyndon. *Feminism, Marriage, and the Law in Victorian England, 1850–1895.* Princeton, N.J.: Princeton University Press, 1989.

Stephen, Sir James Fitzjames. "Keeping Up Appearances." *Cornhill Magazine* 4
    (September 1861): 305–18.
Valverde, Mariana. "The Love of Finery: Fashion and the Fallen Woman in
    Nineteenth-Century Social Discourse." *Victorian Studies* 32, 2 (winter 1989):
    168–88.
Walkowitz, Judith. *Prostitution and Victorian Society.* Cambridge: Cambridge
    University Press, 1980.
Wardlaw, Ralph. *Lectures on Magdalenism.* New York: J. S. Redfield, 1843.

CHAPTER 4

"Boston Marriage" among Lesbians

Are We a Couple If We're Not Having Sex?

Esther D. Rothblum

A discussion about lesbian couples raises a number of questions. First, recent research and writing have emphasized the fluidity and multi-dimensionality of the term "lesbian." Not all women who self-identify as lesbian are currently sexually involved with women; some are celibate, whereas others may be in sexual relationships with men. Women may be sexually involved with women and identify as heterosexual, bisexual, or lesbian or eschew all labels about sexual orientation. Although sexual behavior and self-identity may or may not be congruent, the general public views lesbians as women who have sex with women, so that sexual activity is a critical part of the definition of who is a lesbian.

Secondly, it is not always clear what "counts" as a couple. When couples cannot legally marry, sexual activity may assume importance in defining couple status. Yet women may have romantic and passionate relationships that do not involve genital sex. Are such couples "just" friends? This chapter will examine the overlap among the concepts of sexual orientation, sexual activity, coupled relationships, and nonsexual relationships among lesbians.

Portions of this manuscript were adapted from E. D. Rothblum, "Transforming Lesbian Sexuality," *Psychology of Women Quarterly* 18 (1994): 627–41. Reprinted with the permission of Cambridge University Press.

WHO IS A LESBIAN?

In 1993 the feminist periodical *Off Our Backs* published a review of the diaries of Anne Lister, an English scholar and traveler who wrote at the beginning of the nineteenth century (Johnson 1993). The quotation that was highlighted in italics at the center of the page stated: "In short, there can be no doubt that Anne was a *genuine* nineteenth century lesbian" (23, italics mine). What was "genuine" about Anne's lesbianism was that her diaries contain evidence of genital sex with other women, in contrast to many other historical documents where sex has had to be inferred from love or passion.

How do we decide who "counts" as a lesbian? This question has been particularly challenging for historians, as language about gender, sexual activity, sexual identity, friendship, relationship, and community has changed over the course of the century. Historians Estelle Freedman and John D'Emilio (1990) pose this question as follows:

> What, however, is sexuality? Given its changing meaning over time, what is one looking for in records of the past? The very term "sexuality" is a modern construct which originated in the nineteenth century. As we explained in our book *Intimate Matters,* it is only in the twentieth century that American society became so "sexualized" that the term had clear meaning throughout the culture. In the contemporary era, Americans have come to use "sexuality" to refer to the erotic, that is, to a state of physical attraction to either sex. In the past, however, there was no language of "sexuality" per se. Rather, in pre-industrial America, what is now called sexuality was largely embedded within a reproductive language. (483)

The research on lesbians has not only been sparse, but there have been different (if overlapping) conceptualizations of who is included in studies of lesbians. My recent research has begun to examine the inter-relationships of components of the lesbian experience, in order to answer the question "Who *is* a lesbian?" Most of the psychological studies of lesbians have recruited survey participants by placing announcements in lesbian or gay newsletters, distributing surveys at lesbian organizations or events, or leaving questionnaires at gay bars, feminist bookstores, gay or lesbian churches, or lesbian restaurants (see Rothblum 1994 for a review of methodology). The assumption underlying such recruitment methods has been that women who fill out surveys asking about lesbian issues are lesbians. Jessica Morris and I (1999) obtained a national sample of 2,393 lesbian (89 percent) and bisexual (11 percent) women, of which one-quarter were women of color. We examined the degree to which women who answered a Lesbian Wellness Survey are distributed on five aspects of lesbian sexuality and the coming-out process:

1. Sexual orientation—numerical rating of sexual identity from exclusively lesbian/gay to exclusively heterosexual;

2. Years out—length of time of self-identity as lesbian/gay/bisexual;

3. Outness/disclosure—amount of disclosure of sexual orientation to others;

4. Sexual experience—proportion of sexual relationships with women; and

5. Lesbian activities—extent of participation in lesbian community events.

Statistical analyses found only mild (but statistically significant) overlap among these five aspects, indicating that being lesbian is not a homogeneous experience. For example, women who rated themselves as exclusively lesbian were not necessarily out to lots of people or involved in the lesbian community.

Closer examination by the demographic characteristics of race/ethnicity and age revealed a diversity of experience. African American, Native American, and Latina respondents had more overlap among the five aspects of the lesbian experience. For white and Asian American respondents, the dimensions hardly overlapped at all. The results indicate that researchers who are studying one aspect of the lesbian experience (e.g., outness to others) need to ensure that they are not assuming such behavior based on other dimensions (such as frequent participation in lesbian community activities or years of being out), especially among white and Asian American lesbians.

WHAT IS LESBIAN SEXUAL ACTIVITY?

What is sex? In our society, *sex* is commonly defined as heterosexual intercourse. JoAnn Loulan (1993) has described how adolescents who have engaged in a number and variety of sexual activities but have not had intercourse will say that they haven't "gone all the way." The first time women have genital sex has a powerful definitional value, because it distinguishes the relationship from other, nonsexual relationships (e.g., friend, colleague, acquaintance, neighbor). Even when women recall their first experience of heterosexual intercourse as somewhat disappointing, they know that the experience "counted" (and in fact, most people can recall the number of sexual relationships they have had more distinctly than the number of friends, relatives, and co-workers they have had).

Women in the United States and other Western nations live in a culture of sex. Girls' toys and products for female adolescents focus heavily on their future roles as sexual beings. Susanna Rose (1996) has described how books and magazines intended for girls and women have a romance narrative in contrast to the adventure narrative for boys and men. An enormous amount of attention is focused on women finding the ideal male romantic/sexual partner, celebrating this with a lavish ceremony (the wedding), and staying with that same partner for a long time, preferably "forever." (Of course, since women live longer than men and tend to marry men who are somewhat older, "forever" means that many women will be alone in their old age.) Sex and romance are the themes of songs, movies, and television programs and how-to books and advice columns, especially those intended for women.

It is vital for the appearance-related economy that women feel responsible for their own sexual attractiveness, so that they will purchase products and engage in practices (e.g., dieting, cosmetic surgery, exercise) to enhance sexual appeal (see Rothblum 1992, 1993 for reviews). Billions of dollars are at stake in the media portrayal of women's sexuality. The U.S. economy alone includes an annual $33 billion diet industry, a $20 billion cosmetic industry, a $300 million cosmetic surgery industry, and a $7 billion pornography industry (Wolf 1991). The culture of sexuality and its correlates, the cultures of fashion and pornography, portray women almost overwhelmingly as European American, young, extremely thin, middle or upper class, able-bodied, and heterosexual. For the majority of women who do not fit this narrow demographic profile, privilege comes with being as close to this image as possible. The economy would have much to lose if women stopped being influenced by its messages. This culture of sex, not surprisingly, prioritizes sexual activity, sexual attractiveness, and sexual relationships to the exclusion of all other ways of relating except perhaps for the mothering of children.

How does the culture of sex affect lesbians? Lesbians, too, are socialized as girls and women to value sexual attractiveness. Most lesbians work and socialize with heterosexual people and are similarly influenced by the sexual messages in the media. Lesbian books and magazines, like those for heterosexual women, focus on the romance narrative (Rose 1996). For example, in the Naiad Press novel *Never Say Never,* two co-workers, Leslie who is a lesbian and Sara who is heterosexual, become close friends. Though it is obvious to the reader and to both women that they are sexually attracted to each other, the suspense builds as to whether or not Leslie and Sara will "consummate" their relationship—that is, become genitally sexual. Whether or not the women do "it" will affect the reader's perception as to whether the book has a happy ending (they become lovers) or an unhappy one (they remain "just friends").

What is lesbian sex? Sexual activity, as defined by lesbians, is greatly affected by heterosexual definitions of sexual activity. Two women are considered to have engaged in sex if they perform mutual genital stimulation. A lesbian who has never engaged in this activity will probably not believe that she has had sex with another woman. A lesbian who had an orgasm while watching or kissing another woman, for example, has not "gone all the way."

These definitions of sexual activity, both the heterosexual and the lesbian/bisexual versions, focus on genital activity and thus ignore other, nongenital, sexual experiences that women may have had (Loulan 1993; Rothblum and Brehony 1993). We have no terminology for the early sexual crushes that some girls develop on other people, usually a female friend or female teacher. We have no language for the sexual feelings that arise between adult friends, even when both friends are in sexual relationships with other people. In contrast, if the friends engage in genital sexual activity with each other, we immediately have language; they are having an affair.

A major survey of sexual activity among twelve thousand people (Blumstein and Schwartz 1983) indicated that lesbians are less likely to have genital sex than are married heterosexual, cohabiting heterosexual, or gay male couples. Loulan (1988) surveyed more than fifteen hundred lesbians and found the majority (78 percent) to have been celibate for some period of time. Of those who had been celibate, most had been celibate for less than one year, 35 percent had been celibate from one to five years, and 8 percent for six years or more. The results of both surveys were interpreted as reflecting women's lack of socialization to initiate sexual encounters.

What are the implications of lesbians engaging in genital sex less than heterosexual women or than men, yet at the same time using a genital-based definition to define "sex"? This raises a number of issues. Why do lesbians engage in genital sex less frequently, and what does this say about women's sexuality? Is there a way that lesbian communities should discuss the relative devaluation of alternatives to genital sex? Can we reclaim erotic, nongenital experiences as "real" sex?

WHAT IS A LESBIAN COUPLE?

Heterosexual marriage is defined by a legal ceremony. A married couple is considered to be in a relationship until there is a legal divorce. This is the case even when the married couple is not engaged in genital sex, when one or both partners are engaged in sex with other people, or when the couple is living apart. This is not the case for nonmarried couples. Cohabiting couples, whether heterosexual, lesbian, or gay (as of this writing, lesbian and gay couples cannot legally be married in any U.S. state, with the exception of civil unions in Vermont), are defined as a couple if they are having sex.

This sex-focused definition of a relationship has a number of implications for lesbians and bisexual women in female-female relationships. It focuses on an aspect (genital sexual activity) that is less frequent among lesbian couples than nonlesbian couples, thus overemphasizing sexual activity when this may not be what is important to lesbians in a relationship. Lesbians may feel pressure to have genital sex in order to provide a definition for their romantic feelings for another woman. They may feel pressure to continue having sex in order to view themselves as still being partners. If genital sex ceases, and if one or both partners tells close friends about this, the lesbian community may view the couple as having ended their relationship, and the members of the couple may be considered sexually available by other women (Brown 1993). Lack of sexual activity may be interpreted (by the couple, the lesbian community, and their therapist) as a sign that something is seriously wrong with the relationship, even if all other aspects of the relationship are satisfying.

Often women tell me that I am using a very narrow definition of "sex" and say that they define sex in broader terms. Surveys also indicate that lesbians, being women, place more focus on love, affection, and romance, than on genital sexual activity (e.g., Klinkenberg and Rose 1994). Nevertheless, ask any lesbian couple who are celebrating the anniversary of their relationship what, in fact, they are celebrating—that is, what happened on the day they are counting as the anniversary—

and the majority (but not all) will say it was the day they first had genital sex (actually, they say sex, not genital sex, but we have a very specific social construction of what we "allow" to be included in the word "sex").

Further, the sex-focused definition of what constitutes a lesbian relationship ignores the reality of women's ways of relating. For centuries of recorded history, women have felt strong love, affection, and intimacy for other women, even when both women were married to men. When two unmarried women lived together as "spinsters," they were considered to be in a "Boston marriage," a term that reflected the presumed asexual nature of the relationship (the city of Boston was home to many colleges and universities and thus to some highly educated women who lived together). Lillian Faderman (1981, 1993) has described the passion and love between women in the nineteenth century: "It became clear that women's love relationships have seldom been limited to that one area of expression, that love between women has been primarily a sexual phenomenon only in male fantasy literature. 'Lesbian' describes a relationship in which two women's strongest emotions and affections are directed toward each other. Sexual contact may be a part of the relationship to a greater or lesser degree, or it may be entirely absent" (1981, 17–18).

Interestingly, the lesbian community often assumes that women who expressed love for each other in past decades or centuries were, in fact, genitally sexual. The lesbian novels *The Ladies* (Grumbach 1984) and *Patience and Sarah* (Miller 1969) are fictional accounts based on real women who lived together in past times. Although their sexual activities are unknown (and would have been hidden from society if they existed), the authors have introduced a sexual component into these relationships.

Lesbians may not have genital sex as often as nonlesbians, but we certainly spend a great deal of time thinking about, talking about, and being in relationships. Several years ago, Kathy Brehony and I reclaimed the historical term "Boston marriage" to describe current-day romantic but asexual coupled relationships among lesbians (1993). There are women in our lesbian communities who live together and share long histories together. They may have been sexual in the past, or they may never have had genital sex. They are "lovers" in every sense of the word except for the absence of current genital sexual activity. They are usually viewed as couples by the lesbian community, which may in fact idealize the couples for the longevity and romantic nature of their relationship.

Often, in marked contrast to Boston marriages in previous times, these lesbians keep their asexuality hidden from the community. In order to illustrate some of the diversity of these romantic but asexual relationships among lesbians, I will briefly describe some of the ways in which lesbians form romantic but asexual relationships (from Rothblum and Brehony 1993); all names are pseudonyms.

Lesbians may become sexually attracted to heterosexual women who do not reciprocate the desire for a genital sexual relationship. A young lesbian, Laura, moved to San Francisco and became attracted to her heterosexual roommate Violet. Violet seemed to encourage the relationship in multiple ways, such as having heart-shaped tattoos made with each other's names and telling Laura it was okay that people mistook them for lovers. Laura refers to their relationship as: "When we were whatever we were: Whatever it was that we had." When Laura suggested they become lovers, Violet said she couldn't do it; Laura was devastated.

Lesbian ex-lovers often remain friends (see Becker 1988 for a review), and the passion of the friendship may have the eroticism of the prior genital sexual relationship. Elizabeth and Marianne were briefly genitally sexual, then Marianne broke that off saying that the age difference of twenty years was too great for her. Marianne, the younger of the two, became involved sexually with another woman, Eve, and Elizabeth decided to move away. Elizabeth and Marianne continued their relationship over the telephone, and both agree that they are the most important people in each other's lives.

A lesbian couple may "drift" into celibacy without much actual discussion about this. The following example also illustrates how the lesbian community may view a member of a couple as sexually available when she is no longer genitally sexually involved with her partner: Angie and Cedar met at a women's music festival, became lovers, and were sexual for six months. They moved in together and slept in the same bed. Then they slept in separate rooms one night a week, then half the time, then they slept together only one night a week. They stopped having sex. After three years of celibacy, Angie had an affair. Cedar was devastated, and Angie broke off her affair with Linda. Linda was confused since as soon as she found out that Angie and Cedar weren't having sex, she didn't think they were really a couple. Angie and Cedar entered couples therapy, but decided to lie to the therapist that they were doing the homework assignments to be sexual when in fact they didn't want to be sexual. They have recently celebrated their eighth anniversary and are still "monogamous" (that is, not having sex with each other or with anyone else).

Boston marriages can exist today in multiple ways. Pat is a sixty-year-old retired teacher. She was involved with Cathy for sixteen years, and they were sexual the first four or five years. Cathy has a niece whom they called "Little Cathy." Pat and Cathy often wondered whether Little Cathy and her roommate Barbara were a lesbian couple. One day, Pat discovered that her lover Cathy had become sexual with Barbara (Cathy's niece's roommate). Little Cathy was extremely upset that her aunt had become sexual with her roommate and was considering suicide (even though Little Cathy said she had never been sexual with Barbara). The last Pat heard, Cathy and Barbara had moved to Texas and were currently asexual but still together. Three Boston marriages exist among these women: between Pat and Cathy, between Little Cathy and Barbara, and between Cathy and Barbara.

On the other hand, some lesbians may be open about the asexual nature of their relationship. When Janet and Marty met, they soon became lovers, had sex a few times, and moved in together. Suddenly, Marty announced that she did not want to have sex. The couple built a log cabin together, tells everyone they are asexual and a couple, and have been celibate for eighteen years.

When couples are not genitally sexual, they may need to find new language for sexual activity. Ruth and Iris call what they do together in bed "bliss." Ruth is involved sexually with a man, and Iris with another woman. Both Ruth's and Iris's partners want them to remain monogamous. Consequently, Ruth and Iris have an agreement that they have only a spiritual (rather than physical) connection and say it is ecstasy. Ruth says, "It's like coming to the goddess." They say that it is the most important relationship in their lives, more important than their respective partners, yet they have trouble with people taking it seriously. They see the same therapist, and Iris says of her, "Bless her heart, she's trying!"

Not having genital sex may create confusion about whether women are "really lesbians." Sarah is in her midtwenties and in love with Hannah, who is in her midthirties. They have a primary relationship but without sex. They have an agreement that they can have other lovers, but only men. Sarah is confused because she is a lesbian, and now her friends see her only with male lovers. It has shaken her whole identity as a lesbian. Hannah is primarily heterosexual. They are both afraid that sex would make them even more intense, given their closeness already.

These examples raise the issue of what sexual activity is. When the two members of a couple disagree on what constitutes sex, and thus whether or not they are having sex, they may also differ on whether or not they are in a "real" relationship. Even when both members of the couple agree that their genitally asexual relationship makes them a "real" couple, the lesbian community may disagree with this definition of the relationship. The couple will need to decide whether to disclose their lack of genital sex to other people and what to do if the lesbian community views them as sexually "available" or otherwise denies the reality of their relationship. Validation of a relationship by the lesbian community as well as by the heterosexual macrosociety is important, given the lack of acknowledgment that lesbians have received for their sexual feelings and behaviors as they were growing up or while coming out.

These relationships raise questions about *monogamy,* a term that is difficult to define when the members of a couple are not genitally sexual. In contrast to lesbian relationships during the so-called sexual revolution of the late 1960s, norms of many lesbian communities today idealize lesbians who are in monogamous couples. Is it a "real" relationship when one or both members of a lesbian couple are not genitally sexual with each other but are engaged in sexual relations with other women (or with men)?

When I was doing the interviews for my book *Boston Marriages: Romantic but Asexual Relationships among Contemporary Lesbians,* I began to feel like an imposter because most of my friends told me that they and their partner had sex often, "all the time." Then, when a few of these friends broke up with their lovers, they told me it was because they "never had sex." These were the same women; how could their stories have changed so much? Marny Hall (1998) has written about this phenomenon in her book *The Lesbian Love Companion: How to Survive Everything from Heartthrob to Heartbreak.* She argues that we create stories to make sense of our lives and then change these stories when our lives change.

NONSEXUAL RELATIONSHIPS

One group that continues to have close, passionate, and nonsexual relationships today are female adolescents. Lisa Diamond (1997) has described what she terms "passionate friendships" among adolescent and young adult women. These friendships are portrayed as "love affairs without the sexual element" (5), with elements of romantic love, idealization, obsession, exclusivity, possessiveness, and sexual desire. Nevertheless, such relationships may be viewed (by the young women and by those around them) as a prelude to a future partnership with a man. Similarly, Janice Raymond's (1986) book, *A Passion for Friends,* includes descriptions of women's intimate friendships in non-Western cultures in which women, even if married, spend most of their lives in close contact with other women. Oliva Espin (1993) has portrayed close, intimate but nonsexual relationships among unmarried women in Latin American cultures.

In contrast to a sexual relationship, a friendship is presumed to be independent of sexual behavior and, to a great extent, of sexual feelings and fantasies. Friendships are so secondary in importance to sexual relationships that many women (including lesbians) have had the experience of a friendship decreasing in intensity when one or both women became sexually involved with someone else. When friendships between women are especially close or intense, outsiders suspect the presence of sexual feelings or behavior. One reason for the greater acceptance of nonmonogamy in sexual relationships in the women's communities of the 1970s was the idea that feminists could be close to several other women in the spirit of "sisterhood."

Friendships and sexual relationships are not mutually exclusive. Lesbians often feel that their lover is their friend, even their best friend (as do some heterosexual couples). Similarly, friends may have sexual feelings for one another, though they may or may not acknowledge these feelings to each other (or even to themselves). Discussion of sexual feelings between friends may interfere with the friendship, given the high salience of sex over friendship in our society. Lesbian ex-lovers often remain friends (see Becker 1988 for a review), and the passion of the friendship may have the eroticism of the prior genital sexual relationship.

I have argued previously (Rothblum 1999) that in contrast to the coupled model for sexual relationships in Western society, friendships are permitted to be more permeable. Perhaps this greater flexibility in friendships is precisely because friendships are less salient than sexual relationships.

Being part of a "couple" connotes being part of a twosome, not more and not less. Women who are not coupled may rush into a new relationship just to avoid the stigma of the word "single." Given women's relational capabilities and the multiple ways in which women are interconnected with family of origin, friends, neighbors, co-workers, and, in the lesbian communities, with ex-lovers, the word "single" hardly does justice to this web of kinship ties. Similarly, not all women limit their passion to one sexual partner. Whether openly or secretly, whether temporarily or more permanently, many women have multiple partners. This range of relationships among lesbians has been discussed in the book *The Lesbian Polyamory Reader: Open Relationships, Non-Monogamy, and Casual Sex,* edited by Marcia Munson and Judith Stelboum (1999).

In sum, there has been little feminist debate about women's ways of relating in either sexual or nonsexual ways. Sexual relationships in particular are so influenced by patriarchal definitions that we cannot truly conceive of women relating in ways that feel authentic to us. Women's relationships are so complex and multidimensional that behavior, identity, and affection may not be homogeneous. We know little about how women's sexual and nonsexual relationships change over the lifetime. As we begin the new millennium, there is increasing uncertainty over who is a "woman," given the emerging transgender movement. For a feminist vision of women's sexuality, "sex" would need to be broadened to encompass more aspects of women's bodies, spirituality, love, and passion.

REFERENCES

Becker, C. 1988. *Lesbian ex-lovers.* Boston: Alyson Publications.

Blumstein, P., and P. Schwartz. 1983. *American couples.* New York: William Morrow.

Brown, L. 1993. The Boston marriage in the therapy office. In *Boston marriages: Romanic but asexual relationships among contemporary lesbians,* edited by E. D. Rothblum and K. A. Brehony. Amherst: University of Massachusetts Press.

Diamond, L. 1997. Passionate friendships: Love and attachment among young lesbian, bisexual, and heterosexual women. Paper presented at the Annual Convention of the Association for Women in Psychology, March, Pittsburgh, Pa.

Espin, O. 1993. So what is a "Boston marriage" anyway? In *Boston marriages: Romantic but asexual relationships among contemporary lesbians,* edited by E. D. Rothblum and K. A. Brehony. Amherst: University of Massachusetts Press.

Faderman, L. 1981. *Surpassing the love of men.* New York: Morrow.

———. 1993. Nineteenth-century Boston marriage as a possible lesson for today. In *Boston marriages: Romantic but asexual relationships among contemporary lesbians,* edited by E. D. Rothblum and K. A. Brehony. Amherst: University of Massachusetts Press.

Freedman, E. B., and J. D'Emilio. 1990. Problems encountered in writing the history of sexuality: Sources, theory and interpretation. *Journal of Sex Research* 27:481–95.

Grumbach, D. 1984. *The ladies*. New York: Fawcett Crest.

Hall, M. 1998. *The lesbian love companion: How to survive everything from heartthrob to heartbreak*. San Francisco: Harper Collins.

Johnson, A. Aug.–Sep. 1993. I know my own heart. *Off Our Backs* 23:22–23.

Klinkenberg, D., and S. Rose. 1994. Dating scripts of lesbians and gay men. *Journal of Homosexuality* 26:23–35.

Loulan, J. 1988. Research on the sex practices of 1,566 lesbians and the clinical applications. *Women and Therapy* 7:221–34.

———. 1993. Celibacy. In *Boston marriages: Romantic but asexual relationships among contemporary lesbians*, edited by E. D. Rothblum and K. A. Brehony. Amherst: University of Massachusetts Press.

Meadow, R. M., and L. Weiss. 1992. *Women's conflicts about eating and sexuality: The relationship between food and sex*. New York: Harrington Park Press.

Miller, I. 1969. *Patience and Sarah*. New York: McGraw-Hill.

Morris, J. F., and E. D. Rothblum. 1999. Who fills out a "lesbian" questionnaire? The interrelationship of sexual orientation, years out, disclosure of sexual orientation, sexual experience with women, and participation in the lesbian community. *Psychology of Women Quarterly* 33:537–57.

Munson, M., and J. Stelboum, eds. 1999. *The lesbian polyamory reader: Open relationships, non-monogamy, and casual sex*. New York: Haworth Press.

Raymond, J. 1986. *A passion for friends: Toward a philosophy of female affection*. Boston: Beacon Press.

Rose, S. 1996. Lesbian and gay love scripts. In *Preventing heterosexism and homophobia*, edited by E. D. Rothblum and L. A. Bond. Thousand Oaks, Calif.: Sage Publications.

Rothblum, E. D. 1992. The stigma of women's appearance: Social and economic realities. *Feminism and Psychology* 2:61–73.

———. 1993. I'll die for the revolution but don't ask me not to diet: Feminism and the continuing stigmatization of obesity. In *Feminist perspectives on eating disorders*, edited by S. Wooley, M. Katzman, and P. Fallon. New York: Guilford Press.

———. 1994. I only read about myself on bathroom walls: The need for research on the mental health of lesbians and gay men. *Journal of Consulting and Clinical Psychology* 62:213–20.

———. 1999. Poly-friendships. In *The lesbian polyamory reader: Open relationships, non-monogamy, and casual sex*, edited by M. Munson and J. Stelboum. New York: Haworth Press.

Rothblum, E. D., and K. A. Brehony, eds. 1993. *Boston marriages: Romantic but asexual relationships among contemporary lesbians*. Amherst: University of Massachusetts Press.

Wolf, N. 1991. *The beauty myth: How images of beauty are used against women*. New York: William Morrow.

CHAPTER 5

"You'll Never Walk Alone"

Lesbian and Gay Weddings and the Authenticity of the Same-Sex Couple

Ellen Lewin

Several years ago, I taught a course on lesbian and gay issues at the University of California, Berkeley. One of the books I assigned, Paul Monette's *Borrowed Time,* is the chronicle of the illness and death of the author's longtime lover, Roger, from AIDS. It deals in wrenching and highly emotional detail with the progress of the disease itself, its changing impact on the two men's relationship, and the terrible loss Monette sustained with Roger's death (Monette 1988). During the week the class was reading the book, one of my students, a recently divorced woman in her midthirties, came to see me during my office hours. Her face was puffy, her eyes red, and she admitted that she had stayed up all night weeping as she read the book. I asked her what about the book most affected her, and she said with some amazement, "They loved each other so much. More than me and my ex-husband."

One of the constant problems for those of us who do our work on gay and lesbian family life is the conviction by many, both academics and ordinary people, that kinship and all that it is thought to entail—intense, unconditional bonds of love and lifelong commitment as well as the mundane details of domesticity—cannot be a part of gay life. Gay people's relationships with their lovers are assumed to be transitory and

Portions of this paper appear in Lewin 1998 and were included in talks given at the University of California, Santa Cruz; the University of New Mexico; and the University of Minnesota.

based on sexual caprice; their ties to blood kin are expected to be attenuated and strained, if not totally absent. As Kath Weston has shown in
Families We Choose, notions of kinship tend to privilege so-called blood
relationships as permanent and binding, while discounting "chosen" relationships with friends as easily dismantled (Weston 1991). Not only
does the anthropological study of lesbian and gay kinship cast doubt on
these assumptions, but lesbians and gay men often find that they must
address these views in constituting themselves as members of communities and families.

In the pages that follow, I focus on the ritual enactment of lesbian
and gay couplehood in ceremonies of commitment I studied in the mid
1990s in the San Francisco Bay area and some other locales. I argue that
while the public controversy over same-sex marriage that emerged during the same period focuses on entitlement to specific rights associated
with legal marriage, thus framing the issue as a matter of civil rights,
examination of the ceremonies as dense, multivalent narratives reveals
a different emphasis.[1] Lesbians and gay men who stage these events are
concerned, among other symbolic aims, with establishing claims to couplehood itself, with proving to the assembled guests and to themselves
that their relationship is the "real thing"—a marriage. To succeed at
this, the celebrants must also convey the conviction that the ceremony
is what it claims to be—a wedding. The quest for authenticity can be
pursued using a variety of symbolic and narrative strategies in constructing the ceremony at the time of its performance and in recollections
of the event that occur later.[2]

It is not only with the straight world that same-sex couples who marry
must struggle in the process of establishing their claims to authentic
couplehood. Gay men and lesbians in the United States are anything but
unanimous in their views on marriage, with many regarding the issue
as a classic instance of the struggle between a politics of resistance and
one of accommodation, only the latest round in a long battle over
whether gays and lesbians should embrace or repudiate difference from
the majority.[3]

On one extreme, conservative gay writers like Andrew Sullivan and
Bruce Bawer have extolled marriage as a key index of the progress gays
have made toward acceptance. Bawer argues, for example, that discrimination against homosexuals is most marked when a couple decides to
live together and that the choice to form a joint household is therefore
a courageous stand against bigotry. "When two straight people decide
to marry, everyone celebrates their commitment," he explains. "When

two gay people decide to move in together, they commit themselves to insult and discrimination and attack. . . . Living alone, most gay people can conceal their sexuality; living together, a gay couple advertise theirs every time they step out of the house together. Is it any wonder, then, that so many gay men have historically been promiscuous, shunning long-term relationships in favor of one-night stands?" He elaborates on this topic bitterly, citing incident after incident in which his publicly committed relationship and those of his friends are slighted by presumably well-meaning heterosexuals. "I have longtime professional associates who routinely ask other men, 'How's the wife?' but to whom it never occurs to ask me 'How's Chris?' Recently when a gay friend of mine was singled out to work on a holiday, he had to call off plans with his companion. But a co-worker explained: 'It's only fair. We all have families to go home to' " (Bawer 1993, 262–63).

Bawer is particularly indignant about an experience he and his partner had at a heterosexual wedding they attended together. Despite the fact that they were both very close friends of the bride and groom, they were the only couple in attendance not asked to sit for formal portraits by the wedding photographer. In the ceremony itself, though both men walked in the procession and stood near the altar, the text read by the judge, written in consultation with the couple, stated outright that "marriage between a man and a woman . . . was 'the only valid foundation for an enduring home.' " Bawer and his partner were terribly hurt by what seemed to them to be a pattern that belittled their legitimacy as a couple. "To both of us," he says, "our omission from the 'couples' pictures and the callous wording of their marriage ceremony . . . drew an unmistakable line of demarcation between their relationship and ours"(ibid.).

Andrew Sullivan also focuses on marriage as the most reliable index of gay people's collective civil status, espousing "equal access to marriage" as the "centerpiece" of the next wave of gay and lesbian politics. In Sullivan's view, because marriage is a bond that demonstrates fundamental similarities between heterosexuals and homosexuals, legal same-sex marriage "could bring the essence of gay life—a gay couple—into the heart of the traditional family in a way the family can most understand and the gay offspring can most easily acknowledge. It could do more to heal the gay-straight rift than any amount of gay rights legislation." Gay marriage would also, he continues, counter the fear and shame that gay people have long experienced, offering them a positive future to imagine. "Gay marriage," according to Sullivan, "is not a radical step; it is a profoundly humanizing, traditionalizing step. . . . It is ultimately the only reform that truly matters" (Sullivan 1995, 178, 183–84, 185).

But it is precisely the whiff of conformity to mainstream values that most infuriates many gay critics of same-sex marriage, particularly feminists who recall the long historical association between marriage and patriarchy. Attorney Paula Ettelbrick has argued that an institution grounded in inequality ought to be interrogated rather than embraced, adding that such capitulation to convention flies in the face of the fundamental differences that exist between gay and straight worlds. "Being queer," says Ettelbrick, "is more than setting up house, sleeping with a person of the same gender, and seeking state approval for doing so. It is an identity, a culture with many variations."[4] Taking much the same position, attorney Nancy Polikoff questions the wisdom of claiming this most abusive of patriarchal institutions. Efforts to criticize marriage's essential message—the valorization of only one model for human relationships—will backfire if lesbians and gay men shift their focus from challenging the inequalities institutionalized by marriage to pursuing its privileges.[5]

A third position on same-sex marriage has been taken by other activists, particularly by those influenced by the social-constructionist views of gender and sexuality espoused by lesbian and gay scholars. Attorney Nan Hunter believes that Polikoff's position, and others like it, essentialize marriage as thoroughly as marriage statutes have historically essentialized gender. Like gender, Hunter explains, marriage is a social construction that has no natural existence outside a particular regulatory environment; it is ancient, but its form has changed throughout history. Her support for efforts to legalize same-sex marriage, then, rests on her assertion that such a change "would radically denaturalize the social construction of male/female differentness." She also notes that marriage would be most advantageous for the least affluent members of the gay community insofar as it offers the least costly mechanism for allocating property and other material arrangements in families (Hunter 1995, 109–10, 119).

Political philosopher Morris Kaplan sees same-sex marriage as a type of civil disobedience that could potentially transform public understandings of basic institutions. "The proliferation of queer couples and families," Kaplan asserts, "may help to redefine the social and legal conditions available to sustain intimate and domestic relationships more generally," leading to a larger "democratic contestation of the organization of personal life" (Kaplan 1997, 235).

Attorney Evan Wolfson, a member of the legal team that argued *Baehr v. Miike,* a case challenging the denial of marriage rights to same-sex couples in Hawaii, takes this position further. He denies the argument that seeking marriage rights for gays and lesbians will counter struggles to broaden notions of family and commitment, including efforts to regularize and expand domestic partnership arrangements as alternatives to marriage.[6] But he observes that "domestic partnership fails to resonate with the emotional, declarative, and often religious power most people feel inheres in marriage" (Wolfson 1994–95, 607). Same-sex couples, he points out, feel entitled to more than a limited package of benefits; arguments that reduce their desire for legal marriage to those (admittedly important) advantages miss the essence of what the struggle for marriage is all about. "The brilliance of our movement's taking on marriage is that marriage is, at once and truly, both conservative *and* transformative, easily understood in basic human terms of equality and respect, and liberating in its individual and social potential" (Wolfson 1994–95, 599).

Wolfson's assessment of what same-sex couples are claiming when they seek the right to marry speaks directly to the approach I take to the meaning of lesbian and gay ceremonies of commitment. While the legal struggle to legitimate marriage for same-sex couples winds its way slowly through the courts and the legislatures, both in the United States and elsewhere, couples have been going about the business of staging commitment ceremonies, holy unions—or just plain weddings—regardless of the status, or lack thereof, of such ceremonies. While the eventual outcome of the legal debate is certainly of interest to these couples, they do not require the official authorization furnished by a marriage statute to carry out the process of "getting married." Their ceremonies exist in addition to, or in spite of, the law's limitations and simply assert their validity because they are what they appear to be—weddings.

AUTHENTICATING THE COUPLE

In each of my interviews with same-sex couples who had staged commitment ceremonies or were in the process of planning them, I asked for comments on the view of many people in the gay community that people who have weddings are mimicking a straight institution and that

gays should define their own culture rather than try to imitate heterosexuals. Whenever I brought this subject up, couples nodded knowingly.
Some of them told me about gay friends who were less than enthusiastic
about, or even openly hostile to, their wedding plans; others described
situations where straight people seemed to see their ceremonies as an
invasion of sacred heterosexual ground. "So what do you say to people
when this comes up?" I asked over and over.

"Who says getting married is only for heterosexuals?" Couples voiced
some variant of this response in virtually every interview. "Is it copying
heterosexuals to want some of the good things that straight society offers?" some said. "Isn't love what it's all about?" said others. Still others
reasoned, "If God has brought us together, then we are only fulfilling
His will in making our union public." Couples understood their impulses as marks of their common humanity with heterosexual couples;
they saw their celebrations as legitimate because their bonds as couples
were fundamentally authentic and real.

How did these couples establish their authenticity? In the years since
Stonewall, revelation of one's "true self," the release from secrecy and
concealment that compromises individual integrity, has been at the heart
of the struggle for lesbian and gay liberation, assuming a place of particular importance in the narrative ritual of "coming out."[7] Coming-out
narratives are animated by a conviction that one's real self emerges when
one reveals one's homosexuality to friends and family, and perhaps more
importantly, to oneself. As Bonnie Zimmerman has noted, the theme of
the coming-out story in lesbian fiction is the discovery of one's true self,
often envisioned as a homecoming. In such accounts, coming out—dis-
covering and making public one's lesbian or gay identity—tends to be
imagined almost as an autonomous force, something like gravity that
cannot be suppressed indefinitely (Zimmerman 1984).

How can one be assured of the authenticity of anything in a world
that offers the temptations of artifice and delusion at every turn? Many
of the narratives I gathered drew on couples' accounts of emotional
intensity as evidence of the artlessness of their experience. Assuming that
the real self is lodged within, straining to reveal itself, powerful feelings
are taken as indicators of truth and reality, an assumption enormously
aided by the rise of popular psychotherapeutic models of individual happiness (Herman 1995). In coming-out narratives, for instance, the sen-
sation of being "at home" typically attests to the authenticity of the
revelation, as personal conviction endows experience with an authority
that cannot be contradicted by anyone who, in essence, "wasn't there."[8]

One's relationship with the divine can also offer evidence of authenticity. The discovery of fundamental truth, particularly in the Protestant reading of spirituality that permeates mainstream American culture, can be located in experiences of personal revelation that suggest direct communication with God. People tend to find evidence of such ultimate truths in the feeling of rightness that attaches to ordinary emotional states. For example, the perception that one's identity is simply the only way one can imagine being implies, as well, that it has been mandated by some higher force. Falling in love, similarly, is experienced as imbued with urgency that means it must be beyond one's control. To repudiate it, either by concealing it or refusing to honor it, would amount to an abdication of faith, a failure to recognize that one's earthly condition is a reflection of the image of God in which we were created.

American culture supplies other bases for authenticity, particularly in the construction attached to the concept of "love." In his groundbreaking study of American kinship, anthropologist David Schneider identified the basic cultural elements that give the kinship system coherence and meaning in terms of two basic components—the order of nature and the order of law—out of which all kinship relationships are established and defined. That is, this system offers two ways of defining relatives—"by blood" and "by marriage"—and though only the former of these is thought to be constituted in a natural substance, both are seen as real and bounded by codes of conduct. Because blood ties are understood to have a material basis, Schneider's reading presumes that they are taken to be permanent and hence involuntary; marriage (or by extension, any other tie, such as friendship, defined by a legal or social arrangement) can be terminated and is, therefore, inherently voluntary and potentially impermanent.[9] Both are, however, signaled by or experienced as love—*cognatic* love in the case of parent and child and *conjugal* love for spouses. These two types of love are enacted significantly in sexual intercourse and the kiss, both of which Schneider explicates as symbols of a process whereby opposites are unified in the biogenetic events of reproduction (1968, 39).

The Schneiderian understanding of American culture situates love at its center and argues that love is real because it is experienced as beyond volition, particularly when it involves sexual expression. Love arises normatively between individuals not united by a natural substance (blood), but sexual intercourse seals that bond with other natural substances and with a seemingly irresistible physicality. Insofar as love is perceived to be a profound and mysteriously compelling force, it must then be authentic. Furthermore, as sociologist Anthony Giddens reminds us, the experience of romantic love tends to be idealized in Western cultures, conceptualized as a transcendent state that marks the completion of a quest for one's intended other (Giddens 1992). The popular song "You'll Never Walk Alone" speaks to us in its simple assurance that finding one's place in a couple is simply the most natural and desirable condition.

For gay and lesbian couples, a ceremonial and public avowal of "being in love" may dramatize an implicit opposition between "true" and "romantic love," a contrast rooted in Victorian discourse. As sociologist Steven Seidman has argued, true love has been imagined as idealistic, spiritual, and altruistic, the antithesis of romantic love's foundation in sensuality, egotism, and deception (Seidman 1991). Since (particularly male) homosexuality conventionally conjures up images of promiscuity, a couple that declares their true love for one another refuses, in effect, to be defined by prevailing representations. Insofar as "love" has been most elaborated in American culture as a feminine characteristic (Cancian 1987, 4–6), closely allied with the attachment to others expected in women, its elaboration in same-sex weddings further confounds tendencies to view gay men (and lesbians, perhaps) as more concerned with individual gratification than with relationships and expressive emotionality.

Making the wedding a "public" event may also provide validation of claims to authenticity, for how can the community, particularly representatives of the heterosexual majority, be wrong? Couples I interviewed spoke again and again of the importance of having witnesses to their commitment and of the community's presence as the elements that sealed their union. In effect, the community's approbation counteracts the opposition of the wider society toward homosexual love; the community's readiness to accept the same-sex couple into its midst is particularly powerful when that "community" spans the gay-straight divide. Couples' accounts of planning their ceremonies virtually always report (sometimes heroic) efforts to include gay and straight, young and old, male and female, friend and relative. If groups of heterosexuals recognize the significance of the events, if people assumed not to be biased in favor of homosexuality warrant the sanctity of their bond, then its validity must be beyond dispute. Such approval is particularly important when greater efforts had to be made to assure the participation of the guests; convincing previously skeptical heterosexuals that a same-sex relationship is truly about love is a major victory.

The authenticity of gay and lesbian weddings is further confirmed by the perception by both actors and guests that they are voluntary, rather than the product of social pressure or simple capitulation to convention. Over and over, couples laughed as they reminded me that they could hardly be accused of getting married to please their parents or to get a lot of gifts, while others occasionally joked about "having" to get married to legitimate their offspring. Voluntary behavior is understood, in this construction, to spring from the heart, and to be pure and uncontaminated by the desire to gain some benefit from a course of action. In a world thought to be corrupted by the pursuit of profit and advantage, true love shines as a beacon of authenticity, as something trustworthy, innocent, and beyond disbelief.

Paradoxically, perhaps, authenticity can be ritually demonstrated *either* by self-conscious originality *or* by reliance on traditional forms. On the one hand, some couples see their inventiveness as proof of the individual truth of their feelings. Shunning cliché and rejecting prepackaged sentiments by composing their own vows or contriving some unique ceremonial twist speak to both the uniqueness and the legitimacy of the relationship. Even when the product of these creative efforts bears an uncanny resemblance to boilerplate matrimonial language, couples may still emphasize the creative particulars that found their way into the ritual.

On the other hand, lack of originality can be as effective a demonstration of authenticity as originality. Reliance on "tradition" locates a couple within an existing history or community and therefore makes the ceremonial product a more convincing example of its genre. In these cases, the assertion that the event is *really* a wedding is strengthened to the extent that it conforms to customary requirements for such a ritual occasion.

All these sources of validation and recognition can be further solidified through the bestowal of gifts. While it is unlikely that receiving presents is the primary inspiration of any gay or lesbian (or heterosexual) couple planning a ceremony, gifts, particularly those conventionally associated with weddings, such as china, silver, crystal, and household goods, authoritatively signal the establishment of a sanctioned domestic unit—a family. When such gifts are family heirlooms, moreover, or are given by blood relatives, or when relatives contribute to the cost of the ceremony, they indicate that the same-sex couple has been integrated, symbolically at least, into the constellation of kin. In much the same way, being called upon later to host family holiday celebrations may intensify claims to being part of the wider world of relatives.

THE FAMILY CHINA

About six months after "Karen Newton" and "Andrea Katz" met, they decided to become engaged.[10] Although they had yet to move in together or to plan an actual ceremony, they were convinced that they would marry and began their preparations by having "engagement rings" designed by a local jeweler. When I later met with them in their Berkeley home, they explained every step of the process in detail, with Karen supplying an account of their decisions about the rings. "[They're] yellow gold and white gold and sapphire and amethyst, because . . . I wanted yellow gold and she wanted silver and an amethyst. And we ended up designing something that combined the two. . . . And for our wedding bands, we had a very thin simple gold band designed to go with this. And mine is yellow gold, and hers is white gold. . . . [They] are identical. So it's kind of like this is the merging of the two identities and then there's the individual identities, too."

Karen and Andrea agreed that they encountered few obstacles in putting together plans for a wedding ceremony they celebrated on the terrace of a landmark San Francisco restaurant that was the scene of their first date. From the jeweler who made their rings to the furniture salesman who sold them their new couch, no one with whom they made arrangements indicated that there was anything out of the ordinary about two women getting married. But their families presented some more difficult issues. Andrea's parents have lived all their lives in the same working-class Jewish neighborhood in a large Midwestern city, and their relationships with friends and family in that community run deep. When they first learned Andrea was a lesbian, some years earlier, they had been quite distressed, and Andrea's mother, in particular, did not want her friends to know that her daughter was gay. During all the time that she kept this embarrassing information to herself, Andrea's mother had been attending weddings and showers given by her friends' and relatives' children, all the while secretly worrying that her own daughter would never bring her the *naches* (Yiddish for "gratification") of being the mother of the bride. So once Andrea told her about the wedding plans, her mother began to tell everyone about the coming event. "She thought, 'Damn it, you know. My kid's getting married and I want the same thing.' So she took the initiative on her own. . . . She

took it upon herself because she was . . . just very proud and very happy.
. . . [She thought,] 'I want people to know my kid's getting married, and
I want to share that. And I want people to participate the same way I've
participated in their kids' ceremonies.' "

Andrea's mother was so enthusiastic that she sent the two women a
list of thirty-seven relatives and friends she thought they should invite
to the wedding. A few weeks later, she called Andrea and Karen to tell
them that her girlfriends had decided to throw them a shower in absen-
tia. Andrea reported, "She called . . . and said, 'The girls want to know
if you guys need comforters or a microwave or what is it you need for
your pre-wedding gift?' And you know, they'll want to know what china
we want."

Early in the process of planning their wedding, Karen and Andrea
decided to register for gifts at two San Francisco stores, Macy's and
Gump's (an elegant local store specializing in china, silver, crystal, and
other home furnishings). Andrea laughs as she describes the transformation in her consciousness of herself as a lesbian.

> In my younger more radical-dyke feminist days, [I] would just have plowed
> into Macy's and Gump's [to] get china and break it. And now it's turned
> around that I actually wanted to do this, facetiously, but part of it is I
> want it to be recognized as a real relationship. So I want to go to Macy's
> and Gump's and register. And I want china. . . . I've been to several
> weddings and certainly I know that in the cultural milieu I grew up in and
> that my mother still participates in strongly . . . you go to showers and
> you get gifts. And people register. And I'm just fascinated by the idea that
> we can go to five stores and just, you know, do wish lists and then just
> send this out across the country, and we'll get 25 percent. Things that we
> will use. . . . And there is also the recognition element, that again, this
> is like everybody else does it. And I want that. In some ways it's the campiness
> of it, of just like having that experience, of computerizing across the
> country and telling people, "We want the towels with the red stripes, not
> the blue ones."

But in admitting their desire to acquire china, silver, and crystal—
"nice things"—Karen and Andrea are talking about much more than a
desire for material accumulation. It quickly becomes clear that they are
explaining the process of establishing themselves as a family and of making sure that the larger world understands that their union constitutes
them as a couple that heads a family. They intend to have children
together and host many holiday dinners and other festive occasions in
the dining room of the house they purchased together not long before
their wedding. Karen muses, "I just think it would be really nice to be

able to set up a household with the kinds of nice things that, you know, I'd like to pass on to my kids." Andrea adds that her mother has offered to give her the family china, a gift that has led her to speculate on why having these things is important to her.

> It's where the china and the crystal and the silver come in. . . . And I definitely want china for that reason. . . . My mom's china, which is very, very dear to her, as much as she says, "I hate what you kids did to it," that china shows the wear and tear of Thanksgiving dinners and seders and Rosh Hashanah dinners and Sunday nights with grandma and grandpa and everybody over. It's a real *feeling!* We will get pieces of that china . . . and I want that. And . . . there's a certain formality that I want to be able to have. I don't know that I would associate it with necessarily Shabbat or Jewish holidays, but certainly for Thanksgiving dinner, I want to do that.

Karen adds, "Well, we do Thanksgiving. We do Passover. . . . We *are* the family center here."

For Karen and Andrea, evidence that becoming a married couple will allow them to make claims on being a family is authoritatively conveyed through the symbolic medium of wedding gifts. On one level, registering at department stores and being the beneficiaries of the structured largesse of wedding showers attests to the legitimacy of their assertion that their relationship is for real, as worthy of support as any heterosexual marriage. On another level, possessing these household goods, both the new items they have chosen and the family china, will offer a constant reaffirmation of their status in the years to come. The family china, the formal silver and crystal, and the accouterments of middle-class domesticity symbolize family, encoding stability, tradition, and the fulfillment of intergenerational continuity. To be sure, these possessions signal the achievement of class mobility and professional success, undoubtedly an issue for both women. But beyond this, and more to the point for the present discussion, they also effectively mark the authenticity of Karen and Andrea's union as a *marriage*. The importance of claiming such authenticity is reinforced by both women's bemused understanding of the desire for gifts as a contradiction to the unconventional, counter-cultural sensibilities once central to their expression of lesbian identity.

IN THE SHADOW OF DAVID AND JONATHAN

> Hear these words from the eighteenth chapter of the first book of Samuel (vv. 1–4):

"When David had finished speaking to Saul, the soul of Jonathan was bound to the soul of David, and Jonathan loved him as his own soul. Saul took him that day and would not let him return to his father's house. Then Jonathan made a covenant with David, because he loved him as his own soul. Jonathan stripped himself of the robe that he was wearing, and gave it to David, and his armor, and even his sword and his bow and his belt."

These were the words a San Francisco Baptist minister used to begin his meditation at the 1995 wedding of "Ken Taylor" and "Greg Bowers." The guests gathered in the shadowy chapel of the hundred-year-old landmark Swedenborgian Church, an outstanding example of the arts-and-crafts style of the late nineteenth and early twentieth centuries, set behind a high garden wall in the city's Pacific Heights district. The church had been rented for the occasion. Inside the chapel, a fire crackled in the huge fireplace that spanned its rear wall. The ceiling was supported by bark-covered madrone trunks; the congregation took their seats on woven-rush chairs. Candles illuminated the intimate space.

Ken and Greg are both native Midwesterners from blue-collar families. Now in their early thirties, they own a comfortable hilltop home in one of San Francisco's working-class neighborhoods, which they share with their two dogs. Ken works for a federal agency and travels frequently; Greg is a computer consultant employed by a large software company. They planned their wedding to coincide with their second anniversary.

Although a lot of discussion preceded the final plans for their ceremony, there was little doubt in their minds from the beginning that it would be a religious event. Ken is a lifelong Baptist and he spoke eloquently about how important it was to him that they have a church wedding. Since moving to San Francisco, Ken has been an active member of a Baptist congregation located near the Castro District. The membership in the church is diverse, but it does have a large number of gay members and took the step some years earlier of declaring itself to be "open and affirming" of same-sex relationships. This relatively radical action eventually led to the congregation being expelled from the Southern Baptist Convention and to affiliating with the more liberal American Baptist Church. Ken considers his religion a central part of his life.

It's always been a big part of my life. It's helped me get through some very difficult situations. I feel I have a relationship with Christ personally. I've always grown up with that. And even growing up gay, and growing up in a Baptist church in Oklahoma *and* being gay—there were obviously some issues to deal with there—[but] I've always felt, I still felt very grounded whether I was having problems at home, a relationship, or work or whatever. It keeps me centered and keeps me focused. It's always been a part of my life.

Since both men felt comfortable with the young minister who had recently become the pastor of Ken's church, the decision to ask him to officiate was quite straightforward. But besides having a church ceremony, it was essential in both their minds that other people be present. "It meant a public display of what Greg means to me, what we mean to each other. And it also means—I don't know the right phrase—I don't want to say 'elevate' a gay relationship to a heterosexual ceremony, because that gives the connotation that we're *below*. I wanted to try to maybe just take the next step as far as community is concerned. That we can do this. I mean, most people like myself have been resigned to just accepting [that we could never have a wedding]. Like Greg was thinking that he was never going to have one."

While having a church wedding was only one of the things Ken and Greg were conscious of having been denied because they were gay, it loomed large in both men's thinking. Both associated having a wedding with overcoming the outsider status they had long assumed to be an inalterable fact of homosexuality. Greg was frank about what this meant to him when he first realized he was gay. "Even when I was coming out, I thought, 'This is awful. I'm gay and I can never get married, and I can never be in a relationship like that.' And then as I started being more comfortable with being gay, and was out, and had friends and the community, and it just became my lifestyle, and my life, that's the way I was. . . . I knew that I would like to be in a long-term relationship, but as far as getting married, I never really considered that. So then when he asked me to marry him, it was like, wow, okay."

Ken explained why having a wedding was so important to him. "For me, in a selfish way, I didn't want to deny me and Greg the tradition of going through a ceremony just because we're gay. I guess I had pretty much written off [when I was] younger that because I'm gay, I'll never have a wedding. And so I decided, well, why not? I love this man. Why can't we? It went from there."

Deciding to get married was also the most visible sign of their growing commitment to being out in the wider community. Around the time they began planning the ceremony, Ken launched a gradual, but determined, process of coming out at his job, a process he described as positive and affirming. He became close friends with a woman co-worker who had recently become engaged and her excitement about her wedding stimulated him to share his dreams with her. He confided in her and sought her advice as he arranged a romantic trip to Hawaii, discussing each detail of his plan to propose to Greg. After Greg had accepted, they shared information about weddings in general and about each of their ceremonies, trading hints about where to hold such events as well as about such matters as food, flowers, and music.

Both Ken and Greg felt strongly that their ceremony was not a departure from Christian tradition. The pastor's words affirmed this as he used Biblical quotations to show that there is a precedent for same-sex love in Scripture, a precedent that means that God understands and supports their union.

> It is clear from this scripture that a love relationship occurred between David and Jonathan. A beautiful love relationship that was honored by God. Marriages, by and large, were for convenience. . . . But in the case of David and Jonathan, we have love. Pure and simple love. A love that never ended and that grew in devotion over the years. I dare say that their love was among the purest in the Bible. When Jonathan died, David wept over his grave and said, as recorded in 2 Samuel 1:26: "I am distressed for you, my brother Jonathan; greatly loved were you to me; your love to me was wonderful, passing the love of women."

Greg and Ken's claim to legitimacy was reinforced by its resemblance to the kind of mainstream Protestant wedding a heterosexual couple might also have planned. A tuxedo-clad usher showed guests into the church, seating them to the right or the left depending upon which of the two grooms they were connected to. Two candles were lit on the altar at the start of the ceremony, representing the two separate entities who would be united. The couple, both dressed in tuxedos, made their entrance to an organ fanfare, each proceeding down one of the side aisles until they met at the altar. The minister led them through "vows of intention" in which they promised to face the future together. After the Scripture reading and the minister's homily (on the subject of David and Jonathan), the two men faced each other for the most solemn moment, the pronouncement of their "vows of commitment." They then exchanged rings, which the minister explained as "circles symbolic of eternity," made of precious metal to represent "pure love." Each swore to the other, "I choose you to be my spouse, today and every day." As a vocalist sang "Love Changes Everything," they knelt and prayed, the minister's hands resting on their shoulders. They completed the ritual by using the two candles to light a single "unity candle," indicating their change of status was complete. The minister declared them "joined together forever."

Much as Greg and Ken accentuated the authenticity of their union through the form they adhered to throughout the ceremony, the guests could not fail to be aware that this was no ordinary wedding. Only one relative of the two men, Greg's mother, had come to San Francisco for the occasion, and the program made special note of the fact that she was "in attendance." I overheard the guests seated behind me exclaiming about how "wonderful" it was that she had chosen to come.

But these elements of incongruity were minor, effaced by the many ways in which the event adhered to "tradition." After the ceremony, we moved to the adjoining parish house, decorated with gigantic floral arrangements, for the reception. Piano music was played as the guests filed in from the courtyard. Two professional portraits of the couple adorned the entrance area; elaborately wrapped gifts were piled in the far corner of one room. At one table, bartenders dispensed wine, champagne, and mineral water; another table held an elegantly displayed assortment of appetizers; later, we moved into another room to be served dinner from another lavish buffet. The wedding cake, multitiered and white, topped with two male figures dressed in formal attire, was available for inspection on a central table.

Ken and Greg's wedding confirmed the validity and authenticity of their relationship on a number of levels. To the extent that the ceremony and reception adhered to the familiar forms of other (heterosexual) weddings of their experience, it was clear to them that the occasion was as real as any other wedding. The acceptance they received from numbers of nongay people enhanced this perception, as did the presence of their gay friends, whom they described as their "chosen family."

Each of these sources of recognition, however, paled beside the Biblical recognition the minister provided. By interpreting the story of David and Jonathan as evidence of transcendent acceptance of homosexuality, and by going so far as to assert its historic role as the model for marriage as an institution, the minister attested to the legitimacy of their claims. As long as David and Jonathan's love stands for exemplary devotion, then, his homily uses biblical authority to dare doubters to question the authenticity of Greg and Ken's love or the claim that their relationship is a marriage.

Greg and Ken's belief in God and the importance they placed on their involvement in a spiritual community provided the foundation for their use of Scripture to anchor their claims to authenticity. That is, the choice to situate their ceremony in a church with a minister officiating and to explain their love in the language of familiar Old Testament references work to obstruct any implication that they were playacting or imitating an institution to which they lacked a legitimate claim. Their ceremony manifestly constituted a performance of something anyone from their backgrounds would immediately recognize as a "wedding" and nothing else.

"YOU'LL NEVER WALK ALONE"

Do lesbian and gay weddings represent a radical challenge to conventional gender arrangements or an uncritical effort to acquire some of the advantages marriage confers on heterosexual couples? The two unions I've discussed draw on forms the couples understand to be "traditional" in different ways, each emphasizing different elements of the symbolic complex that is typically played out at such weddings.

In the case of Karen and Andrea, authenticity flowed from their perception that they were being incorporated into a system of exchange in which Andrea's parents had long been players. The enthusiasm that Andrea's mother, in particular, revealed when given the opportunity to launch multiple gift-giving events for her daughter makes clear that legitimacy is, in large part, socially conferred. Gifts, most notably domestic goods that testify to the centrality of the new marriage in a network of kin relations, eloquently confirm the recognition of others. For Karen and Andrea, the prospect of receiving the family china announced to all who could see that they were next in line, designated to accentuate family continuity on holiday occasions. The family china, in essence, testified that Karen and Andrea had become kin and therefore embedded their *love* in the context of kinship. The material logic of American kinship, then, made their relationship a marriage.

Greg and Ken understood themselves to be assured of authenticity by God's will. Not only did their minister firmly believe that the love of two men had provided the prototype for Christian marriage, but their declaration of mutual devotion was witnessed by the same God whose word was revealed in the Bible. According to the minister's reasoning, the purity of their love elevated it beyond the level of mere convenience that in his view commonly sullies heterosexual marriage; since gay unions have no official standing, no one could accuse Greg and Ken—or any other same-sex couple—of choosing to marry to fulfill family expectations or to gain financial or legal advantages. In a sense, it was the transgressiveness of Ken and Greg's union that most unambiguously marked it as an expression of *love,* since only a force as strong as love could enable a couple to stand up to forces that would keep them apart.

Both of these ceremonies speak to a seeming paradox that stands at the heart of lesbian and gay marriage, as it does as well at the center of other dimensions of lesbian and gay family life. As I pointed out in my earlier study of lesbian mothers, motherhood for women who are conventionally assumed to be inappropriate occupants of the maternal role—either because of the conflation of (hetero)sexuality with motherhood or because they are thought to be too sexual to display the altruism associated with motherhood—may be said to make complicated cultural statements when they claim the identity of mother. On one level, by demanding that they be recognized as mothers, they are transgressing common understandings and challenging conventional beliefs about sexuality and procreation. But in other ways, I found lesbian mothers' views about what motherhood meant to be profoundly conventional and even conservative of traditional notions of maternal character. My informants argued that motherhood gave them access to a particularly compelling source of virtue and moral ascendancy over non-mothers, and further, that motherhood was uniquely linked to their femaleness. That is, their understandings of their identities depended in large part on the same sort of naturalized notions of motherhood that are characteristic of the wider cultures' expectations. Their existence simultaneously challenged and reinforced "tradition," suggesting that efforts to distinguish between resistance and accommodation may be less meaningful than many theorists have assumed.[11]

But the struggle to claim authenticity for same-sex unions engages with this problem of resistance and accommodation in a somewhat different way. Because of the ritual, performative context in which the demands couples make for legitimacy are enacted, problems of intent and interpretation can become central. What specific symbolic moves mean to the couple and what they suggest to those who attend or hear about the ceremony may not be the same. In the same way, the meanings that attach to particular symbols—be they ceremonial elements or wedding gifts—cannot help but shift depending on the identity of the actors. So while family china, for example, may invoke images of tradition and conventionality for heterosexual couples who marry, receiving these same dishes may imply the conquest of conventions that restrict marriage to "opposite-sex" couples. And receiving the blessings of God as revealed in the language of Scripture may allow couples not only to situate their relationship within a celestial plan, as do heterosexual couples, but to proclaim that their transgression of convention has been accomplished with the collaboration of the divine.

As long as same-sex couples are unable to directly claim the right to either *blood* or *law* as evidence of kinship, we can expect their unions to accentuate the autonomous power of *love* as a source of legitimacy. Lesbians and gay men draw on the same symbolic universe as heterosexual spouses to assert that they are to be treated as "couples," but the limitations within which they must negotiate their claims means that they must emphasize the single kinship feature to which they have unimpeded access. When one couple I interviewed chose "You'll Never Walk Alone" as the song that would accompany them on their way to the altar, they were doing more than slyly mocking the popular culture that excluded them. They were marking couplehood as a status worthy of attainment and reminding all who witnessed their wedding that they had full access to the basic requirements for achieving a union all would have to recognize as authentic—true love.

NOTES

1. The public debate over same-sex marriage has been associated most visibly with the proliferation of a variety of local statutes and employment benefits known as "domestic partner" policies and with litigation challenging the constitutional basis of limiting legal marriage to heterosexual couples. In response to the possibility that the supreme court of Hawaii might rule that same-sex marriages were legal *(Baehr v. Miike)*, Congress passed the so-called Defense of Marriage Act (DOMA) in 1996, which authorized states to refuse to recognize same-sex marriages performed in other states.

2. A more detailed discussion of these ceremonies is to be found in Lewin (1998).

3. See Vaid (1995), for example, for an argument that this dichotomy is the central strain in lesbian and gay politics.

4. Ettelbrick (1992), 22. Since this essay was written, Ettelbrick's work with the Empire State Pride Agenda has led her to modify her position on marriage. As the Hawaii and Vermont cases moved to the center of gay-rights activism around the country, Ettelbrick has become a persuasive advocate for the legalization of same-sex marriage.

5. Polikoff (1993), 1546; see also Warner (1999).

6. Domestic partnership statutes have been enacted by a growing number of municipalities since Berkeley, California, established the first such provisions in 1984. In some locations, domestic partnership registration or other evidence of joint residence and financial interdependency entitles couples to share in such benefits as health insurance or bereavement leave, but in most the benefits are

purely symbolic and in no way reproduce the advantages that accrue to legally married husbands and wives. Two major challenges to restrictions against same-sex couples obtaining marriage licenses were mounted in the 1990s, the most well-known of which was the *Baehr v. Miike* case in Hawaii, which took the matter of same-sex marriage as far as the state supreme court. Fears in Hawaii, and around the nation, that same-sex marriage was headed for legalization set off a wave of preventive legislative measures. At the federal level, the Defense of Marriage Act (DOMA) offered states the option of not recognizing same-sex marriages performed in other states, thus bypassing the full faith and credit provisions of the Constitution. In 1998, voters in Hawaii approved an amendment to the state constitution that defined marriage as being possible only between a man and a woman. The supreme court of Hawaii ruled that the challenge to the marriage statute therefore did not constitute a violation of the state's rigorous equal gender-rights provisions. Since this writing, a similar case in Vermont, *Baker v. Vermont*, resulted in the passage of a civil union provision in that state, with most of the legal entitlements associated with marriage.

7. Stonewall refers to the historic 1969 riot at New York's Stonewall Inn, an event commonly used to date the start of the gay- and lesbian-rights movement.

8. Testimonies of personal experience also stand at the heart of Second Wave feminist politics; personal narratives convey a sort of "truth" that is absolute because of the uniqueness of individual lives even as their "truth" is also attested to by the discovery that these occurrences seem to be both culturally structured and pervasive. See Jones (1993) and Scott (1992) on the authority of experience; see Personal Narratives Group (1989) on feminist uses of narrative.

9. Schneider (1968), 27, 37; see Weston's revision and extension of this argument in her consideration of how gay men and lesbians create "families we choose" (1991).

10. Couples' names, indicated in their first appearance with quotation marks, are pseudonyms.

11. See Lewin (1993) for a more detailed treatment of this issue.

REFERENCES

Bawer, Bruce. 1993. *A Place at the Table: The Gay Individual in American Society*. New York: Poseidon Press.

Cancian, Francesca M. 1987. *Love in America: Gender and Self-Development*. Cambridge: Cambridge University Press.

Ettelbrick, Paula L. 1992. "Since When Is Marriage a Path to Liberation? " In *Lesbian and Gay Marriage: Private Commitments, Public Ceremonies*, edited by S. Sherman, 20–26. Philadelphia: Temple University Press.

Giddens, Anthony. 1992. *The Transformation of Intimacy: Sexuality, Love and Eroticism in Modern Societies*. Stanford: Stanford University Press.

Herman, Ellen. 1995. *The Romance of American Psychology: Political Culture in the Age of Experts*. Berkeley and Los Angeles: University of California Press.

Hunter, Nan D. 1995. "Marriage, Law and Gender: A Feminist Inquiry." In

Sex Wars: Sexual Politics and Political Culture, 107–22. New York: Routledge.

Jones, Kathleen B. 1993. *Compassionate Authority: Democracy and the Representation of Women.* New York: Routledge.

Kaplan, Morris B. 1997. *Sexual Justice: Democratic Citizenship and the Politics of Desire.* New York: Routledge.

Lewin, Ellen. 1993. *Lesbian Mothers: Accounts of Gender in American Culture.* Ithaca, N.Y.: Cornell University Press.

———. 1998. *Recognizing Ourselves: Ceremonies of Lesbian and Gay Commitment.* New York: Columbia University Press.

Monette, Paul. 1988. *Borrowed Time: An AIDS Memoir.* San Diego: Harcourt, Brace, Jovanovich.

Personal Narratives Group. 1989. *Interpreting Women's Lives: Feminist Theory and Personal Narratives.* Bloomington: Indiana University Press.

Polikoff, Nancy D. 1993. "We Will Get What We Ask For: Why Legalizing Gay and Lesbian Marriage Will Not 'Dismantle the Legal Structure of Gender in Every Marriage.'" *Virginia Law Review* 79(7):1535–50.

Schneider, David N. 1968. *American Kinship: A Cultural Account.* Englewood Cliffs, N.J.: Prentice-Hall.

Scott, Joan W. 1992. "Experience." In *Feminists Theorize the Political,* edited by J. Butler and J. W. Scott, 22–40. New York: Routledge.

Seidman, Steven. 1991. *Romantic Longings: Love in America, 1830–1980.* New York: Routledge.

Sullivan, Andrew. 1995. *Virtually Normal: An Argument about Homosexuality.* New York: Knopf.

Vaid, Urvashi. 1995. *Virtual Equality: The Mainstreaming of Gay and Lesbian Liberation.* New York: Anchor.

Warner, Michael. 1999. *The Trouble with Normal.* New York: Free Press.

Weston, Kath. 1991. *Families We Choose: Lesbians, Gays, Kinship.* New York: Columbia University Press.

Wolfson, Evan. 1994–95. "Crossing the Threshold: Equal Marriage Rights for Lesbians and Gay Men and the Intra-Community Critique." *New York University Review of Law and Social Change* 21(3):567–615.

Zimmerman, Bonnie. 1984. "The Politics of Transliteration: Lesbian First-Person Narratives." *Signs: Journal of Women in Culture and Society* 9(4): 663–82.

CHAPTER 6

The Couple at Home

Education's Contribution

Nel Noddings

People form couples—same sex or opposite sex—for a variety of reasons, but one of the most obvious reasons is to establish a home. Oddly, educational systems in the Western world give little attention to the task of homemaking even though it is a task almost universally undertaken. Philosophy, too, has been remiss in analyzing what it takes to make a home. When the home has been discussed in philosophy, the purpose has usually been to describe the role of the home and family in maintaining the state and its public functions. "Home" is rarely taken as an object of analysis in itself.

The establishment of the modern home as a place of privacy and shelter from the public world increased the separation of women from the public domain. Although women had always been expected to assume domestic responsibilities, many women in premodern times also participated in the wider world of work. Growth in the middle class, with its pride in individual ownership of house and furnishings, actually increased the isolation of many women, and, paradoxically, this isolation was interpreted as a sign of well-being or status in the economic world. Homemaking as a major occupation became an enterprise engaged in full-time by more women, and the education of girls for this activity took place almost exclusively in homes. (The discussion and analysis provided here are restricted to what we call the Western world and, within that, to the mostly white world—one that greatly influenced the lives and aspirations of all women.) Now we are living in a time when both women and men expect to have occupations outside the home. How will young people be prepared for the work of establishing a home? Why is such preparation especially necessary today? What does it *mean* to make a home? Finally, given the immense quantity of material that schools are expected to convey, can preparation for homemaking contribute to cultural literacy?

THE CONCEPT OF HOME

The historian Theodore Zeldin remarks:

> There are few schools in the West which try to teach children to understand other people by making them play the role of another, which in effect is an invitation to widen one's idea of what a home is. If home is where one feels comfortable and understood, but still retains one's privacy and mystery, if it is where one both takes care of others and is taken care of, while also having the right to be left alone, and if it is one of the great personal and collective works of art that all human beings spend their lives attempting to raise up and keep from falling down, then the art of creating homes, as distinct from building houses, still has a long way to go, and still remains within the province of magic. Instinct and imitation are not enough to make a home.[1]

Now, in fact, schools in the United States often use role playing, but its purposes are limited. There is nothing like the study of homes that Zeldin seems to have in mind. Western education, originally designed as an initiation of boys into public life, has never given anything but casual attention to domestic life. Even the building of houses—an enterprise ranked at a less universal level by Zeldin—is largely ignored.

But is there nothing of intellectual interest here? Gaston Bachelard challenges a view often voiced in philosophy. Writing of the *house,* which he calls "one of the greatest powers of integration for the thoughts, memories and dreams of mankind," he says: "Without it, man would be a dispersed being. It maintains him through the storms of the heavens and through those of life. It is body and soul. It is the human being's first world. Before he is 'cast into the world,' as claimed by certain hasty metaphysics, man is laid in the cradle of the house. And always, in our daydreams, the house is a large cradle. A concrete metaphysics cannot neglect this fact, this simple fact . . . to which we return in our daydreaming."[2]

A little later, Bachelard notes that "the house we were born in is physically inscribed in us. It is a group of organic habits."[3] He seems to be talking about a stability that has been almost lost in the postmodern world. Few of us have remained long enough in our birth-homes to develop the physical habits he describes. However, he is not referring exclusively to a physical entity when he speaks of the house we were born in, and he is right in speaking of "organic habits." These develop in homes regardless of moves and changes in the "house" and are influenced by one's physical surroundings. Do young people understand that each member of a couple brings this set of "organic habits" to the relationship?

As we approach the great work of art described by Zeldin, we see that the organic habits each member of the couple brings to the relationship pose one important set of problems for the couple. Another, closely related, is one of creating a new, shared aesthetic. By "aesthetic" I do not mean an elite enterprise—collecting fine art, creating "house beautiful," or exercising formal aesthetic criteria. I mean simply deciding together what the place will look like, what objects will be cherished, how things will be arranged, how important hospitality will be, and so on. To create a shared aesthetic involves a problem of analyzing both the organic habits of the couple and the cultural background from which these habits have emerged. Understanding this problem requires an appreciation of the relation between inhabitant and place. Edward Casey writes:

> Built places . . . are extensions of our bodies. They are not first places, as
> the Aristotelian model of place as a strict container implies, in which these
> bodies move and position themselves. Places built for residing are rather
> an enlargement of an already existing embodiment into an entire life-world
> of dwelling. Moreover, thanks to increasingly intimate relationships with
> their material structures, the longer we reside in places, the more body-like
> they seem to be. As we feel more "at home" in dwelling places, they
> become places created in our own bodily image.[4]

But what if the couple have very different habits and aesthetic visions? The classic contemporary example here is "The Odd Couple," two people with opposite habits of neatness, entirely different senses of the aesthetic, and conflicting emotional patterns. The story makes wonderful entertainment, but in real life such a clash spells trouble for the relationship. Even smaller differences—one collects, the other discards—can cause distress and require negotiation. In addition to being influenced by personal habits, the aesthetic created by a couple is heavily influenced by cultural and economic factors. For some, cultural influences virtually dictate the place in which a couple must dwell. Identity is tightly connected to place. Casey describes the fate of Navajos for whom even a relatively small geographical move has spelled a loss of identity, even a loss of life.[5] Although most of us are not as attached to a geographical place as the Navajo, many of us embed the memory of early places into the aesthetic we build as a couple. Without this continuity, our dwelling places are more like hotel rooms than extensions of our bodies.

Thus, a couple must attend to the antecedents of the aesthetic they will build as well as the vision of a new aesthetic. Some can live comfortably behind dead-bolted doors with drawn shades; others will feel suffocated in such an environment. Our various habits and attitudes also affect the metaphors we construct and use. *House* and *home* are enormously powerful symbols. Bachelard, for example, describes the doubly symbolic meaning of doors: doors open and close; keys lock and unlock. A "mere door," he writes, "can give images of hesitation, temptation, desire, security, welcome and respect."[6] There are, then, both concrete decisions to be made and symbolic understandings to be explored in building a shared aesthetic.

Will the couple live in close connection to the outside world—lots of doors and windows, porches and gardens—or closed off from the world in agreed-upon privacy? How much does it matter? Although it is beyond the scope of the present chapter to consider this question in depth, I should at least note that the problems of impoverished urban couples may well be worse than those of correspondingly poor rural couples on at least this dimension. The rural couple can "open the door" on a broader and less threatening vista. There is a greater incentive to open up than to lock themselves in.

In addition to learning about and accommodating the partner's organic habits, revising one's own, and building a shared aesthetic, couples have to create a home that will provide for individual growth. The home is not only a "group of organic habits," as Bachelard says, but "something deeper, the shelter of the imagination itself."[7] Again, I am not referring to an elite condition characterized by great leisure but, rather, to an arrangement that allows each member to dream, plan, and execute at least some ideas for her or his own growth. Virginia Woolf, in her classic *A Room of One's Own,* saw clearly that to grow and to create, women needed both privacy and a measure of financial independence.[8] Anne Morrow Lindbergh, too, emphasized the need for women to claim solitude and achieve a measure of emotional independence.[9]

In this task—sheltering the imagination—heterosexual couples face perhaps more formidable problems than same-sex couples. That great model of traditional family life, the Victorian home, at its best often provided such shelter for the children of the house, and the era is replete with literature expressing nostalgia for the home of childhood.[10] But the gain for children came at an enormous cost for women. The division of labor was rigid in the middle and upper classes. Males could expect to put into action the plans generated by a sheltered imagination. Females could expect only to nourish the imaginations of others. Today, although most women work outside the home, they must still do most of the work that home maintenance requires. The legacy of the Victorian home with its resident "angel" is alive in current demands for the restoration of "family values." "Liberation" for many women has come to mean holding two full-time jobs, and home is the last place they would look for privacy and a shelter for the imagination. Indeed, several recent polls have suggested that both women and men today often look upon work (a paid job) as an escape from the unremitting demands of home life.

Responses to this problem are often joyless. Many academic women feel they must make a choice between having a career and having a family; they are convinced they cannot have both. Some couples enter premarriage contracts stipulating how the work of the household will be done. Others decide to let many household tasks "slide": beds are unmade, plants disappear, the table is never really "set," few meals are prepared from scratch, household members eat when they can—alone or with television for company. This last response makes a mockery of a shared aesthetic, and the loss creates new strains. If the home provides nothing but a place of physical shelter and junk-food consumption, where will its members find the conditions to support their growth? Must all of life's meaning then be found in paid work?

The modern, Western conception of home as a private place for family life—a place separate from commerce and public life—grew in popularity in the seventeenth century. The Dutch seem to have led the way in this development.[11] They established private homes and separate facilities for business. Their backyard gardens were private in contrast to the public courtyards that characterized houses in the rest of Europe. For the legion of working girls—in "service" or in some industry such as textiles—the great hope was to save enough to marry well. For some, marrying well meant forming an economic partnership with one's husband and continuing some form of paid work in addition to homemaking; for increasing numbers, it meant staying at home and, perhaps, supervising one or two servants.

Home, as an ideal concept, became a place like the one described by Zeldin, a place in which couples expected privacy and in which they might not only raise children but display treasured belongings and express their own aesthetic sense. Starting in the mid-seventeenth century, it was common for the breadwinner to leave the house to conduct business, and it became more difficult (and less acceptable) for women to participate in business life. It also became customary for middle-class women, greatly increasing in number, to nurse their own children and to participate in raising them, often with the help of servants or nannies. Since the private home was now a matter of some pride, they also had much to do in maintaining it and caring for the possessions collected in it.[12] The rise of the middle class, the modern conception of home, and a rigid division of labor (newly redefined) between the sexes developed simultaneously. By the mid-nineteenth century, it was a sign of economic distress when a middle-class wife entered the job market. But even the peasant and working classes were affected by the bourgeois conception of home, and in recent times particular visions—"Ozzie and Harriet," "Father Knows Best," "Leave it to Beaver"—have provided norms for home life in general. More recently still, these visions have come under attack for their neglect of real conflict, their unquestioning acceptance of the patriarchal family, and their universalization of ways of life unavailable (or unacceptable) to many. But as new norms make it not only acceptable but desirable for women to work outside the home, a problem long familiar to many working-class women becomes a problem for all of us: Who will do the work of homemaking and caregiving?

Reading a history of the concept "home," we become aware that the vision most of us have grown up with is a relatively new idea. Further, there is no assurance that the idea will not disappear or undergo drastic revision. The threat is clearly present, and the frequent cries for a return to "family values" are evidence that many people fear the threatened changes. It seems as foolish, however, to drift aimlessly with random change as it is to resist change dogmatically. The task is to assess likely or incipient changes for the goodness of the consequences they are likely to produce. This task, too, is beyond the scope of this chapter. However, if we accept as a fact that at present many people value and will continue to value the home as a "personal and collective work of art," then our task is to analyze ways of promoting this art. In what follows, I build on Zeldin's description of home and on the notions of organic habits, a shared aesthetic, and a shelter for the imagination. I will not be concerned with the particular constitution of couples as families; that is, the couple need not be a man and a woman to be recognized as a family, and discussion of couples does not imply rejection of other family forms. Concentrating on couples here, I consider what has to be learned by any individual who plans to join another in establishing a home. The assumption is that, even if the family changes dramatically in its structure, *home* will remain important.

LEARNING TO CREATE A HOME

Learning to care and to be cared for is a major developmental task. Indeed, we might better speak of two tasks because we now understand that learning to be cared for is a major task in itself, and elementary school teachers find it increasingly necessary to teach children what it means to be cared for. Children who interpret either authoritarian coercion or negligent indulgence as care have not learned what it means to be cared for and are likely to fall into relationships marked by abuse or indifference. But even children who *have* learned to be cared for do not automatically care for others. This, too, must be learned.[13]

The first step in teaching children to care is, of course, to care for them. A child cannot learn to care for others if she does not know what it means to be cared for, and this learning is more physical and emotional than intellectual. Responding appropriately to care is one of the organic habits we carry with us from our childhood homes. However, there must be an expectation, made manifest early on, that children—both girls and boys—will care for others as they become able to do so.

This expectation sounds simple and obvious, but it actually flies in the face of a long tradition that defines females as the caregivers.[14] Discussion of this tradition rarely happens in classrooms, and, when it does, it is likely to be presented as "the way we used to think"; there is no clarification of the "we" who "used to think this way" nor, more importantly, is there discussion of the effects of this tradition on present attitudes.[15] As a result, young people are likely to think that gender discrimination is a thing of the past and that the roles they take on so easily are somehow "natural." Moreover, they are likely to undervalue or even scorn the work of caregiving.

Without a thorough introduction to the history of women's treatment in Western culture, students may point to the growing participation of girls in sports, math, and science as evidence that "all this is behind us." Some progress should certainly be acknowledged. But if we are rightly pleased by the increased participation of women in formerly male pur-

suits, why are we not concerned that there is not a corresponding increase in the number of young men who enter elementary school teaching, nursing, full-time homemaking, and other caring occupations? This
question opens an enormously important question about the valorization of traditionally male occupations and the denigration of "women's
work."

The history of nursing is instructive. Before the semiprofessionaliza-
tion of nursing, to call a nurse was simply to call a woman, and every
woman was expected to answer the call. Even when professional nurses
became available, the expectation remained that a woman would respond when summoned. Susan Reverby remarks: "The responsibility
for nursing went beyond a woman's duty toward her children, husband,
or aging parents. It fell to all available female members. At any time the
family's 'long arm' might reach out to a daughter working in a distant
city or mill, bringing her home to care for the sick, infirm, or newborn.
No form of women's labor, paid or unpaid, protected her from this
homeward pull."[16]

The expectation that women will provide care as needed is still widespread. It is not an exaggeration to say that this expectation is part of
an organic group of habits that are culturally induced. When children
are ill, for example, it is usually the mother who is expected to stay
home—even if her work is in a "male" profession. Although the expectation has been devastating for women's public lives, we have to acknowledge that it arose as one solution to a real problem. When care is
required, *someone* must respond. Paid caregiving is not feasible for
everyone, and, even when families can afford it, it is not always satis-
factory.[17]

I have referred to the expectation that women will provide care as
one of a set of culturally induced habits of mind. It is different from the
"organic habits" that grow out of idiosyncratic family life, and particular couples cannot be expected to solve the problems it has caused;
these are problems for the larger society. But young people need to be
aware of the problems, alert to the possible political remedies, and prepared to cope with them in their own relationships.

Another culturally induced habit of mind that must be studied is the
tendency to devalue women as well as their work. Again, both boys and
girls may react to historical accounts of women's oppression by saying,
"Why study that? It's over!" But they need to understand that the legacy
is alive. Women have been accused of undermining the spirituality of
men, of moral inferiority, of insatiable sexual desire, of not having

evolved mentally, of being emotionally unstable, and even of a special kinship with children because they themselves never grow up.[18] If all of this is "history," why do we regularly hear debates (and doubts) about women as priests, political leaders, and military officers? It is as important for heterosexual couples to understand the social oppression of women as it is for same-sex couples to understand the discrimination that has made it so difficult for them to form publicly recognized families. Yet this material is rarely included in the school curriculum.

This may be a good place to pause for a moment and say something about the odd enterprise we call "education" today. Two major ideologies have long contested what should be taught in schools. One insists that the most important subjects are those traditionally transmitted as disciplines; relevance to present-day life is considered an extra, added attraction if it is considered at all. The other, in direct opposition, wants to teach all of the skills and information required in adult life.[19] What I am suggesting is that, although both approaches capture something important, neither is truly educative. Children do have to be prepared for adult life, and they do need a certain amount of what E. D. Hirsch has called "cultural literacy."[20] But, in response to those who would teach specific life skills, we must insist that it is necessary to probe beneath particular tasks to ask about the symbolic meanings and organic habits that underlie successful accomplishment of these tasks. To teach homemaking in the schools should not mean teaching the specific skills of cleaning, cooking, shopping, and so on. Such skills, if presented at all, should be problematized and treated in considerable depth. Similarly, we need not abandon the traditional disciplines, but they should be mined and combed for their contributions to coping with the great existential questions. The aim is to encourage self-knowledge at both the individual and cultural level.

Thus, every couple needs some understanding of cultural influences on their relationship and how each member has internalized these influences. How society has been genderized is particularly important to understand. But even the new, supposedly enlightened ways should be problematized. For example, should a liberated woman reject domestic tasks entirely, or might she find deep satisfaction in doing some of them? I referred earlier to "joyless" solutions, and one such solution is the treatment of all housework as drudgery to be equitably shared. No wonder so many couples now want to escape from home to the more manageable arena of paid work. But housework, properly understood as one vital part of a full life, can yield great satisfaction, even pleasure. For example, I've never felt the same about polishing furniture since reading this paragraph from Bachelard: "When a poet rubs a piece of furniture—even vicariously—when he puts a little fragrant wax on his table with the woolen cloth that lends warmth to everything it touches, he creates a new object; he increases the object's human dignity; he registers this object officially as a member of the human household."[21]

I do not mean to romanticize household work. Most of us need work outside the home, but those who are fortunate enough to have other satisfying work may well take delight in some household tasks. Further, it seems reasonable to suppose that partners will be more willing to share in tasks that bring some pleasure than in those portrayed as mere labor. In preparing young people for adult life, we should make available a wealth of material that celebrates domesticity.[22]

Part of the joy in creating a home is building a shared aesthetic. A couple can either be unthinking victims of current fashion and consumerism or become thoughtful planners who decide for themselves how they will live. It is sad to read research reports of middle and high school students who mock those who cannot afford or reject brand-name clothing, sports equipment, and the like. Many students even sacrifice time that might have been spent in study, reading, and dreaming to work at routine jobs so that they can buy expensive items now fashionable. In this area, schools are guilty of more than neglect; they may rightly be charged with complicity in promoting the idea that education is mainly aimed at getting a good job that will enable one to buy the wonderful things advertised.

One antidote for infectious consumerism is the careful and joyful study of alternatives in living styles. There is so much in fiction, biography, poetry, and essays on this topic that its neglect seems even more reprehensible. Students should be encouraged to explore a wide range of material and deepen their own sense of the aesthetic of everyday life. On simplicity, they should be exposed not only to Thoreau but also to Quaker writings, accounts of religious asceticism, stories of rural life, regional cookbooks (which often tell wonderful stories), and a host of biographical accounts. In addition, when the usual required readings are studied, time might be taken to discuss the houses, rooms, and gardens that are described. Familiarity with "great literature" thus takes on a point beyond proving that one is a member of the educated class.

The study of homemaking can be intellectually rich as well as personally rewarding, and its study can inform students about matters well beyond their own relationship; such study can then be turned again to the relationship and refresh it. For example, many authors have drawn a distinction between dwelling and wayfaring, and these two ways of being in the world seem to describe deep psychological types. Erazim Kohák, confessing himself to be a dweller, writes:

> I left home at fourteen, an exile, not an emigrant. I bore the posture of dwelling as a deep program within me. I have not traveled light: I sank roots in all the places of my sojourn—and roots nourish. . . . At each move, a part of me was left behind. I could never be in one place and one place only. I have buried too many memories in too many places. And now I have come home, to Prague, to Czechoslovakia, to the land of my childhood, the land of my dreams, living and teaching in the language which for so long had been only my private secret. . . . I am home. Yet so much of me did not come along. It stayed at Boston University, in New Hampshire, on the South Shore, with my memories.[23]

A "deep program" of dwelling is one name for a set of organic habits—habits that pervade body, mind, and spirit—and it is a program that brings with it the beginnings of an aesthetic. Dwellers are likely to want houseplants, permanent furniture, heirlooms, pets, and all sorts of favorite objects, decorations, and utensils. They may become deeply attached to a particular place or region. For dwellers, exile spells great suffering, but one forced into exile at an early age may never know whether he or she is, by temperament, a dweller or a wayfarer.

A first generation in exile suffers the agony of the dweller who cannot dwell. What is longed for is that particular place untouched by time— the fruit trees where they were, the house and all its rooms as they were, the view as remembered, the neighbors as they were. It is an impossible dream, a longing for place, not for ideological satisfaction. Later generations, still in exile, often translate the feelings of parents and grandparents into political movements. Both the original home and the dream are unreal. Katherine Platt writes of the Palestinian refugees, "The personal rituals of mourning were transformed into rituals of protest and militance."[24] There is, in this militance, hope for a future, but what the older generation grieves over can never be replaced. And younger generations, displaced from birth, may never really understand what it means to dwell.

As young people come to understand what home means to many people, they may become more sensitive to the damage done by political solutions that displace people. They may also come to appreciate their own home-places and begin to care for them. Wendell Berry, for one, insists that caring and dwelling are interdependent.[25] Displaced persons either cannot care for the land (or house or region) they love because they are prevented from dwelling there, or they do not care enough to do so; the latter are displaced by choice—absentee landlords and the like. The study of home-places reaches out to the world and comes back again to enrich personal lives.

Young couples, forced to move again and again, may take heart from Kohák's story and put down roots wherever they find themselves. The shared aesthetic they build will be, at least in part, movable. The alternative may be a nagging regret, expressed beautifully by the poet Rainer Maria Rilke:

> Oh longing for places that were not
> Cherished enough in that fleeting hour
> How I long to make good from far
> The forgotten gesture, the additional act.[26]

Creating a shared aesthetic, then, establishes a form of stability, and this stability is part of what is required to shelter the imagination. The following passage from Gladys Taber captures most of the themes discussed here. Writing of home, she says: "It may be full of tensions and anxieties and it may be shabby. But it is a place where we can be ourselves, without pretense. Where we can confide our fears and worries to members of the family. Where we can express our dreams, even if they happen to be impossible to fulfill. . . . A home place is still an anchor. The whole family has a vested interest in the books, the old candlesticks, the cross-stitched luncheon set . . . and dozens of other things."[27]

There is an element of the romantic here, and there should be. If home is a place that has inspired writers, poets, composers, and singers, that is evidence that it has at least sometimes been a place of romance and contentment. We cannot be sure what sort of place home will be in the future. "Home" is a changing concept. But public life has changed dramatically, too, from an arena of participation to one of spectacle.[28] When people retreat from public life, home becomes even more attractive, more romantic. Indeed, Hannah Arendt worried that too much expressive involvement in home-places might destroy the desire to participate responsibly in public life, and this concern, too, should be part of education for private life. She commented:

> Modern enchantment with "small things," though preached by early twentieth-century poetry in almost all European tongues, has found its classical representation in the petit bonheur of the French people. Since the decay of their once great and glorious public realm, the French have

become masters in their art of being happy among "small things," within
the space of their own four walls, between chest and bed, table and
chair, dog and cat and flowerpot, extending to these things a care and
tenderness which, in a world where rapid industrialization constantly kills
off the things of yesterday to produce today's objects, may even appear
to be the world's last, purely humane corner. This enlargement of the
private . . . does not make it public . . . , but, on the contrary, means only
that the public realm has almost completely receded.[29]

It is impossible to predict whether, given the shabbiness of current
political life, Americans will take a turn toward the French or whether,
given the apparent exhaustion Americans express over the demands of
homemaking, the workplace will supplant both home and public life.
This would be a victory for a faceless corporate America but for no one
else. The challenge to American education is enormous. At present, we
are helping those forces that would concentrate all efforts on the workplace. Education for public life—including thorough preparation for the
liberal discourse that provides a foundation for democracy—has given
way to single-minded efforts to raise test scores, and education for home
life has never received appropriate attention. However, as we consider
education for homemaking, we must remain aware not only of the threat
to public life but also to the possibility of inadvertently strengthening
the movement for a return to "family values." The approach suggested
here recognizes the need to prepare all youngsters for both bread win-
ning and caregiving; it does not glorify the patriarchal family.

Lindbergh emphasized women's need for solitude and Woolf our need
for a room of one's own. Perhaps we should be reminded that everyone
needs solitude and privacy. Even children need at least a corner they can
call their own and decorate as they wish, in which they can store their
possessions, and where they can dream.[30] Again, this restoration of
home and its parts might be both concrete and metaphorical. Bachelard
combined the analysis of space in actual houses with rich metaphoric
analysis. For example, doors can open into the world or shut it out; keys
can open spaces and provide new insights or be used literally to lock
things up. We can speak of corners in our minds, windows on our souls,
keys to our hearts, ceilings on our aspirations, and cellar-like moods of
gloom and despair. In a similar vein, Lewis Thomas used "the attic"
metaphorically to store private thoughts and memories. "Bring back the
old attic," he advised. "Give new instructions to [psychiatric] patients
who are made nervous by our times, including me, to make a conscious
effort to hide a reasonable proportion of thought."[31] Thomas was de-

scribing the function of actual attics in which things are kept, but hidden, and the role of mental attics that might do the same sort of thing psychologically. He was pointing to another aspect of the uneasiness that afflicts current life—the temptation, increasingly acted upon, to make everything public. The home cannot shelter the imagination if everything done there, said there, thought there becomes public, and nothing is left to the imagination.

The actual home is not only a shelter for the imagination; images of home have also been prominent in literary and psychological imagination. Bachelard shows how every part of the house has produced images for analysis and poetic expression: doors, windows, cellars, attics, stairs, chimneys, corners, creaky floors, pantries, parlors, bedrooms. Students need to hear about and discuss these images. It might be salutary for them to hear about the man described by Carl Jung. This fellow heard a noise in the cellar one night and hastened to the attic to check things out. Finding no intruder in the attic, he concluded that all was well. The prudent fellow did not dare to face his real fears in the cellar.[32] In a similar vein, students might analyze Robert Frost's "The Witch of Coös" in which a skeleton—carrying itself "like a pile of dishes"—is reported to be trying to escape the attic and return to the cellar "where it came from."[33] The cellar has become, metaphorically, a place of hidden fears and evil intentions, the attic a place of stored memories and secret (often unfulfilled) dreams.

Both Thomas and Lindbergh have provided good advice for couples, although neither intended to give such advice. (Thomas was advising his friends either giving or receiving psychiatric care, and Lindbergh was describing a near perfect day in a relationship.) Thomas said: "Forget whatever you feel like forgetting. From time to time, practice *not* being open, discover new things *not* to talk about, learn reserve, hold the tongue. But above all, develop the human talent for forgetting words, phrases, whole unwelcome sentences, all experiences involving wincing."[34] Give and receive privacy graciously. Be embarrassed when you are wrong and grateful for the other's silence. Exercise your sheltered imagination but do not express it fully or indiscriminately.

Lindbergh uses dance as her metaphor: "A good relationship has a pattern like a dance and is built on some of the same rules. The partners do not need to hold on tightly, because they move confidently in the same pattern, intricate but gay and swift and free, like a country dance of Mozart's. . . . There is no place here for the possessive clutch, the clinging arm, the heavy hand. . . . [The couple] know they are partners moving to the same rhythm, creating a pattern together, and being invisibly nourished by it."[35]

In preparation for eventual healthy relationships, students should be aware of the difficulties of homemaking today, of financial problems, of problems aggravated by heavy workloads, of those made worse by a corrupt and distasteful public life, of those induced by changing patterns of home and family life. But they should also be given something to dream about—the possibility (romantic? I suppose) of real joy in entering a relationship and making a home.

CONCLUSION

The concept of home is dynamic. Whether it will become more or less important in our lives is an open question. But for the foreseeable future, establishing a home will continue to be an important reason for people to form couples. Maintaining a home as a place where one cares for others and is cared for requires an understanding of the organic habits of both partners, the construction of a shared aesthetic, and a continuous effort to provide shelter for the imagination of both members of the relationship. I have suggested that schools could play an important part in preparing young people for homemaking by treating the topic with some intellectual vigor. It may well be that, in the general retreat from public life, people will have to choose between the home and workplace as a place of serenity and nurturance. One hopes that both will be places of fulfillment.

NOTES

1. Theodore Zeldin, *An Intimate History of Humanity* (New York: Harper Collins, 1994), 393.

2. Gaston Bachelard, *The Poetics of Space,* trans. Maria Jolas (New York: Orion Press, 1964), 7.

3. Ibid., 14.

4. Edward Casey, *Getting Back into Place* (Bloomington: Indiana University Press, 1993), 120.

5. Ibid., 35–37.

6. Bachelard, *Poetics of Space,* 234.

7. Ibid., viii.

8. See Virginia Woolf, *A Room of One's Own* (1929; reprint, New York: Harcourt Brace Jovanovich, 1981).

9. See Anne Morrow Lindbergh, *Gift from the Sea* (New York: Random House, 1955).

10. "Home" was an important literary theme in pre-Victorian, Victorian, and post-Victorian literature. See, for example, the works of Jane Austen, Charles Dickens, and Marcel Proust, among many others.

11. See Witold Rybczynski, *Home: A Short History of an Idea* (New York: Viking, 1986).

12. For an account of women's shifting interests from about the mid-seventeenth century, including nursing one's own children and running one's own household, see Olwen Hufton, *The Prospect before Her: A History of Women in Western Europe 1500–1800* (New York: Alfred A. Knopf, 1996).

13. See the essays in Allan M. Hoffman, ed., *Schools, Violence, and Society* (Westport, Conn.: Praeger, 1996), in particular, Nel Noddings, "Learning to Care and Be Cared For," 185–98. There is a growing body of feminist literature outside of education on this topic. See, especially, Sara Ruddick, *Maternal Thinking: Towards a Politics of Peace* (Boston: Beacon Press, 1989).

14. For the effect of this expectation on the lives of women scientists, see Margaret W. Rossiter, *Women Scientists in America: Struggles and Strategies to 1940* (Baltimore: Johns Hopkins University Press, 1982); for the connection to nursing, see Susan Reverby, *Ordered to Care* (Cambridge: Cambridge University Press, 1987); on the general expectation and its effects, see Tish Sommers and Laurie Shields, *Women Take Care* (Gainesville, Fla.:Triad, 1987). Countless biographical accounts also attest to the power of this expectation.

15. Apparently, most such subjects are approached this way—"the way we used to think"—in social studies classes. See Catherine Cornbleth, "An American Curriculum?" *Teachers College Record* 99, 4 (1998):622–646.

16. Reverby, *Ordered to Care*, 12.

17. For informative discussion of the issues, see John D. Arras, ed., *Bringing the Hospital Home* (Baltimore: Johns Hopkins University Press, 1995); also Suzanne Gordon, Patricia Benner, and Nel Noddings, eds., *Caregiving: Readings in Knowledge, Practice, Ethics, and Politics* (Philadelphia: University of Pennsylvania Press, 1996).

18. Many books address the history of women's association with evil, including Bram Dijkstra, *Idols of Perversity* (New York and Oxford: Oxford University Press, 1986); Joseph Klaits, *Servants of Satan: The Age of Witch Hunts* (Bloomington: Indiana University Press, 1985); Nel Noddings, *Women and Evil* (Berkeley and Los Angeles: University of California Press, 1989); John A. Phillips, *Eve: The History of an Idea* (San Francisco: Harper and Row, 1984); Rosemary Radford Ruether, ed., *Religion and Sexism* (New York: Simon and Schuster, 1974).

19. For a comprehensive discussion of this conflict, see Herbert Kliebard, *The Struggle for the American Curriculum* (New York: Routledge, 1995).

20. See E. D. Hirsch, *Cultural Literacy: What Every American Needs to Know* (Boston: Houghton Mifflin, 1987). However, my use of "cultural literacy" is somewhat different from Hirsch's. I would not prescribe a list of particular facts for all children to learn. Rather, I refer to a large body of cultural material from which individual children may learn selectively.

21. Bachelard, *Poetics of Space*, 67.

22. I would include in this category many regional cookbooks, gardening books, biographies, and much poetry.

23. Erazim Kohák, "Of Dwelling and Wayfaring: A Quest for Metaphors," in *Longing for Home,* ed. Leroy S. Rouner (Notre Dame: University of Notre Dame Press, 1996), 30–46.

24. Katherine Platt, "Places of Experience and the Experience of Place," in *Longing for Home,* ed. Leroy S. Rouner (Notre Dame: University of Notre Dame Press, 1996), 125.

25. See Wendell Berry, *Another Turn of the Crank* (Washington, D.C.: Counterpoint, 1995).

26. Rainer Maria Rilke, from *Vergers, XLI,* quoted in Bachelard, *Poetics of Space,* 56.

27. Gladys Taber, *Stillmeadow Sampler* (Philadelphia: J. B. Lippincott, 1959), 140–41.

28. See, for example, the account in Jean Baudrillard, *Fatal Strategies,* ed. Jim Fleming, trans. Philip Beitchman and W. G. J. Niesluchowski (New York: Semiotext(e), 1990).

29. Hannah Arendt, *The Human Condition* (Chicago: University of Chicago Press, 1958), 52.

30. See the fascinating discussion of corners in Bachelard, *Poetics of Space.*

31. Lewis Thomas, *Late Night Thoughts on Listening to Mahler's Ninth Symphony* (New York: Viking Press, 1983), 140.

32. See the story in Bachelard, *Poetics of Space,* 19. It is drawn from Carl G. Jung, *Modern Man in Search of Soul* (New York: Harcourt, Brace and World, 1955).

33. Robert Frost, "The Witch of Coös," in *Complete Poems* (New York: Henry Holt, 1949), 247–52.

34. Thomas, *Late Night Thoughts,* 142.

35. Lindbergh, *Gift from the Sea,* 104.

CHAPTER 7

When One of Us Is Ill

Scenes from a Partnership

Mary Felstiner

In the early years of the women's movement, I thought couples were built on gender and other human-made frameworks. Since everything surrounding two partners was socially arranged, then everything could be *rearranged*. It took me a long time to learn that anatomy stakes a claim in the household and no effort on the part of a couple makes it leave. Among this tenant's effects are illness and disability.

Recently, I found myself asking: How does the company of disease crowd or expand a relationship? Or to put it personally: What happens to a pair of equal partners when one of us is ill?

A chronic disease moved in on us after three years of marriage, just two weeks after the day in 1969 that our daughter was born. In that era of feminist ventures, John and I had fixed on dividing all the labor after birth labor; as newly minted parents our motto was *fair's fair*. It never occurred to us there'd be add-ons to our contract, namely, a baby with breathing problems, severe jaundice, colic—and also a postpartum insult to my joints. Not long after the birth, a sudden, painful stiffening of both my wrists turned out to be rheumatoid arthritis, a disease I heard of then for the first time. Rheumatoid arthritis, called RA, was chronic, I learned, and lifelong; incurable and unpredictable; touched off by hormone upheavals or autoimmune reactions in pregnancy, by trauma, predisposition, bad luck, or all the above. No one could tell whether it might leave a person alone for years—or (in my case) attack all the joints, deal out pain most days, and ration the ability to move. What I did know was this: Two of our bodies had conceived a newborn and just one of our bodies was paying, forever. Meanwhile, the other member of our couple became a chronic swimmer and a runner.

For me one question stayed unanswered: If illness could set partners moving in two directions, what counterforce would keep them parallel?

Three decades later that question struck me again when a friend came face to face with it. She and I were spending a day downtown, browsing bookstores and craft stores and food stores, glad to be on the move. A few hours later we each went limp, as my RA and her MS sent us into deep fatigue.

"At least you know how I feel by late afternoon," she said.

"No one else really gets it, do they?"

"Not this, not how I collapse bit by bit."

"By the time your bus gets back tonight," I reckoned, "you'll be down for the count."

When she arrived home, her husband of many years was waiting at the door. The suitcase he took in hand, though, wasn't hers; it was his. He was leaving, he announced. Moving out. He couldn't take it anymore—her disease, her tiredness, her displacement of him. Apparently he'd braved the onset of her illness but couldn't face the chronic part. After a while (I imagined) some husbands wanted their wives back, their lives back. They'd contracted for better or for worse, not for worse and worse. They longed for a chance to be primary in the couple again.

"The first thing I thought when he left," my friend told me on the phone, "was, what if I get *really* sick?"

I shivered for myself, too. Not frightened—terrified. Might *any* partner leave when illness turned too intense or boring or just stayed too long? I knew I couldn't get cured and I couldn't get by without John helping me. What never left me was precisely the need never to be left.

My friend's phone call triggered hard questions about partnerships. Does illness disrupt the sequence every couple goes through—Bringing It Together, Making It Work, Sticking It Out? If one partner stays less hardy than the other during these stages, how does a couple handle *that*? I was searching, of course, for predictions and reassurances. What I ended up learning caught me off-guard.

BRINGING IT TOGETHER

The stark thought—what if I get worse?—was tough to voice within a longtime couple, so I couldn't imagine asking it in a start-up partnership. Then I read how Kenny Fries questions a new lover: "Do you realize my disability is, over time, not going to get better? It will remain the same or get worse as I get older. 'I know that,' Kevin tells me." Fries asks himself: "Can anyone comprehend that no matter how many times he tells me how attractive I am, so much within me, as well as so much that surrounds me, conspires to tell me otherwise?"[1]

No matter how many times John "tells me how attractive I am," I still remember thirty years before, when I had two working arms to put around him and the only problem with my hips was how I thought they looked from behind. I swooned and loved and married before I got impaired. I can't ask outright, "So John, would we be a couple if I'd had these joints when we met?" How could he reply to my face? How could he know for sure? Then I imagine his answer anyway: "*You're* the one wondering. You're the one thinking you can't be in love and infirm."

Well, I do wonder what value we set on women when feminine traits like mobility, sexuality, and fertility are uncertain or missing or dwindling? In marriage markets everywhere, from dowry dealings to dormitories, what is the worth of a handicapped woman? "What would have happened," one writer asks of our idols, "if Juliet had been blind? Would Romeo still have deemed her worthy of his love? Would Darcy have appreciated Elizabeth Bennett's wit if she had had a disfigured face?"[2] To be chosen at all, would an impaired woman have to be heroic—disfigured by fire while saving a child or blinded while shielding Romeo from the Capulets?

In real life, ill or disabled women are less likely to get married than either men with a handicap or women without one. A young attorney with a serious chronic disease told me what struck her when diagnosed: "Who will ever marry me?" was her very first thought. At a conference on Disabled Women and Development, a Caribbean activist, Evincia Edwards, said: "I am surprised to hear that some disabled women are married. They say that we shouldn't be married and shouldn't have a boyfriend because we can't do nothing." A disability activist, Rosangela Berman Bieler, said everyone assumed her husband had caused an accident "and married me because of guilt. . . . They cannot believe that an able-bodied man could fall in love with a disabled woman."[3]

Would my own impaired body have found a partner? Out of this private doubt I wanted to make some social sense. We'd come together during the 1960s women's movement with one model of a couple: independent in identity, matched in ability, and equal in responsibility. Then chronic disease plowed into us and pushed our partnership off course. We were going to have to make it work when fair wasn't fair anymore.

MAKING IT WORK

How uneven does it get when disability enters the game? In a story told by Michelle Fine and Adrienne Asch, someone sees a woman in a wheelchair and exclaims: "You must be a saint." This is not said to the woman, actually, but to the husband wheeling her along.[4] Now, would we exalt a woman for pushing a man along, for being who she already is—wife, daughter, nurse, domestic, baby-sitter for the young and old? Would we notice a man when he's caring for a child? Pushing a stroller, he's a dad. Pushing a wheelchair, he's a saint.

It happened to John and me one day ambling along a sidewalk. As his arm lifted me over cracks, two people stood aside to let us pass. One said, "What an angel," not looking clearly at either of us. I wanted to throw back, "No, he isn't. He's got *advantages* lugging someone around," but I couldn't think of anything specific at the moment.

"Here," John said, and tucked a hand tighter under me. All at once I felt us lifting off, his wrist sealed to my armpit.

"Angel," I whispered. "You're opening up your wings."

"Oh, I'm opening up, all right," John said. "Opening up your milk cartons, your mail, your bottles, your window, your toothpaste . . ."

"Good God, what expertise."

"I practice every day. It's not elective."

An image came to my mind then, from the week before, when I'd watched John running up a hill. His feet were melting the ground like King Wenceslas's feet in snow, his face held an unearthly smile, rain parted around him. Lifting upward, he sped past some young people who might have called out to him, "What an angel," but instead: "Whudda ya, about sixty?" All *they* saw was a pounding older man.

Partners like mine, I realized, could easily lose sight of their own frailties, feel too strong by comparison. Every so often, after hefting something heavy, John would get spasms in his back and stay paralyzed for days. One day out in the country he'd been rolling a stump down a rough path—to make a seat out of it—when it broke away.

"You chased that stump to the bottom of the hill and heaved it back up, and nothing bad happened to your back?" I asked when he came in.

"Stupidest thing I ever did," John allowed. Yes, but some people never give up hoping they're invincible.

"C'mon," I said. "Let's take a look at what you made." This was visibly absurd. Pulling myself up from the couch, I landed on my swollen right ankle, shifted instantly to the left one, then zigzagged across the floor like a crazed squirrel. Once outside, my ankle turned maybe half an inch over a twig and took such pain I had to skip sideways, plainly getting nowhere fast. But I was game to make it down in honor of John's effort. If I collapsed, he'd roll me uphill like the stump.

"Hold on," John said and lifted my shoulder high so my right side skimmed the path.

"Oh, it's beautiful! You did it. It's a wonderful place to sit." And my knees gave up in a bend.

Just after John pushed me up to the cabin, he suddenly slapped his lower back in pain. "Not now," I cried out. Not a spasm here where no one could lift him up. But as he whipped off his shirt and jabbed at his back, I saw it—a big tick corkscrewing in. I rushed—well, wobbled—to the bathroom for tweezers, calling out, "Counterclockwise pulls a tick out, right? Right?" When my rheumatic hand failed to close the tweezers tight, John grabbed them from me, reached behind himself to manage a hard squeeze, a backwards counterclockwise twist, a steady pull, and it was out. One of us did fine in a pinch.

Would I ever be that one again? This was a question I learned to subdue. For instance, whenever my elbow pressed the kitchen table, bone to wood, it recollected having more upholstery, but I stopped mentioning this aloud. I'd had practice muting certain kinds of news. A friend once looked across the kitchen table and asked us, "How did you manage when you *both* were writing books about the Holocaust?" John shook his head, and I came up with one thing I could recall. "There were years of silence." Through those years John was reading poetry—outpourings really—from Holocaust eyewitnesses, while I was moving through testimony from the Eichmann trial. At the end of each day I was flinching, and John was too. We spared each other any extra rawness from retelling. Staring across our toddler at dinner, we each figured, more or less, what the other had learned about. That practice served me later for absorbing pain and weakness—the raw material in my joints. All I asked was, show me you know it's there (and he did). The rest I would keep to myself.

But silence worked better when *each* of us kept it for the other's sake.

"Do you wonder," I once asked John, "why it's hard to stay fond of a disabled woman? Because half the time she's subduing anger, mostly at you."

"For what?"

"For being the one nearby. For striding out of the house to work when I'm hobbling around—oh, what powers able-bodied men do have." The truth was, those powers were the things I loved in John, so I felt subdivided and unjust.

In a matter of time, I realized what a batch of human problems looked like mine and swapped my private view for a wide-angle lens. Thirty-five million Americans were disabled, I found out. If you were in line with six other people, one of you would have a serious impairment. If able-bodied, you'd be a realist if you said, "I'm in pre-disability; my impairment's on order, though." You could end up disabled because you slipped on an unlit staircase in a housing project—or on the gangway to your corporate jet; because your parents couldn't pay to treat an injury or because you were born with a limb malformed; or simply because you passed the age of sixty-five, like one-third of all Americans with handicaps. If you were among the 7 percent with disabilities in every nation, you'd lack what an ethicist calls equal protection against suffering, fair "access to the economic, political, and psychological resources of the family, the community, the nation, the globe."[5]

At first I assumed this unsheltered suffering must bring the men down with the women. Then I looked a little closer. "Double prejudice is the root cause of the inferior status of women with disabilities," Esther Boylan writes, "making them the world's most disadvantaged group."[6] I thought I was alone, but no, I belong to the world's most disadvantaged group. With a disability, women are likelier to get divorced than men or able-bodied people and then to lose child custody. Women with rheumatoid arthritis, once divorced, remarry less than other women. When disabled women try to support themselves, only a quarter find places in our country's labor force, compared with half of all disabled men. For every man among the world's 40 million mentally ill people, two women suffer from severe anxiety or depression, yet available treatment goes mostly to men.[7] Clearly it's best to be born male before getting impaired.

Studies show first of all that women soft-pedal their disabled husbands' behavior problems and give them most of the care they need, whereas men with disabled wives bring others in to help; and second, that women grow closer than men to their impaired partners, maybe because they've been tutored to give care. "Disability is a great leveler," Robert Murphy writes. "It forecloses an ancient power struggle and puts an end to 'male superiority.' "[8] The trouble is, if a disabled man and an able-bodied woman level out, who's a *disabled woman* equal with?

STICKING IT OUT

Why does this question of fairness continue to bother me long after we've passed through the trials of getting together and making it work? Why not simply fix on being equal to my *tasks* each day, telling my joints: "Morning's here, get this citizen moving"? Maybe because inside the body a closed-circuit system works between the brain and the rest. But inside a couple, I'm sure even the most private transmissions pick up public signals about gender and age. My hidden fear of being all alone, when ill, sounds amplified wherever women talk from experience: They know their life expectancy is about eight years longer than men's, and in those extended years more of them (with less income) will fall ill. "Men die sooner," one demographer sums up, "having suffered fewer years of trouble while alive."[9] My private dread, it turns out, fits a nationwide gender gap that stretches women twice: They endure more sick years within a couple and survive more years alone without it.

Even with enviable privileges—two partners with two jobs and some health insurance—John and I make our daily decisions inside the confines of an ailment. Neither of us wanted to spend our lives this way. John signed on from the beginning to be a nurturer but didn't ask to be a nurse. I bargained on being a freelance person, not a patient. Losing access to our early model of equality, I'm looking for a more imaginative scheme, maybe still to be invented.

My new search starts with the 1990 Americans with Disabilities Act, which has removed more than spatial barriers. With each wheelchair ramp, certain spaces stop belonging to the young and mobile; with each "reasonable accommodation," more people can see the value in a body marked by disease or time. I like to imagine Julia Roberts in *Pretty Woman IV,* a sequel where she's gained a good bit of weight, her knees are going bad, and in spite of thick lenses she's groping around and dropping things. Oh she's still got that smile, and some rewards come to a not-so-pretty woman—like maybe a partner who's used to her groping around.

But it's still a stretch for most people to picture the ill and old parading physical appeal. And the idea that some bodies are unsightly still causes emotional harm among those who aren't either ill or old, as I learned when a student from my Holocaust course called late one night. He'd been reading Nazi propaganda.

"I'm unfit and ugly," he said, almost too low to hear. "I can't imagine why my girlfriend's here."

"What do you mean ugly?"

"All the deformities of Jews, I've got. Big nose, black hair, bent shoulders, *you* know."

"Do you think you could ask your girlfriend how ugly you are?"

He did, and survived to come to class again. But he knew that many millions felt a visceral disgust toward bodies like his. What could I say when disabled bodies like mine also inspire disgust, when everyone dislikes the traits I'm known for, like a nice slow way of doing wash or handling cash?

To change disgust into desire would take a massive shift in outlook, as the revolutionary slogan "Black Is Beautiful" proved. Even my own outlook has had to change: I used to want disgust concealed; now I'm learning to want disgust *reversed.* I used to believe that just because John helped me, I was the dependent one. Now I'm thinking the able-bodied partner is dependent too—on my *skill* in taking suffering day by day. I'm trying to discard a tight equation (disabled = dependent) because it keeps alive a false corollary (able-bodied = independent). In the new math of disability rights, independent balances dependent to the decimal point: By relying on help, I do for myself all I can.

I started seeing how the "most disadvantaged group in the world" poses moral dilemmas in just the right way: a need for independence versus a right to assistance from others, the value of caring versus the burden of one-way caregiving, the inherent benefits of being in a couple versus the excess benefits that couples get in social respect. So what I've learned after thirty years of feminism is a paradox. Feminism prizes social and physical power, but feminists also rename power as prejudice: It can exclude people by race and age and health. If more wisdom is pressed on us, feminists will finally sack the presiding belief that being able-bodied is normal, right, and well deserved. Then a disabled woman will give and take love *with* her disability. Not in spite of it, not because of it.

WHAT HELPS

Whenever doubts come at me, what helps is talking with a friend of mine whose young partner, I know, is going deaf.

"Can we have lunch at your place?" I ask ahead. "It's quieter there." Hearing-loss isn't my problem but voice-loss is, since my vocal cords, like my joints, are always inflamed. Before lunch that day I damage my voice even more by teaching in a room so hot we push all the windows open in hopes of a breeze; outside a power mower is going at its job, and I try with my small microphone to yell over it. By the end of class I can't speak at all.

So I just listen as my friend describes her partner: "The things she does now to handle her hearing loss are exactly the things that attracted me at the start. She plans ahead, she asks her colleagues to adjust, she takes it all as a challenge."

That's it: That's the solution to my private doubt. One should be loved and love oneself more than ever just for handling the condition at hand.

I whisper to my friend as we eat sandwiches, "Would any partner *gladly* take what's in store here?"

"I've got the answer to that one. Yes," she says. Straight at me. "Yes."

What helps my own partnership as things get harder is to give up the ideal of sameness, which was always a scuffle at best. Now we're on separate tracks and separate isn't equal in this event. For one thing, John is fresh and spry—up to now. He wonders how soon his body will get weak, but I can't afford to. I wonder what full speed feels like, but he doesn't have to. We both wonder how we'd handle more suffering, but here the edge is mine. I already live with what he fears. He wants to know what happens if his body loses hard-earned strengths. I want to know, what if my weakness keeps some friends away. He'd like to be sure of help if he gets helpless. I'd like to know how on earth I'd *be* of help to him. His desire: to go on able as he is. Mine: to grow weaker with a touch of dignity. His ambition: to keep active. Mine: to stay zesty. He wonders how long he can outrun any impairment, straight ahead. I wonder how long before we're circling slowly, side by side. Our common partnership is built on different stores of fear and fatigue, dependence and rage; it's topped up with resilience and compassion. And, yes, it's good for some laughs.

I noodle around with possible drawbacks of *not* having a disease. Without MS, for instance, my friend whose husband left her at the door would not have witnessed him and his suitcase walk back in, one year later, committed as never before and dripping with remorse. Without RA, for another instance, I might not have found a straightforward reason for resenting John. Without RA, a hardworking marriage might have seized up. I might have missed my partner's quick way of grabbing my arm on a set of stairs, a stony path, a lightless night. And one thing's for sure. Subtract RA, and I'd never have picked up an *otra cosita,* a little something else, along the way: a faith. Simply, when one of us is ill, two of us will take the heat.

If one morning I wake up padlocked into pain, if an iron switches on between my bones, I can say, "John. Feel my arm, the upper part. Chilly, right? Now feel the elbow joint."

"OW-W-W," he shouts out, alarmed after all these years that anything so tropical lives in a temperate frame.

My faith is in that shout. When he leans over and kisses the outer corner of my arm, I think: "OK, I'll get started right now on this day."

NOTES

I would like to thank Ruth Rosen, Nina Jo Smith, Estelle Freedman, Alek Felstiner, and the Women Writers Group in San Francisco for generous assistance.

1. Kenny Fries, *Body, Remember: A Memoir* (New York: Penguin, 1997), 216, 220.

2. Deborah Kent, "Disabled Women: Portraits in Fiction and Drama," in *Women and Disability,* ed. Esther Boylan (London: Zed Books, 1991), 14.

3. Susan Sygall, "Caribbean Interview" and "Interview with Rosangela Berman Bieler of Brazil," in *Women and Disability,* ed. Esther Boylan (London: Zed Books, 1991), 13, 87.

4. Michelle Fine and Adrienne Asch, "Introduction: Beyond Pedestals," in *Women with Disabilities: Essays in Psychology, Culture, and Politics,* ed. Michelle Fine and Adrienne Asch (Philadelphia: Temple University Press, 1988), 18.

5. Elizabeth V. Spelman, *Fruits of Sorrow: Framing Our Attention to Suffering* (Boston: Beacon Press, 1997), 8; Benedicte Ingstad and Susan Reynolds Whyte, eds., *Disability and Culture* (Berkeley and Los Angeles: University of California Press, 1995), 5; Joseph P. Shapiro, *No Pity: People with Disabilities Forging a New Civil Rights Movement* (New York: Times Books, 1993), 6.

6. Esther Boylan, ed., *Women and Disability* (London: Zed Books, 1991), 1.

7. Fine and Asch, 10; Nortin M. Hadler and Dennis B. Gillings, eds., *Arthritis and Society: The Impact of Musculoskeletal Diseases* (London: Butterworths, 1985), 44; Sue Tuckwell, "The Hidden 40 Million," in *Women and Disability*, ed. Boylan, 11–12.

8. David Mechanic, *Medical Sociology* (New York: Free Press, 1978), 272–73; Robert Murphy, "Encounters: The Body Silent in America," in *Disability and Culture*, ed. Ingstad and Whyte, 152.

9. Lois M. Verbrugge, "Pathways of Health and Death," in *Women, Health, and Medicine in America: A Historical Handbook,* ed. Rima D. Apple (New York: Garland, 1990), 79.

CHAPTER 8

Wives and Husbands Working Together

Law Partners and Marital Partners

Cynthia Fuchs Epstein

Family members working together characterized the economic unit in much of human history. On the farm, in small craft shops, and in businesses, family members—husbands and wives, sons and daughters—have labored together. Only after the industrial revolution when the site of most work was transferred to central locations—factories and office buildings—did family members engage in the economic sphere as individuals. Yet, although the percentage of individuals engaged in family businesses has decreased, a substantial number of families in the United States and elsewhere continue to engage in economically productive activities together—on family farms, in family-run businesses, and in professional partnerships. It was, and is, the pattern for a significant percentage of immigrant husbands and wives to work together (Foner 1999). The place of women in such family enterprises has often gone unnoticed, both officially and in the minds of the public. For example, in the past, the United States Census classified husbands as "farmers," but wives were regarded as "unemployed" when both worked on the family farm. Similarly, wives in "mom-and-pop" stores were not counted as shopkeepers or businesswomen. The historian Alice Kessler-Harris (1981) has noted that women's economic activity often went unrecorded because they did not share ownership of businesses run by their

Parts of this chapter appeared in Cynthia Fuchs Epstein, *Women In Law*, 2d ed. (Chicago: University of Illinois Press, 1993).

husbands or did not draw money as a salary although they worked hard in them.

Attention to the work of women, for pay or without pay, has increased. But even today, scholars of "women-and-work " issues and journalists of the media do not observe or pay much research attention to the extent to which husbands and wives share business lives. Even today there are no reliable statistics on how many husbands and wives work together. Indeed, much more attention has been devoted to the analysis of the sharing of housekeeping and child care rather than shared work lives.

Although the overall percentage of small businesses is declining, however, and traditional mom-and-pop grocery stores and pharmacies, for example, have been replaced by large chain stores in most of the United States, family businesses in which husbands and wives participate still exist and are common among immigrants from Asia, Latin America, Korea, India, the Caribbean, and Eastern Europe. They, like generations of immigrants before them (Foner 1999), struggle to make a living in cities and towns where their access to jobs in established sectors of the marketplace is limited because of language barriers, prejudice, and lack of connections. These businesses are highly visible in cities across the nation and include grocery stores, dry-cleaning establishments, newspaper kiosks, and ethnic restaurants, to mention only a few of the types owned and run by husbands and wives.

Among the family "businesses" of the past were the professional practices of male lawyers, doctors, accountants, and dentists who, as solo practitioners, depended on their wives to be receptionists, bookkeepers, assistants, and secretaries. Excluded from becoming professionals themselves, women (we will never know just how many) were clustered in these subsidiary positions. These, of course, were not real partnerships. Only for the few women who overcame many obstacles and completed professional degrees was it possible to become a formal partner, although, as I note, they were far from equal partnerships. Women attorneys faced employment discrimination, which resulted in limited job opportunities. Only a very few broke through the barriers, so a number of women subsequently turned to small family practices with husbands or fathers or entered the profession with the express purpose of helping their husbands. Like immigrant families, these practices provided opportunities in an otherwise inhospitable world.

In the course of studying the obstacles and facilitating factors that women faced in the legal profession (Epstein 1981, 1993), I encountered about a dozen husband-wife law partnerships. Of a sample of sixty-five lawyers chosen at random among lawyers working in New York City and its suburbs, about 16 percent worked in a family firm. At the time I first studied them—in the late 1960s and 1970s—most women attorneys had fewer options in professional life than they have now. However, their experiences provide a model for understanding husband-wife business partnerships more generally. Further, I followed up this sample in 1980, and in more recent research assessing women's mobility opportunities in the law (Epstein 1995; Epstein et al. 1999), I found certain patterns remaining. This chapter will explore some of the dynamics of husband-wife law partnerships that I studied in the past three decades and their consequences for women's equality in the home and in the workplace.

What advantages and disadvantages did women experience in fusing their marital relationship with a professional relationship in which their husband was a partner? First of all, in the past, it was often the only employment they could obtain. Today, that is no longer the case for women in the professions, but many women choose to work with their husbands for many reasons, among them dissatisfaction with employment opportunities and time pressures reconciling child care and work.

HUSBAND-WIFE PRACTICES AS A RESPONSE TO DISCRIMINATION

My first study of women attorneys revealed extensive discrimination both in law school admission and in employment. In the late 1960s they were just about 3 percent of law school students and 3 percent of all lawyers. This was before a number of lawsuits opened the doors of law schools that had placed quotas on female recruitment, and the doors of law offices—large and small—that were closed to women attorneys. Today, women constitute about a quarter of all lawyers and more than 40 percent of all law school students. In my first study, most women attorneys who were not in practice with their husbands or fathers worked for the government, in law schools (usually as research assistants or librarians), or for firms, or had their own solo practices. I followed some of them later on and encountered new ones in the late 1970s. The couples I encountered in the succeeding decades tended to work in firms with other attorneys because that was where the growth in the legal profession was and because antinepotism policies were no longer operative. However, lawyer couples still exist (although we do not know how many there are).

As I noted above, most women worked in law partnerships with their husbands because they couldn't get jobs elsewhere or believed they could not. Many of their husbands encouraged this arrangement because it was advantageous to them. For a male independent practitioner, having his wife as a partner meant he had a devoted and a far better than average attorney. Most women who had graduated from law school in the 1960s and 1970s had to surmount many obstacles. Yet, they usually entered law school with higher Law School Aptitude Test (LSAT) scores on average than men, got higher grades in their law school classes than men, and were dedicated to professional life. They were the survivors in an usually punishing environment in which only the brilliant and hardy women survived.

For the women attorneys, partnerships with husbands were a safe harbor in a hostile professional world. Other male lawyers might be suspicious of a woman lawyer and doubt her capacities, her femininity, and her motives, but the lawyer to whom she was married did not.

However, most of the partnerships studied in the mid 1960s and 1970s were not characterized by equality either ideologically or in practice. Yet, given the contribution of both husband and wife to the family income, they probably were more egalitarian than most other marriages of their generation. Husband and wife law partners depended on each other, felt a common stake in the their firm, and were less competitive than other partners.

Yet, husband-wife partnerships tended to adapt the sex division of labor within their firms to that of the profession. Not unlike many workplaces today, including larger firms, the men usually did the "outside" work such as client contact, courtroom appearances, and other high-profile work. The women typically did the less visible work, such as writing briefs and researching cases. They also tended to the office management—the "housekeeping" of the firm.

Neither partner saw these arrangements as problematic or as sexist. In the mid 1960s and 1970s, it was still unusual for women to handle litigation or argue cases in court—it was believed that women did not want to do those things and were not good at them. Wife-lawyers accepted the prevailing cultural view about sex differences in interests and ability. Thus, they thought it was more appropriate for their husbands to go to court while they did the "backroom" work of the law firm because they believed men were more assertive than women. Most were content to share their husbands' glory vicariously.

Wife-lawyers usually defined themselves as their husbands' "help-mates" and saw their professional roles as part and parcel of their family roles. They used this definition to explain their presence in a "masculine" occupation and at the same time to prove they were still feminine. Because they defined their activity as helping their husbands, it was socially acceptable to be in a "masculine" profession.

DOING THE HOUSEKEEPING OF THE FIRM

Many of the women interviewed in partnerships with a husband (or in a small firm with a husband and unrelated partners) reported that they were performing the practice's nonlegal administrative tasks—hiring secretaries, running the office, and keeping the work calendar. Performing these tasks came at a price. These "sex-appropriate" duties unfortunately did not develop the attorney's skill or contacts and usually condemned her to professional obscurity. In addition to performing the "housekeeping" tasks, women in partnerships with their husbands were limited to the same specialties as other women lawyers of the time—matrimonial cases, probate work, and real-estate law. In a diversified practice this prevented the women from competing with their husbands. It also often gave husbands an opportunity to avoid work they did not care to do—the more mundane or "emotional" hand-holding counseling work lawyers are often called upon to perform but which is not highly regarded in the profession. One consequence of this division of labor was that women did not build an independent client base, had a lower chance of getting referrals, and had low visibility in the profession.

Although theoretically husbands and wives were equal partners and drew equal shares, in fact, women tended to earn less money or ceded control over the money to their husband-partners. Further, wife-attorneys usually felt wedded not only to their husbands but to their joint firm, and therefore unable to leave when a better opportunity came along.

Nevertheless, women lawyers in such practices had real jobs in the law and many of their peers did not. They were subject to fewer role strains because the demands of their work were not in conflict with their domestic duties. Husbands knew when their wives had a hard week at the office and, because it was a joint family enterprise, they were not likely to complain. Furthermore, husbands could and did cover for their wives when their children were sick or needed attention. Wife-partners could put their careers on hold when their children were small and not worry about losing tenure in the firm. In partnership with their husbands, women could work fewer hours than their peers and still maintain a steady relationship with the firm and their profession.

Most wife-partners I interviewed in the 1960s and 1970s presented a rosy picture of their work situations and even those who were dissatisfied showed resignation more than resentment. Yet when I interviewed other lawyers who knew the couples, they sometimes provided insights into their relationships. Colleagues reported that husbands could and did take advantage of their wives. Some wives complained to friends that their husbands used them as secretaries, for example. "He says it's easier to give me the things to do than to explain them to a secretary" was a common observation.

Yet most of the wife-partners suppressed their resentment because the need to maintain good family relations was paramount, and there was no place else to go. Rebels were scarce, but they did exist. One unusually dissatisfied lawyer-wife turned the problem into an advantage, reported a friend. "She complained that it was always 'Darling, get me this form or that one from the file,' until she was so disgusted, she went out and got herself a judgeship." Of course, she could do this only as women began to be appointed to the judiciary in a changing social environment.

COMPETITION

Career competition between husband and wife can put a partnership under enormous strain. If competition on the part of the wife is intense and unmasked, it can become a central threat to both partnerships, professional and marital. Although high career aspiration has been culturally approved for the husband, the career-ambitious wife faced disapproval in the past, and there are still residues of this ideology today. Thus when the wife-attorney is not only in the same field as her husband but engaged in practice with him, her hopes to move upward professionally may be thwarted, which can result in friction in the marriage and disapproval from outsiders. Ambition and achievement on the part of a wife are tolerable and appreciated more easily only when the husband is equally or more accomplished. Incompetence of either husband or wife is a source of strain, and the two partnerships in which it was reported to me by wives criticizing their husbands, the marriages dissolved later. Of course, charges of incompetence may really be an expression of personal animosity in marriages rather than work. The two lawyers who claimed their husbands were not as competent as themselves went on to different kinds of practices—one became a district attorney, an enormous accomplishment at the time, and later married a judge. The other attorney later married a man in an entirely different field and developed a successful independent practice.

Competition is potentially so disrupting to the husband-wife partnership that arrangements develop to physically separate the partners or the spheres in which they work. The division of labor within the firm certainly reduces competition. The husband's hierarchic position as primary decision maker and the wife's more limited career aspirations and underlying "helpmate" ethos traditionally served to control competitiveness. Further, the structure of partnerships as nominal (if not actual) relationships of equality served to reduce potential conflict.

It would be difficult to assess how much competition was reduced because women's work with husbands was defined as "help" and not the contribution of an equal. Although women in partnerships who began practice after the 1970s felt strongly that a woman should not be merely considered helpers but true partners, a division of labor within the family usually served to reduce the potential for competition. But self-selection also played a role. Very competitive women rarely wished to practice with their husbands, and those who tried it soon turned to other kinds of practice.

It was hard to know what women's feelings were about the effects of their partnerships on their careers and their aims and hopes. A few of the women interviewed—those who aspired to judgeships, for example—indicated that if they were given a second chance they might not choose to work with their husbands. They believed the family partnership had restrained their career development. Most of the women in family partnerships admitted to modifying their initial ambitions in law, typically setting their sights lower. (But this was true also of many women professionals of their generation, no matter what their type of practice.) It was noteworthy, however, that in all my studies of lawyers, the most successful women were married but not in partnerships with their husbands.

It is difficult to determine whether the family partnership serves to restrict the women anymore than the profession at large. For those women who might have dropped entirely out of law to raise families—as some did—the family partnership served to maintain their identity as a lawyer and keep professional connections alive. Driving professional ambition has not been common among American women. And even where it does exist, there are strong cultural taboos about acknowledging it. Of course, women who entered partnerships with their husbands were also committed to being wives and mothers. Some would have completely forsaken their career ambitions to pursue the usual feminine roles if they had been forced to choose.

THE IMPACT OF SOCIAL CHANGE

While the number of dual husband-wife practices has been diminishing, today it is not uncommon to find husbands and wives working in the same firm or partnership along with other lawyers. In these situations, the wife's role is not as helpmate but as full partner. Women lawyers are alert to the need to establish reputations now and are less willing to do work that might impede them. They resist being moved into work traditionally considered to be "women's specialties," and they don't willingly do invisible work in back rooms. As a result, more and more women are handling litigation in the courtroom and engaging in client contact. Some lawyers in practice with their husbands have come into the partnership with established reputations. The following accounts provide an insight into some "new" partnerships I studied in the 1990s.

Katherine Marshall (not her real name), an Illinois lawyer, commented on her own family partnership, formed after she had launched a successful career in a major U.S. Attorneys' office: "The problem of not having the option or inclination or opportunity to participate in the active litigation of the law firm has not been a problem in our firm. Perhaps it is the case because I came out of a very highly litigation-oriented United States Attorney's office. As a matter of fact, many clients came to me in the area of litigation because of my presumed expertise."

Another women reported that the sex division of specialties continued to shape her partnership, though she and her husband had quite different abilities. "I bring in more business clients than my husband does, although he handles more of that type of legal work for the firm than I do. By the same token, he probably brings in more family law problems than I do, although I handle all that type of work for our firm."

One couple who decided to go into practice together found themselves in traditional specialties. The wife, a lawyer in feminist public interest work, reported that

"He had background in corporate work and I had background in Title VII. Neither of us had background in matrimonial work. So we both read everything there was to read on matrimonial work because we suspected that's where most of our clients would be coming from. I learned it by the practice, really."

"Does your husband handle matrimonial cases with you?"

"He hates it even more than I do, so I do most of it and he is trying to build up the corporate end of the practice."

Wives in husband-wife partnerships today, even if they started out together in the past, are far more evaluative of their positions in the firm than their predecessors had been. An established lawyer who went into partnership with her husband in the late 1970s said she felt "her identity oozing away" when her husband's male clients made remarks such as "I see you have the little wife here." She could not be an "associate to my husband" she said, because "it sticks in my craw." It was mainly in this partnership that she realized "how much it means to me to be a hotshot lawyer."

Another couple evaluated their partnership as "being ideal for the family, because it's our own outfit with our own hours and our own thing." In this partnership the wife took off a day a week to take courses that interested her. "What about competition?" I asked. "People always ask about competition," she said. "It's never an issue. If he does well I am delirious. The same is true for him."

Couples who had been in practice for a long time, and those followed up ten years after the first study, had undergone changes. Some were ideological changes, some were life-cycle changes, and some developed because of the new opportunities created by changes in the law as well as the women's movement. The women partners were doing much better in their professional lives than they had been previously. One had become much more active in bar association activities, had developed her reputation, and was bringing in business independently. The firm had grown, and she now had a number of younger attorneys working for her. She claimed to have been affected by the women's movement and seemed also to be assessing her marriage anew. The children were now grown, giving her considerably more freedom.

Sarah Leiber (not her real name), an attorney in a labor relations firm, had developed a specialty in sex-discrimination cases independently of her husband and another partner. She, too, had a heightened sense of career. Because her children were grown, she now had the time to engage in high-profile cases with intensity and developed a national reputation.

New and old partnerships have thrived when opportunities for women have expanded. In fact, husbands and wives both benefit from them. Kathryn Marshall illustrated this in a note about her husband: "I have had the distinct pleasure of hearing my husband discuss the awesome benefits of having his wife as a law partner. He tends to emphasize how his comfort level is increased because of the absolutely unquestioned loyalty that he knows is part of his relationship with his law partner. He also emphasizes his security in working with a known quantity and with someone whose abilities and capabilities he has no doubt about."

Work in a family law firm may also permit women attorneys to take advantage of new opportunities in playing public roles. This is true whatever their ideological commitments. Consider the case of Phyllis Schlafly, an active opponent of the Equal Rights Amendment, whose public-speaking engagements have taken her far from home. Schlafly, who received her law degree in 1979 when she was fifty-three years old, went to work part-time in her husband's firm, Schlafly, Godfrey and Fitzgerald, and continued to pursue her political activity.

It is significant that husband-law partners today share the new ideology of sharing. When their wives have come forward, expressing the desire to take more visible roles in the firms, they usually have gained their husbands' support. One prominent lawyer, well known for his work on cases highlighting social causes, practiced with his second wife until his recent death. Friends of the couple noted that the wife started out in classic style "carrying his briefcase." As time went on, however, the husband promoted his wife's career and gave her a more prominent role to play in court.

It is clear the norms have changed in the past thirty years. Women who work with their husbands do so by choice because they have other options. Women lawyers no longer are satisfied doing the firm's housekeeping or taking on invisible roles, and lawyer-husbands accept this. Moreover, the benefits are shared. Now that women's contributions to family firms have become more visible, men can more easily refer cases to their wives without fear of the disapproval of their clients. Of course, the benefits and rewards in husband-wife partnerships ultimately depend on the personalities involved and the social contexts in which they practice. Other family members, friends, and professional associates can

have an important effect on the relationship, either strengthening it or
undermining it. The quality of networks and the quality of environments
are two factors that lead to constructive or destructive aspects of a marital and work relationship.

MARITAL PARTNERS AND
BUSINESS PARTNERS — CONTINUITIES

One indicator of interest in couple business-partnerships is the number
of books advising couples who work together in partnerships on issues
of conflict, division of responsibilities, and time problems that have
come out (James and James 1997; Marshack, Scott, and Jaffee 1998),
and there is a website, www.couplesatwork.com, sharing information.

Today, with a new entrepreneurial spirit, husbands and wives are
going into business together in enterprises springing up all over the country. These include professional legal and medical partnerships, cinema
management, music production, book and magazine publishing (Davies
1998), and large-scale businesses such as the $50-million-a-year bakery
chain Cinnamons, based in Kansas City (Nelton 1989). From the outsider's perspective, the new husband-wife partnerships can be viewed as
prototypical of a new and useful equality between marital partners and
other professional partners. Sharon and Frank Barnett (1988), authors
of *Working Together: Entrepreneurial Couples,* have coined the term
"copreneurs" for husband-wife partnerships. They point to the benefits
that accrue to couples who are similarly and equally engaged in a family
business because of the sensitivity each has to the other's work demands,
problems, and aspirations. In a work environment in which firm loyalty
to employees is decreasing (Epstein et al. 1999; Sennett 1998), many
people, among them couples, are deciding to start their own businesses.
The number of couples in nonfarm sole proprietorships rose by nearly
a quarter of a million—from 257,899 to 482,933 between 1977 and
1985 (the last period for which I could obtain data) (Nelton 1989). No
doubt there are substantially more today.

As I noted earlier, family businesses are common among immigrant
families although I have not been able to locate research on professional
partnerships. Studies of Korean immigrants seem to be most plentiful.
They illustrate the issues that successive waves of immigrant couples face
who go into business together. A 1996–97 survey of Koreans indicates
that 38 percent of employed Korean women worked together with their
husbands in small businesses (Min 1998). Other studies of Korean im-

migrants in New York, Chicago, Los Angeles, and elsewhere in the country also show the large participation of women in family businesses (Espiritu 1999; Park 1989; Yoon 1997). Like the women lawyers of the past, however, in those businesses, husbands usually control the money and management of the businesses and in some cases may act as the "most immediate and harshest employers" (Bonacich, Hossain, and Park 1987). These business relationships recall the exploitative experiences women lawyers faced before there was opportunity for women to go out on their own. Immigrant women today, facing the same structural conditions of prejudice, limited access to employment, and limited skills, find that they too are isolated from public life, find it difficult to integrate into American society, and find that work is regarded as an extension of their domestic responsibilities. Yet when the family gains economically by the joint labor of husband and wife, and women develop alternative employment opportunities, there is often a recalibration of power within the family and movement toward greater equality. Thus, there is the possibility that women who work in family businesses that are not real partnerships will benefit in the long run, as did women attorneys in the past who were able to take advantage of a widening opportunity structure.

CONCLUSION

Husband-wife partnerships, professional and entrepreneurial, are age-old and continue in today's economy. They provide the opportunity for a true egalitarianism between husband and wife in a joint enterprise. We have seen the development of equal professional partnerships over the past thirty years in the United States. In the most positive situation, husbands and wives are interdependent and equal as they depend on each other to provide labor and emotional resources. But, as in the past, husband-wife businesses may foster gender inequality by reproducing traditional hierarchical domestic roles in the family in which husbands exploit the labor of their wives. Much depends on women's opportunities in the marketplace, the reduction of ethnic, racial, and gender stereotypes that limit employment possibilities, and the exposure of the family to an ideology of equality.

REFERENCES

Barnett, Frank, and Sharon Barnett. *Working Together: Entrepreneurial Couples.* Berkeley, Calif.: Ten Speed Press, 1988.

Bonacich, E., M. Hossain, and J. Park. "Korean Immigrant Working Women in the Early 1980's." In *Korean Women in Transition: At Home and Abroad,* edited by E. Yu and E. M. Philipps. Los Angeles: California State University, Center for Korean American and Korean Studies, 1987.

Davies, Jim. "Sleeping Partners." *Management Today* (Oct. 1998):112–14.

Epstein, Cynthia Fuchs. *Women in Law,* 2d ed. Chicago: University of Illinois Press, 1981; New York: Basic Books, 1993.

Epstein, Cynthia Fuchs, with Robert Sauté, Bonnie Oglensky, and Martha Gever. "Glass Ceilings and Open Doors: Women's Mobility in the Legal Profession." *Fordham Law Review* 64, 2 (1995):291–449.

Epstein, Cynthia Fuchs, Carroll Seron, Bonnie Oglensky, and Robert Sauté. *The Part-time Paradox: Time Norms, Professional Life, Family, and Gender.* New York: Routledge, 1999.

Espiritu, Yen Le. "Gender and Labor in Asian Immigrant Families." *The American Behavioral Scientist* 42, 4 (Jan. 1999):628–47.

Foner, Nancy. "Immigrant Women and Work in New York City: Then and Now." *Journal of American Ethnic History* 18, 3 (1999):95–113.

Jaffe, Azriela. *Honey I Want to Start My Own Business: A Planning Guide for Couples.* New York: Harper Business, 1996.

James, E. W., and Janet James. *Couples at Work: How Can You Stand to Work with Your Spouse?* Denver, Colo.: Boomer House Books, 1997.

Kessler-Harris, Alice. *Women Have Always Worked: A Historical Overview.* Old Westbury, Conn.: The Feminist Press, 1981.

Marshack, Kathy, Cynthia D. Scott, and Dennis T. Jaffe. *Entrepreneurial Couples: Making It Work at Work and at Home.* Palo Alto, Calif.: Davies Black, 1998.

Min, Pyong Gap. *Changes and Conflicts: Korean Immigrant Families in New York.* Needham Heights, Mass.: Allyn & Bacon, 1998.

Nelton, Sharon. "Partners in Entrepreneurship." *Nation's Business* 77, 3 (Mar. 1989):38.

Park, Kyeyoung. "The Korean-American Dream: Impact of New Productive Activities on the Organization of Domestic Life: A Case Study of the Community." In *Frontiers of Asian-American Studies,* edited by G. Nomura, R. Endo, S. Samda, and R. Leong. Pullman: Washington State University Press, 1989.

Sennett, Richard. *The Corrosion of Character: The Personal Consequences of Work in the New Capitalism.* New York: Norton, 1998.

Yoon, In-Jin. *On My Own: Korean Businesses and Race Relations in America.* Chicago: University of Chicago Press, 1997.

CHAPTER 9

Grounds for Marriage

Reflections and Research on an Institution in Transition

Arlene Skolnick

"Is Marriage Finally Dead?" In August 1999, *Redbook Magazine* published the responses of a group of journalists to that question. One of the speakers agreed that the institution had breathed its last breath; most thought that while ailing, it was not yet in a terminal state. Worry about the impending collapse of marriage and the family has persisted in Western culture for at least a century. For a much longer time, marriage has also been the butt of countless jokes, cartoons, aphorisms, and old saws about henpecked husbands, unfaithful wives, and the general folly of those—especially the men—who allow themselves to be roped into it. Those who lamented the sorry state of marriage in earlier eras would be surprised to learn that in the twenty-first century, the institution is still here and shows no signs of disappearing.

Despite today's high divorce rates, more births to the unmarried, the rise in one-parent families, and other trends, the United States today has the highest marriage rate among the advanced industrial countries. The Census Bureau estimates that about 90 percent of Americans will eventually marry. Same-sex couples are also claiming the right to legal marriage, not merely "back of the bus" recognition as "domestic partners" (Graff 1999.)

The combination of high marriage and high divorce rates seems paradoxical but actually represents two sides of the same coin: the centrality of the emotional relationship between the partners. Marriage for love was not unknown in earlier eras. Nevertheless, in most times and places, marriages have been grounded in property, status, and the concerns of parents and kin rather than in the feelings of the couple.

In the West, however, for at least two hundred years, being in love has come to be the only acceptable grounds for marriage. And love, or the emotional quality of the couple relationship, has also become increasingly important as the principal reason for staying together. Yet, even in the heyday of the marital "togetherness" ideal of the 1950s, researchers found that so-called empty shell or disengaged marriages were widespread. Such couples lived under one roof but seemed to have little or no emotional connection to one another. Some people in such relationships even considered themselves happily married; others, particularly women, lived in quiet desperation but saw no alternative.

Contemporary couples usually hold higher expectations. American attitudes toward marriage changed dramatically between the 1950s and the 1970s as part of what has been called a "psychological revolution"—a transformation in the way people perceive marriage, parenthood, and their lives in general (Veroff, Kulka, and Douvan 1981). Surveys taken by the University of Michigan found that, by the 1970s, people had become more psychologically oriented, reportedly seeking emotional warmth and intimacy in marriage.

This shift correlates to higher educational levels. In the 1950s, a psychological approach to relationships was found among the relatively few college-educated Americans. By the 1970s the psychological approach to marriage and family life had become, as the authors put it, "common coin."

In an era when divorce has lost its stigma and remaining married has become nearly as much a choice as entering marriage, it is not surprising that a loving and rewarding relationship has become the gold standard for marital success. Even when they know the statistics, few if any couples initiate marriage expecting that their own relationship will break down. Indeed, research on newly married couples shows few expect the divorce statistics to apply to themselves. How do relationships become unhappy? What transforms happy newlyweds into emotional strangers? In this chapter, I discuss my own research in the context of what others have been learning in answer to these questions.

THE STUDY OF MARRIAGE THEN AND NOW

Over the past three decades, rising divorce rates and other dramatic changes in sexual norms, gender roles, and family life awakened a new interest in marriage and couple relationships across the social sciences. Until then, the study of marriage and the family was carried out mainly by sociologists. There were many studies of what was called marital "adjustment," "happiness," "success," or "satisfaction." These studies were usually based on large surveys asking people to rate their own marriages; researchers would then examine the correlates of satisfaction. The best established ones were demographic factors, such as occupation, education, income, age at marriage, religious participation, and the like. There was little theorizing about why these links might occur.

Self-reported ratings of happiness or satisfaction to study marriage were widely criticized. Some researchers argued that the concept "marital happiness" was hopelessly vague. Others questioned the validity of asking people to rate their own marriages, particularly since the high ratings most people gave to their own marriages seemed at odds with high divorce rates.

There were also deeper problems with these earlier studies. Even the best self-report measure can hardly capture what goes on in the private, psychosocial theater of married life. In the 1970s, a new wave of marital research began to breach the wall of marital privacy. Psychologists, clinicians, and social scientists began to observe families interacting with one another in laboratories and clinics, usually through one-way mirrors. The new technology of videotaping made it possible to preserve these interactions for later analysis. Behavioral therapists and researchers began to produce a literature on the kinds of statements and actions that differentiated between happy and unhappy couples. At the same time, social psychologists began to study close relationships of various kinds.

During this period I began my own research on marriage, using couples who had taken part in the longitudinal studies carried out at the Institute of Human Development (IHD) at the University of California at Berkeley. One member of the couple had been part of the study since childhood and had been born in either 1921 or 1928. Each spouse had been interviewed in depth in 1958, when the study members were thirty or thirty-seven years old. They were interviewed again in 1970 and 1982. The interviews were carried out by experienced clinical psychologists, who later rated each spouse on a large number of personality items and five aspects of marital adjustment. The participants also supplied a great deal of other information about themselves, including self-reports of marital satisfaction.

Despite the richness of the longitudinal data, it did not include observations of the spouses interacting with one another—a research method not available until the study was decades old. On the other hand, few of the new observational studies of marriage have included the kind of in-depth material on the couples' lives that the longitudinal study did. It seemed to me that the ideal study of marriage—assuming cost was not an issue—would include both observational and interview data as well as a sort of ethnography of the couples' lives at home. A few years ago, I was offered the opportunity to be involved in a small version of such a project in a study of the marriages of police officers. I discuss this study later.

The new wave of research has revealed a great deal about the complex emotional dynamics of marriage and, perhaps most usefully, showed that some widespread assumptions about couple relations are incorrect. But there is still a great deal more to learn. There is as yet no grand theory of marriage, no singular road to understanding marriage, no "one size fits all" prescription for marital success. But we have gained some important insights into marital (and marriage-like) relationships. And there seems to be a striking convergence of findings emerging from different approaches to studying couples. Here are some of these insights.

For Better and for Worse

The sociologist Jesse Bernard argued that every marriage contains two marriages—the husband's and the wife's (1972), and that his is better than hers. Bernard's claims have been controversial, but in general, her idea that husbands and wives have different perspectives on their marriage has held up over time. And on a variety of subtle measures of marital satisfaction—for example, would you like your children to have a marriage like yours?—men do seem more content with their relationships than their wives (Skolnick 1993).

But apart from gender differences, marital relationships also seem to divide in another way: Every marriage contains within it both a good marriage and a bad marriage. Early studies of marital quality assumed that all marriages could be lined up along a single dimension of satisfaction, adjustment, or happiness—happy couples would be at one end of the scale, unhappy ones at the other, and most couples would fall somewhere in between. More recently, marriage researchers have found that two separate dimensions are needed to capture the quality of a marriage—a positive dimension and a negative one. In effect, the ultimate determinant has to do with the balance between the good marriage and the bad one. The finding emerges in different ways in studies using different methods.

In my own research, I came across this same "good marriage/bad marriage" phenomenon among the Berkeley longitudinal couples (Skolnick 1981). First, we identified couples ranging from high to low in marital satisfaction based on ratings of the marriage each spouse had made, combined with ratings made by clinical interviewers who had seen each separately. Later we examined transcripts of the clinical interviews to see how people who had scored high or low on measures of marital quality described their marriages.

In the course of the interview, each person was asked about his or her satisfactions and dissatisfactions in the relationship. Surprisingly, it was hard to tell the happily married from their unhappy counterparts by looking only at statements about dissatisfaction. None of the happy spouses were without some complaints or irritations. One husband went on at length at what a terrible homemaker his wife was. The wife in one of the most highly rated marriages reported having "silent arguments"—periods of not speaking to one another—which lasted about a week. "People always say you should talk over your differences," the wife said, "but it doesn't work in our family."

What did differentiate happier marriages from the unhappy ones could be found in the descriptions of satisfactions. The happy couples described close, affectionate, and often romantic relationships. One man remarked after almost thirty years of marriage, "I still have stars in my eyes." A woman said, "I just can't wait for him to get home every night; just having him around is terrific."

The most systematic evidence for this good marriage/bad marriage model emerges from the extensive program of studies of marital interaction carried out by Gottman and Levenson (1992) and Gottman et al.(1998). Their research is based on videotaped observations of couple discussions in a laboratory setting. These intensive studies not only record facial expressions, gestures, and tone of voice but also monitor heart rates and other physiological indicators of stress. The partners also watched a videotape of their conversation and were asked to use a rating dial to provide a continuous report of how they felt during their interaction.

Surprisingly, these studies do not confirm the widespread notion that anger is the great destroyer of marital relationships. Gottman and his colleagues found that anger in couple interaction does not predict whether a marriage would eventually become distressed. Among the indicators that do predict marital distress and eventual divorce are high levels of physiological arousal or stress during the interaction, a tendency for quarrels to escalate in intensity, and a refusal to respond to the other person's efforts to "make up" and end the quarrel.

Ultimately, the key factor in the success of a marriage is not the amount of anger or other negative emotion in the relationship—no marriage always runs smoothly and cheerfully—but the balance between positive and negative feelings and actions. Indeed, Gottman gives a precise estimate of this ratio in successful marriages—five to one. In other words, the "good" marriage has to be five times better than the "bad" marriage is bad.

It seems as if the "good" marriage acts like a reservoir of positive feelings that can defuse tensions and keep arguments from escalating out of control. In virtually every marriage and family, "emotional brushfires" are constantly breaking out. Whether these flare-ups develop into major bonfires depends on the balance within the marriage that makes it a good one or bad one.

Gottman identifies a set of four behavioral patterns—he calls them "the four horsemen of the apocalypse"—that constitutes a series of escalating signs of marital breakdown. These include *criticism* (not just complaining about a specific act but denouncing the spouse's whole character); which may be followed by *contempt* (insults, name calling, mockery); then *defensiveness* (each spouse feeling hurt, mistreated, and misunderstood by the other); and finally, *stonewalling* (one or both partners withdraws into silence and avoidance). Eventually, the couple may end up leading separate lives under the same roof.

Tolstoy Was Wrong: Happy Marriages Are Not All Alike

The most common approach to understanding marriage, as I have shown, is to compare or correlate ratings of marital happiness with other variables. However, some studies over the years have looked at differences among marriages at a given level of satisfaction. Among the first was a widely cited study published in 1965. John Cuber and Peggy Harroff interviewed 437 successful upper-middle-class men and women about their lives and marriages. These people had been married for at least fifteen years to their original spouses and reported themselves as being satisfied with their marriages. Yet the authors found enormous variation in marital style among these stable, contented upscale couples.

Only one out of six marriages in the sample conformed to the image of what marriage is supposed to be—that is, a relationship based on strong emotional bonds of love and friendship. The majority of others were what Cuber and Harroff called "utilitarian" relationships. These fell into three types: first, "conflict habituated" couples resembled the bickering, battling spouses often portrayed in comedy and tragedy—the kind of relationship that would today be called "dysfunctional." Yet these couples were content with their marriages and did not define their fighting as a problem.

A second group of couples were in "devitalized" marriages—they had started out in close, loving relationships but had drifted apart over the years. In the third "passive congenial" type of relationship, the partners were never romantically in love or emotionally close. They regarded marriage as a comfortable and convenient way to live while they devoted their energy to their careers or other social commitments.

The most recent studies of marital types come from the research of John Gottman and his colleagues, described earlier. Along with identifying early warning signs of later marital trouble and divorce, Gottman also observed that happy, successful marriages were not all alike. He also found that much of the conventional wisdom about marriage is misguided. Many marital therapists and much of the public believe that a couple who argue and fight a lot have an obviously "dysfunctional" relationship. On the other hand, those spouses who sweep their conflicts under the rug and avoid communicating with one another about troublesome issues are also in a dysfunctional marriage.

Many marital counselors and popular writings on marriage advocate what Gottman calls a "validation" or "active-listening" model. They recommend that when couples have a disagreement, they should speak to one another as a therapist speaks to a client. One spouse, for example, the wife, is supposed to state her complaints directly to the husband, in the form of "I" statements; for example, "I feel you're not doing your share of the housework." Then he is supposed to calmly respond by paraphrasing what she has said and empathize with her feelings: "Sounds like you're upset about this."

To their surprise, Gottman and his colleagues found that very few couples actually fit this therapeutically approved, "validating" model of marriage. Gottman et al. found, like Cuber and Harroff, that people can be happily married even if they fight a lot; Gottman calls these "volatile" marriages. "Avoidant" couples, those who did not argue or discuss their conflicts openly, also defied conventional wisdom about the importance of "communication" and could enjoy successful marriages.

In my own study, I too found a great deal of variation among the longitudinal couples. Apart from the deep friendship that all the happy couples shared, they differed in other ways. Some spent virtually twenty-four hours a day together, others went their own ways, going off to parties or weekends alone. Some were very traditional in their gender patterns, others egalitarian. Some were emotionally close to their relatives, some were distant. Some had a wide circle of friends, some were virtual hermits.

They could come from happy or unhappy families. The wife in one of the happiest marriages had a very difficult relationship with her father; she grew up "hating men" and planned never to marry. Her husband also grew up in an unhappy home where the parents eventually divorced. In short, if the emotional core of marriage is good, it seems to matter very little what kind of lifestyle the couple chooses to follow.

Marriage Is a Movie, Not a Snapshot

Heroclitis once said that you can never step into a river twice because the river is always in motion. The same is true of marriage. A variety of studies show that over a relatively short period of time, families can change in the ways they interact and in their emotional atmosphere. In studies of police officer couples, described in more detail below, the same marriage could look very different from one laboratory session to the next, depending on how much stress the officer had experienced on each day. The IHD longitudinal studies made it possible to follow the same couples over several decades.

Consider the following examples, based on the first two adult follow-ups around 1960 and the early 1970s (Skolnick 1981).

Seen in 1960, when they were in their early thirties, the marriage of Jack and Ellen did not look promising. Jack was an aloof husband and uninvolved father. Ellen was overwhelmed by caring for three small children. She had a variety of physical ailments and needed a steady dose of tranquilizers to calm her anxieties. Ten years later, she was in good health and enjoying life. She and Jack had become a close couple.

Martin and Julia were a happy couple in 1960. They had two children, an active social life, and were fixing up a new home they had bought. Martin was looking forward to a new business venture. A decade later, Martin had a severe drinking problem that had disrupted every aspect of their relationship. Thinking seriously about divorce, Julia said it all had started when Martin began to have trouble with his business partner.

Perhaps the most striking impression from following these marriages through long periods of time is the great potential for change in intimate relationships. Those early interviews suggest that many couples had "dysfunctional" marriages. It seemed at the time to spouses, as well as to the interviewers, that the source of the marital difficulties was psychological problems in the husband or wife or both, or else that they were incompatible.

For some couples, these explanations were valid. Later interviews revealed the same emotional or personality difficulties and incompatibilities. Some people had divorced and married again to people with whom they were a better fit. One man who had seemed emotionally immature all his life finally found happiness in his third marriage. He married a younger woman who was both nurturing to him and yet a "psychological age mate," as he put it.

Although close to a third of the IHD marriages eventually did end in divorce, all of those couples were married years before the divorce revolution of the 1970s made divorce legally easier to obtain as well as more common and socially acceptable. Many unhappy couples remained married long enough to outgrow their earlier difficulties or to advance past the circumstances that were causing the difficulties in the first place. Viewed from a later time, marital distress at one period or stage in life seemed to be rooted in situational factors: problems at work, trouble with in-laws or money, bad housing, too many babies too close together. In the midst of these strains, however, it was easy to blame problems on the basic character of the husband or wife or on their incompatibility. Only later, when the situation had changed, did it seem that there was nothing inherently wrong with the couple's relationship.

The Critical Events of a Marriage May Not Be Inside the Marriage

The longitudinal data, as noted, revealed a striking amount of change for better or worse depending on a large variety of life circumstances. While the impact of such external factors remains a relatively unacknowledged source of marital distress, there has been growing interest in the impact of work and working conditions—especially job stress—

on family life. One of the most stressful occupations, police work, also suffers from very high rates of divorce, domestic violence, and alcoholism. In 1997, Robert Levenson and I took part in a collaboration between the University of California and a West Coast urban police department (Levenson, Roberts, and Bellows 1998; Skolnick 1998). We focused on job stress and marriage. This was a small, exploratory study using too few couples—eleven—for statistical analysis, but it yielded some striking preliminary findings.

Briefly, Levenson's part of the study looked at the impact of stress on couple interaction in the laboratory. His procedures called for each spouse to keep a stress diary every day for thirty days. Once a week for four weeks, the couples went to the laboratory at the end of the work day, after eight hours of being apart. Their interaction was videotaped, and the physiological responses of each spouse were monitored continuously.

In my part of the project, we used an adaptation of the IHD clinical interview with officers and their wives in their homes. (The sample did not include female officers or police couples.) The aim was to examine their perceptions of police work and its impact on their marriages, their general life circumstances, and the sources of stress and support in their lives. I discovered that these officers and their wives were making heroic efforts to do well, against enormous odds, in their work and family. The obvious dangers and disasters police must deal with are only part of the story; sleep deprivation, frustration with the department bureaucracy, and inadequate equipment were some of the other factors adding up to enormous stress.

Moreover, some of the ways people in other occupations relieve stress were not easily available to these officers. The department offered counseling, but there was a stigma attached to using it. The officers feared any troubles they had would get back to their superiors, and they would be "hung out to dry." Socializing with other officers was difficult because of an aspect of police culture described by the police novelist Joseph Wambaugh as "choir practice"—that is, drinking and womanizing. The men we interviewed felt they had to steer clear of this culture to protect their marriages.

Despite their difficult lives, these couples seemed to have good, well-functioning marriages, at home and in the laboratory—except on high-stress days. Levenson's study was able to examine the direct effects of different levels of stress on the face-to-face interaction of these couples—something that had not been done before. The findings were striking.

Variations in the husband's work stress had a marked impact on both couple interaction and the physiological indicators of emotional arousal.

More surprising, it was not just the police officer who showed evidence of stress but the partner as well. Even before either partner had said a word, while they were just sitting quietly, both the officer and the spouse showed signs of physiological arousal. In particular, there was a kind of "paralysis of the positive emotion system" in both partners (Levenson, Roberts, and Bellows 1998). Looking at the videotapes, you didn't need the physiological measures to see what was going on. The husband's restless agitation was clear, as was the wife's tense and wary response to it. The wives seemed frozen in their seats, barely able to move. In fact, just watching the couples on videotape is enough to make a viewer also feel tense and uneasy.

Recall that these couples did not look or act this way on the days they were not under high job stress. However, in these sessions, the couples' behavior revealed the same warning signs that Gottman and Levenson had found in their earlier studies to be predictors of who was likely to be divorced. The "paralysis of the positive emotion system" means that the "good" aspects of the marriage were unavailable just when they were most needed. Repeated often enough, such moments can strain even a good marriage; they create an emotional climate in which tempers can easily flare, hurtful things may be said, and problems go unsolved. Police work may be an extreme example of a high-pressure occupation, but it is far from the only one. "What's the difference between a stressed-out business executive and a stressed-out police officer?" asked a New York columnist not long ago, after a terrible case of domestic violence in a police family. The officer, he went on, "brings home a loaded gun."

CAN MARRIAGE BE SAVED?

On June 2, 1986, *Newsweek Magazine* featured a cover story that proclaimed that a woman over forty had a greater chance of being "killed by a terrorist" than of getting married. The story set off a media blitz and a wave of alarm and anxiety among single women. However, *Newsweek* had reported on a study that was later criticized by other researchers for relying on trends in earlier generations to make predictions about today's women. That is, before the 1970s, when the great majority of women married in their early twenties or even earlier, a woman who was single when she reached forty was likely to remain so. But patterns of marriage and remarriage have changed so much since then that simply projecting the old trends into the future is not very useful.

In the summer of 1999, the National Marriage Project Report produced another alarming study of the state of marriage. Exhibit A was a finding that, between 1960 and 1990, the marriage rate among young adults had declined by 23 percent. Again, a widely publicized "finding" had to be corrected. The problem this time was the inclusion of teenagers as young as fifteen as "young adults" in 1960 and 1996. Teenagers were far more likely to marry in the 1950s than in the 1990s—or at any previous time in American history.

These periodic alarms clearly resonate with a public deeply concerned that divorce, cohabitation, single parenthood, and other recent trends signal moral decline and the unraveling of the social fabric. Many family scholars agree with these pessimistic conclusions. Other, more optimistic, scholars argue that marriage and the family are not collapsing but becoming more diverse as they adapt to new social and economic conditions.

A third possibility is that we are passing through a difficult transitional period. We are in the midst of a cultural lag between the traditional norms of marriage, which assigned sharply contrasting roles to men and women, and a rapidly changing world outside the home, which has moved toward greater gender equality. Schools, businesses, the professions, and other institutions have become increasingly neutral about gender.

Legal and political trends in modern democracies have militated against gender and other forms of castelike inequality, at least in principle. To be sure, women have not yet achieved full equality. But we have become used to seeing women in the workplace, even in such formerly all-male institutions as the police, the military, Congress, and the Supreme Court.

The family remains the one institution based on separate and distinct roles for men and women. Despite the vast social and economic changes that have transformed our daily lives, the old gender roles remain deeply rooted in our cultural assumptions and definitions of masculinity and femininity. At the same time, a more equitable or "symmetrical" model of marriage is struggling to be born. Surveys show that most Americans, especially young people, favor equal rather than traditional marriage.

But the transition to such a model has been difficult, even for those committed to the idea of equal partnerships. In a study of "peer," or egalitarian, marriages, Pepper Schwartz found that the difficulties of raising children and men's continuing advantages in the workplace make it hard for all but the most dedicated couples to live up to their own ideals (Schwartz 1995).

Intersecting with the gender revolution are the economic shifts of recent years—growing economic inequality, the demise of the well-paying blue-collar job, the end of the stable career of the 1950s "organization man." The long hours and working weeks that have replaced the nine-to-five professional or corporate workplace take their toll on relationships.

Traditionally, marriage has always been linked to economic opportunity—a young man had to be able to support a wife to be considered eligible to marry. The high rates of marriage in the 1950s were sustained in part by rising wages and a relatively low cost of living; the average thirty-year-old man could afford to buy an average-priced house for less than 20 percent of his salary. Recent research shows that economic factors still play a large role in determining when and if a man or woman will marry. As a result, marriage is becoming something of "luxury item," as Frank Furstenberg puts it, a form of "having" available mainly to those already enjoying economic advantages (1996). In his research on low-income families, Furstenberg finds that men and women would like the "luxury" model but feel they can't afford it.

Inside marriage, conflicts stemming from gender issues have become the leading cause of divorce (Nock 1999). Studies of couples married since the 1970s reveal the dynamics of these conflicts. Arlie Hochschild (1997), for example, has found that the happiest marriages are those in which the husband does his share of the "second shift"—the care of home and children. Another recent study shows that today's women also expect their husbands to do their share of the emotional work of marriage—monitoring and talking about the relationship itself; this "marital work ethic" has emerged in middle-class couples married since the 1970s, in response to easy and widespread divorce (Hackstaff 2000).

Dominance is another sore point in many of today's marriages. Gottman and his colleagues (1998) have found that a key factor in predicting marital happiness and divorce is a husband's willingness to accept influence from his wife, but many men experience a loss of dominance in marriage not as equality but as a shift in power that leaves their wives dominant over them. Studies of battered women show that domestic violence may be the extreme form of this common problem—it often reflects the man's attempt to assert what he sees as his prerogative to dominate and control his partner.

Still, change is happening, even while men lag behind in the gender revolution. Today's men no longer expect to be waited on in the home the way their grandfathers were by their grandmothers. Middle-class norms demand a more involved kind of father than those of a generation ago. The sight of a man with a baby in his arms or on his back is no longer unusual.

In sum, marriage and family life today are passing through a difficult transition to a new economy and a new ordering of gender relations. Those who sermonize about "family values" need to recall that the family is also about bread-and-butter issues and back up their words with resources. And while some people believe that equality and stable marriage are incompatible, the evidence seems so far to show the opposite. As one therapist and writer puts it: "The feminist revolution of this century has provided the most powerful challenge to traditional patterns of marriage. Yet paradoxically, it may have strengthened the institution by giving greater freedom to both partners, and by allowing men to accept some of traditionally female values" (Rubenstein 1990).

REFERENCES

Bernard, Jessie. *The Future of Marriage.* New York: Bantam Books, 1972.

Cuber, John F., and Peggy Harroff. *Sex and the Significant Americans.* Baltimore: Penguin, 1965.

Furstenberg, Frank. "The Future of Marriage." *American Demographics* (June 1996):34–40.

Gottman, John M., and Robert W. Levenson. "Marital Processes Predictive of Later Dissolution: Behavior, Physiology and Health." *Journal of Personality and Social Psychology* 63 (1992):221–33.

Gottman, John M., et al. "Predicting Marital Happiness and Stability from Newlywed Interactions." *Journal of Marriage and the Family* 60 (1998):5–22.

Graff, E. J. *What Is Marriage For?* Boston: Beacon Press, 1999.

Hackstaff, Karla. *Marriage in a Culture of Divorce.* Boston: Beacon Press, 2000.

Hochschild, Arlie. *The Time Bind.* New York: Henry Holt and Co., 1997.

Levenson, Robert W., Nicole Roberts, and Sally Bellows. "Report on Police Marriage and Work Stress Study." University of California, Berkeley, 1998.

National Marriage Project. *Report on Marriage.* New Brunswick, N.J.: Rutgers University Press, 1999.

Nock, Steven L. "The Problem with Marriage." *Society* 36, 5 (July/August 1999):20–30.

Rubinstein, Helge. *The Oxford Book of Marriage.* New York: Oxford University Press, 1990.

Schwartz, Pepper. *Love between Equals: How Peer Marriage Really Works.* New York: Free Press, 1995.

Skolnick, Arlene. "Married Lives: Longitudinal Perspectives on Marriage." In *Present and Past in Middle Life,* edited by D. H. Eichorn et al., 269–98. New York: Academic Press, 1981.

———. "His and Her Marriage in Longitudinal Perspective." In *Feminine/Masculine: Gender and Social Change.* Compendium of Research Summaries. New York: The Rockefeller Foundation, 1993.

———. "Sources and Processes of Police Marital Stress." Paper presented at the National Conference on Community Policing, Arlington, Va., November 1998.

Veroff, J. G., Elizabeth Douvan, and Richard A. Kulka. *The Inner American: A Self-Portrait from 1957–1976.* New York: Basic Books, 1981.

CHAPTER 10

Divorce, American Style

Deborah L. Rhode

As the essays in this volume reflect, issues concerning couples have long occupied a crucial and contested place in American culture. Few issues have been so celebrated in public rhetoric and devalued in public policy as those implicating "family values." And nowhere is the gap greater between our professed principles and our legal practices than on matters involving divorce.

That gap is a matter of profound social importance, given recent demographic trends. Close to half of all American marriages end in divorce, and most American children will spend some time living in single-parent families. Many of those families will suffer substantial economic hardship, largely because prevailing public policy has misdescribed the problems and misconceived the solutions.

Popular perceptions of divorce law reflect comfortable myths. One family fantasy is that before "women's so-called liberation," marriages stayed together, homemakers stayed home, and almost everyone benefited, especially the children. Then along came feminists, agitating for divorce on demand, sex-neutral statutes, and full-time careers, and look what happened: impoverished families, displaced homemakers, and fatherless kids with messed-up lives.

The women's movement is blamed for being both too hard on men and not hard enough. Contemporary champions of divorced homemakers claim that feminism has left them unprotected; the push for gender equality in formal law has ignored gender inequality in daily practice. According to accounts like Nicholas Davidson's *The Failure of Feminism* and Carolyn Graglia's "The Housewife as Pariah," the early women's movement "forced through 'no-fault' divorce laws that trampled on homemakers' hard-earned rights to share in the fruit of [long-standing] marriages. . . . The actions of [these] feminists led to real suffering for hundreds of thousands of women with little or no compensating benefit."[1]

By contrast, many divorced men and their increasingly vocal leadership insist that feminism has trampled *their* rights and that the justice system is biased against *them*. In principle, they claim, the law may promise equal treatment between the spouses, but in practice, it doesn't work out that way. According to fathers'-rights groups, ex-husbands are now experiencing the modern equivalent of "taxation without representation": They are denied visitation, impoverished by support payments, and given no say in how their money is spent. Vindictive ex-wives reportedly keep fathers away from piano recitals and keep child support away from children. Funds that should go for kids' needs end up subsidizing mothers' lavish lifestyles. No wonder many men don't want to see or support their former families. From this perspective, "deadbeat dads" look like mainly "working-class men who must get by on very modest incomes to begin with." At the other end of the scale, affluent men allegedly pay through the nose upon divorce.[2]

Some judges hold similar views. As one Colorado court put it, "These women who stay home and cook and clean and do whatever it is they do, and think they're entitled to the money that their husbands go out and work for, have another think coming."[3] What such women need to learn, a California judge agreed, is that marriage "is not a ticket to a perpetual pension." These alimony drones should just shape up and get a real job. According to the chair of the American Bar Association Family Law Section, "A lot of judges are saying, 'You wanted to be equal, here you go.' "[4]

All that's missing from these indictments of women and the women's movement is evidence. Although feminists get much of the blame for the legacy of no-fault divorce, they were not prominent in most states' reform efforts. Few of the legislators, lawyers, and family law experts who *were* responsible for reform focused on equality for women. Rather, reformers' principal objective was to reduce the fraud, acrimony, and unnecessary expense that resulted from restrictive fault-based requirements. When gender equity surfaced in legislative debates, the concern usually was equity for men, who were supposedly staggering under excessive alimony payments.[5]

This problem turned out to be vastly overstated. Researchers estimate that even during the predivorce reform era, only about a fifth of women received regular spousal support. Since the 1970s, the number has declined still further. But until quite recently, the absence of systematic data allowed judges and legislators to rely on misleading anecdotal experience. Although women's-rights advocates are now prominent in the campaign for divorce reform, their message meets resistance on several fronts.[6]

The problem is not a lack of evidence concerning gender inequality following divorce. Recent research consistently finds that the income of divorced women substantially falls and that of divorced men substantially rises. Although the economic situation of most divorced women eventually improves, especially if they remarry, more than half go through periods of considerable hardship and many older women remain in poverty.[7]

State divorce laws typically promise either "equality" or "equity" between the spouses, but in practice women receive neither. Part of the problem lies in contemporary approaches to marital property. Many courts mandate fifty-fifty splits of existing assets or give preference to the spouse who "earns" them. Yet as gender-bias commissions often note, it is scarcely "equal" when the husband receives half of the marital property and the other half is shared by the wife and children. The inequity escalates when judges overestimate women's likelihood of remarriage and underestimate their career sacrifices. Wives assume about 70 percent of household obligations in the typical marriage and pay the price in lowered earning capacity. Yet many courts and legislatures are highly insensitive to the plight of older displaced homemakers with few marketable skills.[8]

Seldom are decision makers as candid as one Colorado judge who aired his disgust at the "Pekingese Problem"—a "generation of women bred for show," unwilling to leave the "gravy train" for a real job. But the same devaluation of women's domestic contributions underlies other rulings. For example, many courts refuse to award continuing financial assistance to homemakers who have made irreversible career sacrifices. Although four-fifths of women believe that they will get spousal support if they need it, only about a sixth of divorced wives actually receive such payments. Two-thirds of these awards are for brief periods, the amounts are usually modest, and only half are fully paid. A judicial survey involving hypothetical cases illustrates the problem. One question featured a nurse who had supported her husband through eight years of college, medical school, and residency, and then, after divorce, wanted to attend medical school herself. Less than a third of surveyed judges would have been willing to grant her four years of support; most thought it "unfair" to saddle her affluent ex-husband with such expenses when she was already self-sufficient.[9]

Courts' preference for a "clean break" rather than continuing spousal assistance institutionalizes gender disadvantages. Since more than half of divorcing couples have no significant property to divide at the time of divorce, many women end up with no compensation for career sacrifices. The problem is compounded by the inability of many wives to afford legal battles over settlements and by the willingness of some husbands to use custody as a bargaining chip in financial negotiations. Although men's-rights activists deny that this occurs, surveyed attorneys suggest otherwise. They estimate that in more than a fifth of divorce cases, one parent, almost always the mother, experiences pressure to make financial concessions in order to prevent custody battles.[10]

Inadequate child support adds further difficulties. Much of the inequality of divorced women stems from one central fact. After most marriages end, men become single, and women become single mothers. About four out of five divorces involve minor children, and women have physical custody in close to 90 percent of these cases. The result is that divorcing wives end up with greater needs and fewer resources than their husbands.[11]

Despite almost two decades of reform effort, America has made highly inadequate progress in increasing either the size or the reliability of child support. Some $30 billion in support awards remain unpaid. About 40 percent of single mothers receive no court-awarded assistance, and only half of the rest ultimately obtain full payment. The average amount of child support ordered is well below the actual costs of child-rearing and a third to a half of what experts estimate that fathers could afford. Yet men are over fifteen times more likely to default on child support than on car payments. About half of all divorced fathers drop out physically as well as financially from their children's lives. Within a few years after divorce, fewer than a fourth of noncustodial fathers continue weekly visits.[12]

Of course, some mothers discourage contact, especially in circumstances presenting a high risk of conflict or abuse. But many fathers exit without such prompting. Men who avoided major child-care responsibilities during marriage often are even less willing to undertake them after divorce. More than 40 percent of surveyed women report that they would prefer more visitation and that their ex-husbands are not fulfilling even the minimal responsibilities specified in their custody agreements.[13]

Yet the most popular recent reform proposals mischaracterize both the problem and the remedy. According to a growing number of state legislators, the culprit is no-fault divorce law, and the appropriate response is to make it harder for couples to end a marriage if one partner objects. A majority of Americans support such reforms, and an increasing number of state legislatures are considering them. The most widely discussed proposals would deny divorce in cases involving children or one spouse's objection, unless the other spouse could prove fault, such as adultery, desertion, or extreme cruelty. Yet we have tried such initiatives before, and we should not yearn to relive the experience.[14]

Proposals to restrict the availability of divorce rest on two assumptions. The first is that divorce brings a wide range of problems, particularly for children, who have disproportionate rates of poverty, delinquency, substance abuse, and educational difficulties. Although virtually no one denies the seriousness of these problems, the question is what to do about them. And there is no persuasive evidence for a second key assumption: that limiting the grounds for divorce will discourage hasty, ill-considered breakups and promote children's well-being.

Some proponents of such limitations even deny that evidence is necessary: According to David Blankenhorn, president of the Institute for American Values, it is "intuitively obvious [that] ... if you make it quicker and easier to break a marriage commitment ... [then] more people will take that opportunity." Other proponents note that divorce rates have increased following no-fault reforms.[15]

Yet such arguments confuse cause and effect. As almost all experts in the field agree, changes in divorce law were a response to, not the trigger for, changes in public attitudes and behaviors. Divorce rates were rising even before no-fault legislation; the temporary increase following statutory reforms largely reflected legal formalization of separations that already had occurred. Careful cross-cultural research finds no significant causal relationship between the stringency of marital laws and the frequency of marital breakdowns. Making divorce harder does not keep couples together; it just makes the process of formal separation more costly and acrimonious. And according to the most systematic research, what harms children is high levels of conflict, low incomes, and poor-quality parenting, not divorce per se.[16]

Certainly this nation's experience with restrictive fault-based divorce statutes has little to recommend it. These statutes created wide dispari-ties between the law in form and the law in fact and between divorce for the rich and divorce for the poor. Individuals with sufficient re-sources could subvert their state's fault-based requirements by traveling to more permissive jurisdictions or by staging courtroom charades closer to home. The latter approach produced certain standard stories. In New York, for example, where adultery remained the only ground for divorce until 1966, court records revealed countless reenactments of the same carefully scripted melodrama, with the same supporting cast of paid "mistresses" rented for the occasion. As one judge noted, these women always seemed to be wearing a "sheer pink robe. It was never blue, always pink." Parties without funds for expensive courtroom dramas often resorted to self-help measures: domestic violence, desertion, or unenforceable mail-order divorce decrees.[17]

This is not an era we should strive to re-create. Nor would children's lives be better if we did. Most evidence indicates that a high-conflict marriage results in more problems for a child than a no-fault divorce. Of course, few would disagree with Hillary Clinton's much-publicized opinion in *It Takes a Village* that "people with children need to ask themselves whether they have given a marriage their best shot, and what more they can do to make it work before they call it quits." But how often do parents fail to ask those questions now? For couples who do, what makes us think that restrictive fault-based divorce statutes would improve the situation?[18]

Proponents of such legislation claim that current law is too permis-sive. According to matrimonial lawyer George Stern, people can now say, "What the heck, we'll run down to the courthouse and we'll get a divorce." Since wives normally initiate most divorce proceedings, they attract special criticism for satisfying their own concerns at the expense of their children's. Sponsors of restrictive statutes want to restrain these "walkaway wives" and end an era in which it is "easier to [escape] a marriage than . . . a contract for a household appliance." Yet researchers who have actually studied divorcing families paint a quite different pic-ture of both divorce law and those who invoke it. Unlike other contracts, divorce settlements must be approved by a judge, and their enforcement is no simple matter. Few mothers who choose to end their marriages do so casually. According to the divorced women in Demie Kurz's study *For Richer, for Poorer,* more than two-thirds of their former husbands were violent, a fifth were committing adultery, and about 15 percent had substance abuse or similar problems. With the benefit of hindsight, these women generally did not view their decisions as ill-considered. Five years after the divorce, only a fourth had negative feelings about the choice, and many of these reactions were connected only to its economic consequences.[19]

Of course, the vast majority of these women could probably have proven fault under recent reform proposals. But doing so would have been costly, acrimonious, and, for women in abusive marriages, potentially dangerous. Even if persuasive evidence suggested that too many divorces are impulsive, the most logical response would be waiting periods, not fault-based requirements. Given the already high costs of divorce, both emotional and economic, adding further legal hurdles is hardly the answer.

Reformers have identified real problems but tackled them at the wrong end. The best way to prevent divorce is to prevent the problems that help cause it. And when that fails, the way to minimize the costs of marital breakdowns is to ensure adequate economic support and social services for divorcing families. Recent proposals for mandatory waiting periods and counseling before marriage are promising strategies. So are proposals to increase resources for domestic-violence prevention and substance-abuse treatment. But we also need to focus more directly on the gender inequalities accompanying divorce and on society's responsibility to address them.[20]

As long as we continue denying that basic responsibility, we will end up with "cheap-fix" strategies like restricting divorce. Such strategies are attractive because they do not involve substantial societal resources. But for divorcing couples, they will be neither cheap nor a fix. A better alternative is to change both the law and the attitudes of those applying it. Marital property and support law should promote greater equality in standards of living for divorced spouses. When one partner has made irreversible career sacrifices, the couple's income should be shared for a period proportional to the length of their marriage or of their children's dependency. More legal assistance, more adequate child-support awards, and more effective enforcement of financial decrees are also critical. Promising proposals include increased sanctions for noncompliance, expanded prosecutorial resources, and centralized collection authority in a federal agency. If we invested significant resources as well as rhetoric in our campaigns against deadbeat dads, we could greatly reduce the hardships for single moms.[21]

Yet it is naive to assume, as do most Americans, that we can solve all our child-support problems through better enforcement. In many cases, fathers lack sufficient assets or the costs of collection are prohibitive. Particularly when marriages end after a relatively short period or the couple lacks adequate income, ex-husbands cannot be expected to compensate for all the difficulties facing their former wives. Experts increasingly agree that, in the long run, we would be better off with a national "child assurance system" like the ones in Scandinavian countries. Under such a system, the government, rather than individual mothers, collects child-support payments and provides supplemental subsidies when parental resources are insufficient.[22]

So, too, we cannot address all the gender disadvantages associated with divorce simply by changing divorce law. Many of these disadvantages stem from deeper structural inadequacies in employment, welfare, health, and child-care policies. Support for families in the United States is much less adequate than in most Western countries. The stakes in addressing these problems involve fairness not just for women but also for their children. The challenge is to make family values a commitment not just in political rhetoric but also in policy priorities.

NOTES

1. For critiques of formal equality, see Joan Williams, *Unbending Gender: Why Family and Work Conflict and What to Do about It* (New York: Oxford University Press, 2000), 114–41; Lenore J. Weitzman, *The Divorce Revolution* (New York: Free Press, 1985), xi, 357–401; Martha Albertson Fineman, *The Illusion of Equality: The Rhetoric and Reality of Divorce Reform* (Chicago: University of Chicago Press, 1991), 53–75. For criticism of feminists, see Nicholas Davidson, *The Failure of Feminism* (Buffalo, N.Y.: Prometheus, 1988), 315; F. Carolyn Graglia, "The Housewife as Pariah," *Harvard Journal of Law and Public Policy* 18 (1995): 509, 510.

2. For "taxation without representation," see Warren Farrell, *The Myth of Male Power* (New York: Simon and Schuster, 1993), 368. For other claims, see Randy Salzman, "Deadbeat Dad Divorces Fact from Fiction," *Wall Street Journal*, 3 Feb. 1993, A14; Kathleen Gerson, *No Man's Land: Men's Changing Commitments to Family and Work* (New York: Basic Books, 1993), 130–31. For the economic plight of deadbeat dads, see Davidson, *Failure of Feminism*, 315. See also Thorn Weidlich, "Divorce Turns Ex-Husbands into Crusaders," *National Law Journal*, 24 July 1995, A1, A22.

3. Colorado Supreme Court Task Force on Gender Bias in the Courts, *Final Report* (Denver, Colo., 1990), 18.

4. California judge, quoted in Graglia, "Pariah," 511; Laura Mansnerus, "The Divorce Backlash," *Working Women* (Feb. 1995): 42.

5. Herma Hill Kay, "Equality and Difference: A Perspective on No-Fault Divorce and Its Aftermath," *Cincinnati Law Review* 56 (1987): 1, 67; Deborah L. Rhode and Martha Minow, "Reforming the Questions: Questioning the Reforms: Feminist Perspectives on Divorce Law," in *Divorce Reform at the Crossroads,* edited by Steven D. Sugarman and Herma Hill Kay (New Haven: Yale University Press, 1990), 191, 195.

6. Weitzman, *Divorce Revolution,* 17–18, 32–33.

7. For income comparisons, see Williams, *Unbending Gender,* 115; Katharine T. Bartlett and Angela P. Harris, *Gender and Law: Theory, Doctrine, Commentary* (Boston: Aspen Law & Business, 1998), 421–22. For poverty, see Demie Kurz, *For Richer, for Poorer: Mothers Confront Divorce* (New York: Routledge, 1996), 3; *Women Work, Poverty Persists: A Status Report on Displaced Homemakers and Single Mothers in the United States* (Washington, D.C.: Women Work, 1995), 16.

8. California State Senate, "Final Report of the California Senate Task Force on Family Equity," reprinted in *Hastings Women's Law Journal* 1 (1989): 9, 23; Joan Williams, "Is Coverture Dead? Beyond a New Theory of Alimony," *Georgetown Law Journal* 82 (1994): 2227, 2232–34, 2251.

9. For expectations, see Lynn A. Baker and Robert E. Emery, "When Every Relationship Is above Average: Perceptions and Expectations of Divorce at the Time of Marriage," *Law and Human Behavior* 17 (1993): 439, 443. For actual payments, see Rhode and Minow, "Reforming the Questions," 202. For the judicial survey, see Weitzman, *Divorce Revolution,* 35.

10. For inadequate compensation, see Lorraine Dutsky, *Still Unequal* (New York: Crown, 1996), 306–15; Fineman, *Illusion of Equality;* Williams, "Coverture," 2258–66. For denials of custody blackmail, see Judith Bond Jennison, "The Search for Equality in a Woman's World: Fathers' Rights to Child Custody," *Rutgers Law Review* 43 (1991): 1141, 1180; Gerson, *No Man's Land,* 130. For surveys, see Scott Altman, "Lurking in the Shadow," *University of Southern California Law Review* 68 (1995): 493, 497–504; Nancy D. Polikoff, "Why Are Mothers Losing? A Brief Analysis of Criteria Used in Child Custody Determinations," *Women's Rights Law Reporter* 14 (1992): 175, 182–83. In Demie Kurz's study, one-third of women reported that they feared violence or retaliation for pressing legal claims; Kurz, *For Richer, for Poorer,* 137.

11. Richard E. Behrman and Linda Sandham Quinn, "Children and Divorce: Overview and Analysis," *The Future of Children* 4 (1994): 4, 6, 10.

12. Marcia Mobilia Boumil and Joel Friedman, *Deadbeat Dads* (Westport, Conn.: Praeger, 1996), 36–37, 119; Irwin Garfinkel, Marygold S. Melli, and John G. Robertson, "Child Support Orders: A Perspective on Reform," *The Future of Children* 4 (1994): 84, 85; Pay Wong, *Child Support and Welfare Reform* (New York: Garland, 1993), 4, 13; Paula G. Roberts, "Child Support Orders: Problems with Enforcement," *The Future of Children* 4 (1994): 101. For experts' estimates, see Sonia Nazario, "The Second Wife," *Los Angeles Times Magazine,* 3 Dec. 1995, 24; Paul R. Amato, "Life-Span Adjustment of Children to Their Parents' Divorce," *The Future of Children* 4 (1994): 143, 151;

Frank F. Furstenberg Jr., "History and Current Status of Divorce in the United States," *The Future of Children* 4 (1994): 29, 37; Behrman and Quinn, "Children and Divorce," 12. For car payments, see Susan Estrich, "Marcia Clark Deserves Better," *USA Today*, 9 Mar. 1995, 11A. For visits, see Furstenberg, "Divorce," 36.

13. Gerson, *No Man's Land*, 131; Kurz, *For Richer, for Poorer*, 163, 166–71.

14. John Leland with Steve Rhodes and Susan Miller, "Tightening the Knot," *Newsweek*, 19 Feb. 1996, 72.

15. David Blankenhorn, quoted in Barbara Vobejda, "Critics, Seeking Change, Fault 'No Fault' Divorce Laws for High Rates," *Washington Post*, 7 Mar. 1996, A3.

16. Leland, "Tightening the Knot," 72 (citing experts); Max Rheinstein, *Marriage Stability, Divorce and the Law* (Chicago: University of Chicago Press, 1972), 277–311, 406–8 (cross-cultural comparison); Caryl Rivers, *Slick Spins and Fractured Facts* (New York: Columbia University Press, 1996), 172–75.

17. Justice M. Steinbrink, testimony before the New York Legislative Committee on Matrimonial and Family Law, *New York Herald Tribune*, 1 Oct. 1965, A19; Walter Gellhorn, *Children and Families in the Courts of New York* (New York: Dodd, Mead, 1954), 285–86.

18. Kurz, *For Richer, for Poorer*, 206; Leland, "Tightening the Knot," 72; Hillary R. Clinton, *It Takes a Village* (New York: Simon and Schuster, 1996), 43.

19. George Stern, on Joi Chen, *CNN News*, 10 Mar. 1996; Maggie Gallagher, *The Abolition of Marriage* (Washington, D.C.: Regnery, 1996), 50, 207; John Paul Akers, "Walkaway Wives," *American Enterprise* 7 (May–June 1996): 35; Jesse Dalman, quoted in Ruaridh Nicholl, "America's Romance with Divorce Is Over," *The Observer*, 24 Mar. 1996, A25; Kurz, *For Richer, for Poorer*, 52–56, 187–91.

20. Leland, "Tightening the Knot," 71; Nicholl, "Romance with Divorce," 25.

21. Susan Moller Okin, *Justice, Gender and the Family* (New York: Basic Books, 1989), 165, 183; Williams, "Coverture," 2258–66; Roberts, "Child Support Orders," 101; Garfinkel, Melli, and Robertson, "Child Support Orders."

22. See Garfinkel, Melli, and Robertson, "Child Support Orders"; Sara McLanahan and Gary Sandefur, *Growing Up with a Single Parent: What Hurts, What Helps* (Cambridge, Mass.: Harvard University Press, 1994), 150; Rhode and Minow, "Reforming the Questions," 208.

CHAPTER 11

What's a Wife Worth?

Myra H. Strober

What's a wife worth? What's a wife worth in a marriage that started with zero assets but after thirty years of marriage has assets of about $100 million, which came from the husband's earnings and stock options? What's the "equitable distribution" at the time of divorce of that approximately $100 million when, during most of the marriage, the wife has been a full-time homemaker, mother, and corporate wife? In other words, how should we think about valuing women's unpaid, invisible work?

In the 1996 Connecticut divorce case of *Wendt v. Wendt,* the facts were precisely those I just described. Since I testified in that case in December 1996, I have served as an expert witness in four additional high-asset divorce cases, where, as in the Wendt case, I have been asked to value the unpaid work of wives who were full-time homemakers in long-term marriages and to give an opinion as to how the couple's assets should be divided. These cases have led me to think at some length about

A version of this chapter was originally presented at the annual meetings of the International Association for Feminist Economics, Taxco, Mexico, June 19–22, 1997. I am grateful to Lawrence Friedman for suggesting several revisions. A second version was presented as a talk at the Radcliffe Public Policy Institute in May 1998 and was later published by the institute as "Feminist Economics 101: Valuing the Invisible Work of Women."

how economists should conceptualize the economics of marriage and
divorce.

In this chapter I discuss three questions.

1. What theoretical framework should economists use to value the
    unpaid work of full-time homemakers in a marriage?

2. What theoretical framework should economists use to determine
    the proportion of assets husbands and wives should get at the
    time of divorce?

3. Why does there seem to be resistance to thinking about marriage
    from an economic point of view?

THE WENDT CASE AND DIVORCE LAW
IN THE UNITED STATES

The Wendts

Lorna and Gary Wendt met in a small-town high school in central Wisconsin, and both attended the University of Wisconsin. They were engaged during Ms. Wendt's junior year in college and married in 1965
when she graduated. She had a bachelor of music degree and he a bachelor's degree in civil engineering. Neither had any money to speak of.
After graduation, they moved to Cambridge, Massachusetts, where he
attended Harvard Business School. She worked briefly at MIT during
his first year and then as a music teacher in Sudbury during his second
year.

After he received his MBA, they moved to Texas, where he took his
first job as a real estate developer. She continued to teach music for a
little over a year but stopped when their first child was born in 1968.
Over the next several years, the couple moved from Texas to Georgia,
and then to Florida, each time for job-related reasons. In 1972, their
second child was born. In 1975, he took a job with G. E. Capital in
Stamford, Connecticut, and the family moved again. He remained with
G. E. Capital, rising to CEO in 1986, and they continued to live in
Stamford.

In 1995, after thirty years of marriage, Mr. Wendt asked for a divorce
and offered his wife $10 million, saying that surely was more than she
"needed" to be comfortable. While accountants for the two parties disagree on the value, it seems that the estate was worth about $50 million

in 1995. Thanks to the stock market, that amount doubled in size over the two years between their separation and divorce.

Ms. Wendt said that equitable distribution of assets was not about "need," but about the value of her contribution to the marriage and that $10 million dollars, 20 percent of their assets, did not constitute equitable division. She then sued to obtain 50 percent of the estate.

Divorce Law in the United States

All states in the United States now have some provision for no-fault divorce. That is, neither the divorce itself, the distribution of property, nor the arrangements for child support or spousal support depend upon which side had legal "grounds" for divorce. However, the conceptual frameworks for determining the distribution of property and spousal support vary by state (American Law Institute 1996).

Eight states have community property laws, where essentially all property except separate property brought into the marriage by either spouse or separate property inherited during the marriage by either spouse is considered to be community property, regardless of who holds title to it. In three of the eight community property states, California, Louisiana, and New Mexico, in case of divorce, state law mandates that the courts divide the community property, regardless of its value, equally between the two spouses. In the other five community property states and in all of the remaining forty-two so-called common-law states, courts are instructed to divide property "equitably," rather than equally (ALI 1996, 2).

At the present time, in all states, regardless of whether they are community property or common-law states, in divorce cases involving property value less than about $10 million to $12 million, the property is divided equally. However, in cases where the value of the property exceeds $10 million to $12 million, women often do not get half of the property, unless they live in one of the three states that mandates equal division. If the husband was the primary breadwinner and the wife a homemaker, the courts usually revert to the old principle, "He who earns it, owns it." They argue that, in these large-asset cases, it would not be equitable to give the wife half of the property (Oldham 1996).

In the five other community property states and the common-law states that seek to divide property "equitably," the value of the contributions that each party made to the marriage is one of the factors the court considers in making determinations about property division at the time of divorce. The contributions of the breadwinner are valued by the sum of earnings, bonuses, stock bonuses, and stock options. In some instances, the present value of future earnings, bonuses, and options are also included in valuing contributions. However, measuring the contributions of the full-time homemaker and their value is more difficult.

Ms. Wendt's Unpaid Work

Ms. Wendt's unpaid work as a homemaker, wife, and mother included the following tasks: first and foremost, providing companionship, sexual partnership, and emotional support in the context of an intimate relationship and raising two children; then, managing the household: cooking, cleaning, grocery shopping, doing laundry, and gardening; budgeting, record keeping, and bill paying; purchasing her husband's clothing, packing it for travel, and having it properly cleaned and maintained; maintaining relationships with family members; and creating and maintaining relationships with friends and neighbors. Also, in later years, her duties included hiring and supervising household help. Much of this work was invisible, behind the scenes, often unnoticed, and generally taken for granted. (For additional discussion of the work performed by women in the upper class, see Ostrander 1984.)

In addition, Ms. Wendt did unpaid work associated with being in what Hannah Papanek (1973) and Rosabeth Kanter (1977) have called a two-person career, a situation where the breadwinner's career is so demanding that it requires not only the breadwinner's efforts to succeed but also the efforts of the spouse. The spouse's contributions in a two-person executive career are of several types: intellectual, status maintenance, public performance, and the provision of emotional aid (Papanek 1973). These contributions vary by stage of the breadwinner's career (Kanter 1977) and age of the couple's children (if any). In the early years, the spouse generally provides what might be termed "technical support," such as typing term papers and arranging travel schedules. As the breadwinner moves up the career ladder, technical support is generally provided by the employer, and the spouse's efforts turn more toward expert skills in people handling, including assistance in recruiting and entertaining personnel and clients. Once the breadwinner reaches the upper regions of management or entrepreneurship, spousal duties change again; expert people handler remains on the list of necessary skills, but now additional high-level diplomatic functions are added to the unpaid job description. In the last ten years of marriage, the women in whose cases I was involved traveled extensively with their husbands for business reasons (often on very short notice), were involved with complex planning of social activities that involved their husbands' business associates and clients, and provided their husbands with opinions, when they were sought, on key personnel and other business decisions. Often they were one of a very few people from whom their husbands felt they could seek counsel in considering major business decisions.

Many people, including feminists, when hearing this list of duties, say: "Yes, these women certainly had a great deal on their plates. But are you *really* saying that performing these duties, even performing them in an outstanding manner over a long marriage, is worth half of the couple's assets, worth something like $50 million?"

VALUING UNPAID WORK

How should economists value the unpaid work of a homemaker/wife/mother in a two-person executive career? The two methods usually used, the opportunity-cost method and the market-replacement method, are, in my view, not appropriate for valuing the work of executive wives. In my expert witness work, I suggested a new method. Here, I review the two usual methods and then introduce the new method.

Traditional Methods

The opportunity-cost method of valuing unpaid labor proceeds from the assumption that if the homemaker chose not to engage in paid employment, she and her family must have believed that the value of her homemaking contributions were at least as high as what she would have earned in paid employment. So, using this method, the annual value of a homemaker's unpaid labor is said to equal the average annual earnings of women with her same education level and in her same educational field.

There are three problems with this method of valuing unpaid work. First, because the opportunity-cost notion says that a full-time homemaker must be worth *at least* what she could earn in the marketplace, it provides an estimate of only her lowest possible value. And the estimate gives us no clue as to the amount by which this lowest possible value understates the true value to the family.

Second, the opportunity-cost estimate forces us to assume that, had the homemaker in question remained in the labor force, she would have had the same motivation, talents, opportunities, work experiences, and earnings as those of the average woman with her same level of education and field who did in fact remain in the labor force. There really is no basis for such an assumption, nor is there any basis for determining the direction of bias resulting from it.

Third, using earnings foregone as the measure of unpaid work transfers to the household all of the gender bias experienced by women in the market. Given the extent of occupational segregation and earnings discrimination against women in the labor market, why would we think that women's market earnings provide a useful measure of the value of women's unpaid labor in the home?

A second way of valuing unpaid work is by estimating the market-replacement value, determining what it would have cost to replace the services provided by the homemaker if we hired substitutes. To make such an estimate, we would start by estimating the number of minutes per day the homemaker devoted to various unpaid tasks. We would then call an employment service and get wage rates for hiring people to do each of these tasks. Multiplying the number of minutes per day for each task by the wage rate for that task and summing the results, we would know the total cost of using hired labor to replace the wife's unpaid labor.

This method, too, is unsatisfactory. In the first place we would have to decide what kind of labor would replace the wife's labor. For example, what sort of person would we use to replace her cooking skills? Would we use a high-class chef or a short-order cook? What sorts of people would we seek to hire to replace her managerial, clerical, and chauffeuring skills?

But even more important, for many services it would be impossible to replace the wife's labor. There would simply be no adequate market equivalent for her work. Raising children, providing love, sex, and emotional support and companionship both at home and during periods of travel are valuable precisely because the wife does it herself. In this connection, it is interesting that in all of the cases in which I was involved, after the husbands separated from their wives and lost their unpaid services, they did not attempt to buy these services in the marketplace. They all chose to live with another woman in a new intimate relationship.

Human-Capital Theory and a Partnership Theory of Marriage

Finding the opportunity-cost and market-replacement methods of valuing unpaid work unsatisfactory, I valued the invisible labor of the women with whom I worked by combining human-capital theory and a partnership theory of marriage.

The concept of investment in human capital is an old one, having originated with Adam Smith; it has been revived in recent years by the work of Theodore Schultz (1961) and Gary Becker (1964). It begins with the proposition that investments in education (as measured by educational attainment and quality of educational institution) and investments in on-the-job training (as measured by work experience) result in economic rewards throughout one's life. At any point in time, these rewards are measured by adding three numbers: current income, current assets, and the present value of future income.

Human-capital theory is usually applied to the situation in which an individual makes an investment in his or her own career and the rewards of the investment accrue to that same individual. But it is also applied when outside parties invest in an individual and some of the rewards accrue to that outsider—for example, state governments, businesses, or parents.

The human-capital investments that the state makes in an individual are solely in the form of money and solely for the purpose of formal education or (less usually) for formal on-the-job training. The human-capital investments that parents make in their children also are mostly in the form of money for formal education, although some parents may also contribute significant emotional support during their children's education.

When I think about the economic aspects of marriage, what I see are two people who make human-capital investments in themselves, in one another, and in their marriage. The investments are both monetary and emotional and go on throughout the marriage. When a full-time homemaker wife cooks meals or a breadwinner husband works in the marketplace, those activities are human-capital investments in his career, her unpaid career, and the marriage.

In a breadwinner/homemaker marriage, there is an asymmetry in the economic returns from the two parties' human-capital investments (Cohen 1987). By providing monetary support to his wife, the breadwinner husband invests in her homemaking. The returns from his investment in her homemaking come early in the marriage; indeed, in many cases, the payoff occurs precisely at the same time that the homemaking activity occurs. She prepares meals, and they are eaten immediately. On the other hand, much of the payoff she receives from her investment in his career tends to come much later in the marriage when his earnings increase.

As noted earlier, at any point in time, the total economic return on the two parties' investments in themselves, in each other, and in the marriage is equal to the sum of current income, current assets, and the present value of future income. The difficult question is how this sum should be divided between the two parties.

Determining how to divide the economic returns from the two parties' human-capital investments is easy if they spelled out their intentions on this matter in their marriage contract. However, until recently, when formal prenuptial agreements began to be increasingly used, the vast majority of couples entering marriage did not formally spell out their economic intentions or expectations, so we are left to infer the property agreements that were implicit in their marriage contracts. In my view, in the absence of any agreement to the contrary and prior to the time that prenuptial agreements became popular, it is fair to say that couples assumed that their marriage was a fifty-fifty partnership.

It is instructive, in this regard, to look at business partnerships in which, if there is no explicit understanding to the contrary, the presumption is that the partnership is fifty-fifty. When business partnerships dissolve and divide their assets, unless specific contrary arrangements were specified in the partnership agreement, each partner gets an equal share of the assets. Neither the partners nor the court asks, for example, whether the contributions of the partner with expertise in marketing were greater in quantity or value than those of the partner with expertise in production. It is assumed that the partners were in partnership because each thought the other's contribution was necessary to make the partnership work.

The same is true in a marriage. When parties begin their marriage with no understanding to the contrary, the default presumption is that they have a fifty-fifty partnership. And the fact that they stayed married for a long period of time should lead us to the conclusion that each was satisfied that the other's contribution was necessary to the successful functioning of the marriage and the two-person career.

In the Wendt case, and indeed in the other four cases as well, I argued that in a long homemaker/breadwinner marriage, say one that lasts fifteen years or more and in which no contract contradicts the implicit presumption of a fifty-fifty partnership, it is plausible to value the wife's unpaid contributions to the marriage using human-capital theory to calculate the return that each party should receive from his or her investment in the two-person career marriage. Thus, the value of the wife's contribution is half the value of the sum of marital assets plus a declining percentage of future returns from the investments she made during the marriage.

I also argued that, using a human-capital framework and a partnership theory of marriage, giving the wife half of the estate and a declining portion of her husband's future earnings should not be viewed as a gift to her. Nor should it be seen as related to her economic need. Rather, it should be seen as her earned right. Since her investment in her husband's career had paid off handsomely, she should now receive her economic due.

The Judge's Ruling in the Wendt Case

The Wendts' divorce complaint was dated December 1995. Their divorce trial began a year later, in December 1996. The trial took eighteen days, with each party calling multiple expert witnesses. In December 1997, Judge Kevin Tierney handed down a 519-page opinion (*Wendt v. Wendt* 1997). He gave Ms. Wendt half of the so-called hard assets—that is, personal property, real estate, cash, stocks, bonds, mutual funds, and Mr. Wendt's fully vested qualified pension plan. In reaching his decision, he used neither the human-capital framework nor the partnership theory of marriage. Indeed, he did not use any economic theory or methodology, a point to which I return in a moment.

The judge awarded Ms. Wendt considerably less than half of the couple's other assets, which were Mr. Wendt's supplementary pension plan, restricted stock, special long-term performance award, and vested and unvested stock options; and he awarded her none of the value of Mr. Wendt's deferred executive compensation. In total, Ms. Wendt got about $20 million, considerably less than the approximately $50 million that would have constituted about half of the estate.

Ms. Wendt was also awarded unmodifiable alimony of $252,000 per year, to continue until her death or remarriage. But the judge did not give her these alimony payments as ongoing returns on the investment she made in Mr. Wendt's career. In fact, he offered no rationale for awarding continuing alimony.

From a feminist economist's point of view, several aspects of the judge's reasoning are quite interesting. His decision not to rely on any economic theory or methodology in making the property awards was quite intentional. In rejecting the human-capital framework, he used the work of two feminist legal scholars, Ann Laquer Estin and Margaret Radin. He quoted Estin in his opinion to the effect that thinking of marriage as a set of mutual investments has "the effect of objectifying both husband and wife and their relationship" (Estin 1995, 1087) and "pushes the institution of marriage from a relationship based on love and obligation toward one based on self-interest" (ibid. 1064). Moreover, he used Radin's concept of commodification (Radin 1987, 1849, 1851) to say that valuing human-capital investments and dividing them at divorce ultimately "commodifies" marriage—that is, creates a commodity out of a noncommercial item (*Wendt v. Wendt* 1997, 80).

The views of Estin and Radin are not dissident voices among feminist legal theorists. Legal theorist Deborah Rhode says she is uncomfortable with the human-capital metaphor as a way of looking at marriage and divorce (Rhode 1998). Joan Williams (1994), in an article not cited by Judge Tierney, says: "The proponents of human capital theory rely on commercial analogies that seem jarring and out of place when applied to family relations" (2227) and "human capital theorists' highly commercialized language . . . threatens undesirable commodification of intimate relations" (2276).

Nor is Tierney the first judge to find human-capital theory distasteful when applied to marriage. Williams quotes a West Virginia court in *Hoak v. Hoak* as follows: "characterizing spousal contributions as an investment in each other as human assets demeans the concept of marriage" (1994, 2276).

The judge was also hard on the concept of marriage as a partnership. After reviewing the testimony of legal scholar, Martha Fineman, who, as one of Ms. Wendt's expert witnesses, also argued that marriage is a partnership, the judge concluded that in Connecticut, marriage is not a partnership and that he was unwilling to "engraft this commercial standard into the vagaries of family life" (1997, 233). These were his words: "Although early humans once roamed postglacial Connecticut, there has been no Connecticut evidence of 'Homo Economicus.' This court will dig no further into the moraine to discover such a being, for the first to discover 'Homo Economicus' can then declare 'marriage is a partnership,' but, until that day dawns, no. Marriage is not a commercial partnership in Connecticut (1997, 234)."

Judge Tierney also cited legal scholar Bea Smith (1990) on this point, from an article entitled "The Partnership Theory of Marriage: A Borrowed Solution Fails." The borrowing referred to is borrowing from the commercial realm, the realm of the market.

RESISTANCE TO THINKING ABOUT MARRIAGE FROM AN ECONOMIC POINT OF VIEW

What should we make of all this? Judge Tierney of course was under no compulsion to use economic theory to value Ms. Wendt's unpaid labor. In effect, he said that the Connecticut legislature left it to him to decide on what basis to determine an equitable division of property, and that the legislature did not require him to use economic theory, or indeed any other theory, to do so. In fact, he indicated that he thought it was wise of the legislature to give courts considerable discretion in making equitable property divisions. He simply was not seeking a systematic way to think about the value of Ms. Wendt's unpaid labor.

Feminist economists are, I think, more interested in developing theory in this arena. But there has been very little writing by feminist economists on these matters. It is interesting to ask why many feminist legal scholars, courts, and, from anecdotal dinner party and classroom evidence since my testimony, numerous others seem to be allergic to the application of human-capital theory to marriage and divorce. For many people, it appears to be threatening to think about marriage as an economic endeavor at all, even in part, and more threatening to think about it as a series of mutual human-capital investments.

Why? The myth of marriage as romance dies hard. Listen to the songs on the radio—still! Watch TV or movies, talk to young people. Many of them continue to believe that marriage is mostly about falling in love or being in love. Some will tell you that marriage is a spiritual union. But distasteful to many are economic analyses of marriage markets, talk about the benefits of prenuptial agreements, or recognition by husbands and wives that they bargain with each other all the time.

In her survey of dual-career couples in San Francisco, Wenda O'Reilly (1983) was told repeatedly by both women and men that "we never bargain; I bargain with my boss, but not with my spouse." Despite their protestations, O'Reilly found they bargained about numerous aspects of their marriage—where to live, whose career to favor, when to move, when to have children, and how and when to spend money. But thinking about marriage as ongoing bargaining was simply not very romantic, so, while they did it, they refused to acknowledge it.

Romance has been hard to hold on to in recent years. With the rapid rise in the divorce rate beginning in the 1960s and the more recent on-going disclosures of domestic violence, one needs greater and greater doses of delusion to hold on to the myth of marriage as a haven in a heartless world.

Perhaps resistance to economic analyses of marriage is strong right now precisely because the rise in the divorce rate and increasing reports of domestic violence have made it difficult to hold on to the romance myth. Perhaps collective resistance to acknowledging the realities of the economics of marriage is directly proportional to the degree to which the view of marriage as romance is challenged by daily observation.

Yet there is more going on here. Resistance to economic analyses of marriage is, in part, resistance to the growing influence of economic rhetoric in the society as a whole. This is, in part, the basis of Radin's work. Increasingly, economic rhetoric is being applied more and more broadly. For example, it used to be that we rationalized foreign aid, at least in part, as helping poor people in poor countries. No more. Foreign aid is now sold as good policy because it builds trading partners. It used to be that we saw colleges and universities as nonprofit organizations, utterly unsuited to governance by for-profit principles. No more. We now have boards of trustees and state legislatures that regularly ask why a university can't be more like a firm. We used to have countries that presented alternatives to the market capitalist model: socialist countries in Eastern Europe, the Soviet Union, and China, and welfare-capitalist countries such as Sweden. But socialism has mostly been converted to market capitalism and the welfare part of welfare capitalism seems in great danger. Market capitalism appears to have become hegemonic. People may resist applying any kind of economic model to marriage as a way of resisting this hegemony, as a way of having at least one part of their lives not governed by the market paradigm.

At some level, I think people do in fact recognize that economics plays a major role in marriage. Protests against commodification and application of the commercial model to the household are in part attempts to change that situation or at least keep it from growing. Note some additional words from the West Virginia court whose opinion in *Hoak v. Hoak*, against using human-capital theory as a conceptual underpinning for marriage, I cited earlier: ". . . this court would be loathe to promote any more tallying of respective debits and credits than already occurs in the average household" (Williams 1994, 2276). I read this as saying: "Stem the tide, hold the line, let's not make things any worse than they already are."

Where does this leave feminist economists? Divided, not of one mind. There are of course some things on which all of us agree: that the invisible work of women has value; that being a full-time homemaker is an exceedingly risky job, as Barbara Bergmann (1986) has argued, probably one of the most risky; and that men and women entering into marriage ought to see prenuptial property agreements as simply good hygiene. But in talking to feminist economists about the Wendt case, I find a good deal of disagreement.

Some don't like the fact that I'm spending my time defending "rich women." They don't think it is fair that anyone, husbands *or* wives, should be permitted to earn such high returns on their human-capital investments. They question how much of these very high returns actually are returns to any human-capital investment by anyone and how much are essentially windfall gains, the result of luck and the vagaries of the stock market. I share some of these concerns. But it is my view that in a society that allows people to retain very high gains from investments, the same rules must apply to wives as to husbands.

Some of my feminist colleagues think that it is bad public policy to reward women who have spent their lives as full-time homemakers because that will encourage younger women to do likewise. They think that feminist economists ought to be in the business of designing public policies to discourage women from full-time homemaking, that the essence of feminism is to get women to be economically independent. I disagree. My work on the graduates of Stanford University, who were in their early thirties at the time I surveyed them, convinces me that women who are married to men in super-high-powered careers may well continue to be full-time homemakers. Not only can these women afford to do so, but also, their family's lifestyle, with frequent geographic moves, frequent demands for spur of the moment business travel, and absent husbands who provide precious little in the way of fathering, leaves them few alternatives. (See Strober and Chan 1999.) Feminist economists are critical of the notion of choice, but they don't always recognize that women married to men in high-powered careers often cannot have careers of their own unless they leave those marriages. Their choices are in fact quite constrained. I am interested in changing the system so that women can be in super-high-powered careers. And I am interested in changing super-high-powered careers so that people in them can have a life and share child rearing and household management and tasks. But until the system changes, I am also interested in protecting the wives of men in super-high-powered careers should they one day get divorced.

Refusing to acknowledge that rich women also face gender bias is a type of discrimination. Feminists resist when other social scientists tell us that we should work on the problems of minorities, that those problems are much more serious than those of women. We should also resist those who tell us that certain groups of women are automatically more deserving of our analyses than others.

CONCLUSION

Ms. Wendt appealed Judge Tierney's decision. She wanted the appellate court to make equality in marriage, as she put it, a principle of Connecticut law. However, the court of appeals affirmed the original decision in every respect (*Wendt v. Wendt*, 2000).

None of the other four cases in which I was involved came to court, although several came close, with settlements arrived at only after numerous days of depositions. In each of the cases, which were settled in the 1996–97 period, details of the property division were not made public. However, each of the four attorneys involved told me that the final distribution was very close to fifty-fifty.

In the summer of 1998, six months after the Wendt decision, the New York court was faced with a case quite similar to the Wendts', *Goldman v. Goldman*. The Goldmans had been married for thirty-three years at the time Mr. Goldman filed for divorce, and Ms. Goldman had been a full-time homemaker in all but the first three years of their marriage. In that case, Judge Walter B. Tolub Jr. awarded Vira Hladun-Goldman 50 percent of the $100 million estate she owned with her husband, Robert I. Goldman, including $44 million in restricted stock in the Congress Financial Corporation. *Business Week* quoted Tolub as arguing, "In a long-term marriage the distribution of marital property should be equal or as close to equal as possible" (Symonds, Burrows, and Forest 57).

The valuing of women's invisible work appears to vary greatly both across states and within states. Basing decisions on well-developed theories of human-capital investments and marriage as fifty-fifty partnerships would go a long way toward increasing consistency of judicial reasoning and providing couples with a clearer understanding of the economic consequences of a decision to divorce. Permitting judges discretion in their decisions to take account of special circumstances is wise. But beginning with a presumption of a fifty-fifty split of accumulated assets, unless there is a prenuptial agreement to the contrary, may be the best way to ensure that unpaid labor in the context of a long marriage is duly rewarded.

REFERENCES

American Law Institute (ALI). 1996. *Principles of the Law of Family Dissolution: Analysis and Recommendations, Tentative Draft No. 2.* Philadelphia: The American Law Institute.

Becker, Gary. 1964. *Human Capital.* New York: Columbia University Press.

Bergmann, Barbara. 1986. *The Economic Emergence of Women.* New York: Basic Books.

Cohen, Lloyd. 1987. "Marriage, Divorce, and Quasi Rents; Or, 'I Gave Him the Best Years of My Life.'" *Journal of Legal Studies* 16, no. 2 (June): 267–303.

Estin, Ann Laquer. 1995. "Love and Obligation: Family Law and the Romance of Economics." *William and Mary Law Review* 36: 989–1087.

Hoak v. Hoak. 1988. 370 S.E. 2d 473 (West Virginia).

Kanter, Rosabeth. 1977. *Men and Women of the Corporation.* New York: Basic Books.

Oldham, Sarah. 1996. Personal communication.

O'Reilly, Wenda. 1983. "Where Equal Opportunity Fails: Corporate Men and Women in Dual-Career Families." Ph.D. diss., Stanford University.

Ostrander, Susan A. 1984. *Women of the Upper Class.* Philadelphia: Temple University Press.

Papanek, Hanna. 1973. "Men, Women and Work: Reflections on the Two-Person Career." *American Journal of Sociology* 78, no. 4: 852–871.

Radin, Margaret. 1987. "Market Inalienability." *Harvard Law Review* 100, no. 8 (June): 1849–1937.

Rhode, Deborah. 1998. Personal communication.

Schultz, Theodore. 1961. "Investment in Human Capital." *American Economic Review* (March): 51.

Smith, Bea A. 1990. "The Partnership Theory of Marriage: A Borrowed Solution Fails." *Texas Law Review* 68, no. 4 (March): 689–743.

Strober, Myra H., and Agnes M. K. Chan. 1999. *The Road Winds Uphill All the Way: Gender, Work, and Family in the United States and Japan.* Cambridge, Mass.: MIT Press.

Symonds, William C., Peter Burrows, and Stephanie Anderson Forest. 1998. "Divorce Executive Style." *Business Week,* August 3.

Wendt v. Wendt. 1997. Stamford/Norwalk Judicial District at Stamford, Conn., March.

Wendt v. Wendt. 2000. Stamford/Norwalk Judicial District at Stamford, Conn..

Williams, Joan. 1994. "Is Coverture Dead? Beyond a New Theory of Alimony." *The Georgetown Law Journal* 82, no. 7 (September): 2227–2290.

CHAPTER 12

Toward an Understanding of Asian American Interracial Marriage and Dating

Jeanne L. Tsai, Diane E. Przymus, and Jennifer L. Best

We want our children to marry Chinese, but it's because
we're Chinese; we forget that *they're* American.

A Chinese father

One of the hottest issues confronting the Asian American community today is the increasing number of interracial dating and marital relationships, especially among younger generations of Asian Americans. Whatever the forum—anthologies of Asian American literature, conferences on Asian American studies, documentaries on local Asian American communities—interethnic dating and marriage are topics of considerable interest and heated debate. Within the Asian American community, some fear that by coupling outside their culture, Asian Americans will lose their Asian heritage. Others in the community argue that coupling across racial and cultural lines will end racial segregation.

Asian American interracial relationships are relevant to persons outside of the Asian American community as well. To individuals committed to combating racism and discrimination, the disapproval and outrage that such relationships evoke illustrate that racial prejudice and discrimination still thrive at the beginning of the twenty-first century. To persons interested in race and culture, children of interracial unions challenge existing conceptions of race and culture that do not account for mixing between groups. Finally, to those interested in racial, cultural, and psychological influences on human behavior, interracial relationships demonstrate how human behavior is multiply determined. For instance, although interracial contact and exposure may influence whether individuals couple across racial lines, factors such as gender expectations, cultural identity, and personality may also play a role.

Despite the relevance of Asian American interracial relationships to these inquiries, our current knowledge base is quite limited. In this chapter we review the meager literature on Asian American interracial relationships and then propose ways in which feminist psychological methodology might advance our understanding of them. We present preliminary data that illustrate how such research might be conducted. Finally, we discuss issues that arise when one applies a feminist methodology to understand interpersonal processes in different racial and cultural groups. We begin by presenting a brief description of the Asian American community and its history regarding intermarriage and dating.

WHO ARE ASIAN AMERICANS?

The group Asian Americans is comprised of individuals of East Asian (e.g., Chinese, Japanese, Korean), South Asian (e.g., Indian), Southeast Asian (e.g., Vietnamese, Hmong, Cambodian, Laotian), and Filipino descent. In 1990, there were approximately 7.3 million Asian Americans residing in the United States, incorporating 2.9 percent of the total U.S. population (a 107.8 percent increase from the Asian American population in 1980) (Uba 1994). Asian Americans are expected to make up 11 percent of the population by the year 2050 (U.S. Bureau of Census, 1992). Most Asian Americans reside in California, New York, or Hawaii, where Asian immigrants first settled in the early nineteenth century (Lee and Yamanaka 1990). Census data from 1990 reveal that among Asian Americans, most are Chinese (22.6 percent), followed by Filipino (19.3 percent), Japanese (11.7 percent), Asian Indian (11.2 percent), and Korean (11 percent) groups (Uba 1994). The rest are Southeast Asians and Pacific Islanders. Two-thirds of Asian Americans are foreign born, that is, immigrants or refugees who came to the United States for a variety of social, economic, political, and educational reasons (Min et al. 1995).

Although tremendous diversity exists among specific Asian American groups, Min and others (Espiritu 1992; Kibria 1997) argue that they are united by a "pan Asian American" ethnicity. The term "Asian American" grew out of the Civil Rights Movement as an attempt to recognize cultural similarities and engender political and social unity among the various Asian American groups. Many Asian American groups share similar cultural values and beliefs, including collectivist orientation, filial piety, respect for authority and the elderly, emotional moderation and control, emphasis on educational achievement, the role of shame as a behavioral influence, and familialism. Asian Americans also share a similar political and social position in American culture. That is, they are grouped together in census and other statistical databases and are often treated as one group in American public policy (Min et al. 1995). In addition, because Asian Americans have similar racial features, members of one specific Asian American group are often mistaken for those of another. For example, acts of racism and discrimination intended against one specific Asian group are often acted out on members of another (Min et al. 1995). These common experiences have resulted in the emergence of a relatively unified Asian American culture (Kibria 1997; Min et al. 1995). As a result of these similarities, much research has grouped Asian Americans together. Thus, in this chapter, we discuss Asian American interracial coupling, differentiating among specific Asian American groups whenever possible.

ASIAN AMERICAN INTERRACIAL COUPLING

As recently as 1901, marriages between Asians and European Americans were illegal. Antimiscegenation laws were ruled unconstitutional by the Supreme Court in 1967, after the passage of the Civil Rights Act and the removal of restrictive immigration quotas (Min et al. 1995). Thus, the small number of Asian Americans in the United States, combined with the illegitimacy of Asian American interracial marriage, may explain why relatively few studies of Asian American interracial coupling existed prior to the 1960s. Since the 1960s, the studies that have examined Asian American intermarriage and dating have revealed four major trends.

First, census data suggest that Asian American intermarriage increased steadily from the 1960s and 1970s to the 1980s. This trend was consistent with rates of intermarriage in other racial and ethnic groups (Lee and Yamanaka 1990; U.S. Census Bureau 1960, 1970b). However, from 1980 to 1990, Asian American intermarriages dropped from 25.4 percent to 15 percent of all Asian American marriages. Interestingly, this trend was not consistent with that of other racial and cultural groups for which intermarriages continued to increase (Lee and Fernandez

1998). Second, specific Asian American groups vary in their likelihood to intermarry. Since the 1960s, Japanese Americans have consistently intermarried more than Filipino Americans, who have intermarried more than Chinese Americans (Lee and Fernandez 1998). Third, when Asian Americans do intermarry, they are more likely to marry European Americans or individuals of the Caucasian race than any other racial/cultural group (e.g., African Americans, Latino Americans). Finally, among Asian Americans, females are more likely to intermarry and interdate than are males (Fujino 1997; Lee and Fernandez 1998).

POPULAR THEORIES REGARDING ASIAN AMERICAN INTERRACIAL COUPLING

Researchers have proposed different theories to explain these patterns. These theories are (1) group size, (2) assimilation, (3) status exchange, and (4) sex-ratio imbalance. Group-size theory proposes that intermarriage is inversely related to group size (Blau, Blum, and Schwartz 1982). That is, the smaller the Asian American group, the greater contact its members have with other racial and cultural groups and the more likely they will intermarry. Conversely, the larger the Asian American group, the less contact its members have with members of other groups and the less likely they will intermarry. This theory may explain why from 1980 to 1990 there was an increase in the Asian American population and a decrease in Asian American intermarriage.

Assimilation theory makes the opposite prediction. Proponents argue that intermarriage is an index of group assimilation (Spickard 1989). Thus, the longer Asian groups are in the United States, the more assimilated to American culture they become and the more they couple across racial lines. This argument has been used most frequently to explain differences in rates of intermarriage among specific Asian ethnic groups. For example, Japanese immigrants, unlike Chinese immigrants, were encouraged by the Japanese government to assimilate to American culture (Takaki 1989). This was particularly true after World War II, when Japanese Americans were unjustifiably interned and their loyalty to the American government unfairly questioned (Nagata 1989). As a result, Japanese Americans may have intentionally increased their contact with, adopted the cultural traditions of, and encouraged intermarriage with European Americans more than other Asian American groups.

Status-exchange theory (Merton 1941) is perhaps the most controversial of theories used to explain interracial relationships. This theory was originally proposed to explain the greater frequency of White fe-male–Black male marriages compared to Black female–White male mar-riages in the 1940s. According to status-exchange theory, females of higher racial status marry males of lower racial status if in other ways the males have higher status than their female partners (e.g., socioeco-nomic class). In the case of White female and Black male marriages, Merton (1941) proposed that White females married Black men if the men were of higher socioeconomic status than they were. Since 1941, status-exchange theory has been adapted and applied to marriages be-tween members of other ethnic and racial groups. For example, this theory has been used to describe marriages between American military men and Korean women they met during the Korean War: In this case, Asian American women exchanged their status as exotic symbols for the higher financial status of their European American husbands (Kim 1998). This theory, however, has received little direct empirical support. That is, no study has demonstrated that such status discrepancies exert any direct influence on one's decision to couple across racial lines.

Finally, sex-ratio imbalance theory has been used to explain gender differences in Asian American intermarriage. This theory suggests that since the 1940s there have been more Asian American females than males, and, therefore, Asian American females have had to look for non–Asian American partners. Findings from studies of Asian Indian inter-marriage do not support this theory. That is, Asian Indian males out-marry more than do Asian Indian females (Hwang, Saez, and Aguirre 1997).

Despite the prevalence of these theories in the literature, they are limited in their empirical support and in what they tell us about Asian American interracial relationships. For instance, the assimilation and status-exchange theories make predictions about the psychological state of individuals involved in interracial relationships, but few studies have actually tested these hypotheses explicitly. Similarly, the group-size and sex-ratio imbalance theories propose that the sheer number of available partners influences Asian American intermarriage, but they tell us little about the cultural and psychological influences that may be at play.

RETHINKING ASIAN AMERICAN INTERRACIAL COUPLING

Given the limitations in our current knowledge and understanding of Asian American interracial relationships, researchers have much to gain from assuming a feminist psychological research perspective. Feminist psychological research methodology assumes a person-centered approach. Landrine and Klonoff (1992), in their article on cultural diversity and methodology in feminist psychology, define person-centered research as research that investigates the intentions and subjective meanings of the research participants, regards the research participant as the primary interpreter or his/her own experience, and combines qualitative and quantitative methods. Furthermore, feminist methodology acknowledges the importance of placing individuals in their surrounding sociocultural context and of viewing individuals holistically (Hare-Mustin 1978).

Most of the existing research on Asian American interracial relationships does not study the subjective experiences of individuals within these relationships but instead makes assumptions about the roles that race and culture play in their relationships. These studies also tend to overlook individual differences within cultural groups that may moderate the influence of cultural values, norms, and stereotypes. Finally, most theories and studies do not view these relationships holistically; that is, they do not consider the dynamic aspects of race, culture, and intimate relationships and how these may change over time. In the next section, we propose a different way of examining Asian American interracial relationships that stems from feminist research methodology. We present preliminary data on Asian American interdating and intermarriage to illustrate our points.

Our preliminary data come from one dating sample and one married sample. The dating sample comprised fifty-four heterosexual dating couples (twenty-two Chinese American female–Chinese American male; twenty European American female–European American male; twelve Chinese American female–European American male), of which at least one partner in each was a student at a large Bay Area university. Couples were involved in committed, monogamous dating relationships lasting, on the average, one and a half years. Couples were recruited from flyers for a larger study of culture and emotion in intimate relationships; only a subset of these findings are reported in this chapter.[1]

The married sample comprised ten interracially married couples, and, therefore, analyses of this sample were not comparative. All ten wives in this sample were Asian American; nine of the ten husbands were European American. The tenth husband was African American.[2] These couples had been married for an average of 13.56 years (SD = 2.31) at the time they participated in our exploratory study; three of the twenty spouses had been previously married. Couples were middle to upper-middle class and well educated; all had attended college, and most had attended some form of graduate school. This sample was recruited from a small Midwestern community organization focusing on social and political issues. Couples completed questionnaires about their relationships, and a subsample was interviewed for approximately one hour about their relationships. For both samples, we attempted to recruit both Asian female–non-Asian male *and* Asian male–non-Asian female dyads, but we received only one response from a couple of the latter configuration. Therefore, we did not include Asian male–non-Asian female dyads in our analyses. Although our samples are small and lack adequate representation, they illustrate a new way of studying and understanding Asian American interracial relationships.

THE SUBJECTIVE EXPERIENCE OF BEING "INTERRACIAL" AND/OR "INTERCULTURAL"

As argued by Jones and Thorne (1987), in order to understand the psychological and phenomenological aspects of interracial and intercultural relationships, we must "rediscover the subject" or examine the subjective experience of individuals within these relationships. Interracial couples may vary in the degree and salience of racial and cultural differences and in the influence they have on their relationships. In the existing literature, however, few researchers have asked couples how they view the roles of race and culture in their relationships. In fact, few studies have assessed whether individuals even see their relationships as "interracial." For example, a European American male in our married sample stated, "It never occurred to me, oddly enough, that we were an interracial couple . . . just that she was Chinese and I was Caucasian, and that was fine. But to be an interracial couple . . . it's very interesting *to be defined* that way."

It is possible that by labeling relationships as "interracial," researchers are presupposing differences that might not exist, and in effect, imposing their interpretations onto their research participants. As a result, these terms may obscure other sources of similarity or difference between partners that may have a greater influence on couples than race or culture. For example, Ahren et al. (1981) found that males and females in interracial marriages were more similar in their scores on personality tests than those who married within their racial groups. The impact of these personality similarities may be significantly greater than the influence of race on the daily workings of the relationship.

These sources of similarity or difference may be more salient to the couple than their racial or cultural affiliations. For example, when asked what the first thing was that they noticed about their partners, married couples listed a variety of characteristics, ranging from "his funky glasses" to "her personality"; *none* reported characteristics that were explicitly racial or cultural. It is possible that some of the characteristics reported by the couples are conflated with cultural stereotypes (e.g., "she was shy" may be related to cultural stereotypes of the submissive Asian female), but it is unclear from couples' responses whether this was in fact the case. Interestingly, when asked to describe their ideal mates, only three of the twenty respondents in the married sample mentioned characteristics related to culture. Of these responses, some were general (e.g., "comfortable in more than one cultural context"), whereas others were more specific (e.g., "not of European descent"). It is possible that the subjective experience of being "interracial" differs for couples for whom race and culture were salient constructs during the commencement of their relationships than for couples for whom they were not.

Other assumptions made by social scientists include the confounding of race and culture; "interracial" couples are often assumed to be "intercultural." Although cultural differences are often associated with racial differences, in certain domains of experience, they may not be. For example, interracial unions may occur between individuals of different racial groups that share particular cultural values and beliefs. Fong and Yung (1995/1996) propose that many Asian American women married Jewish American men because both Jewish American and Asian cultures possess high levels of familialism. In our dating sample, interracial Chinese American–European American couples did not differ from Chinese American couples or European American couples in their reported levels of disagreement in areas vulnerable to cultural conflict, that is, the amount of affection in their relationships, their philosophies of life, or their modes of communication. Similarly, couples in our interracial married sample reported little cultural conflict in their relationships (mean = 2.81 [SD = 1.61], on a scale from 1 = not at all, 4 = neutral, and 7 = extremely).

INTERACTION BETWEEN CULTURE AND THE INDIVIDUAL

All individuals are influenced to some degree by aspects of their culture. How individuals respond to these aspects of culture, however, may vary. A feminist psychological perspective acknowledges that both cultural factors and individual characteristics influence behavior. In this section, we suggest potential cultural influences and individual characteristics that may influence interracial relationships.

Sources of Cultural Influence

Values Cultural contexts influence individuals and their intimate relationships in a number of ways (Berscheid 1999). Culture influences conceptions of romantic love. For example, Ting-Toomey (1994) argues that in collectivistic cultures such as China and Japan, less emphasis is placed on passionate and romantic love than in individualistic cultures. Culture may also influence conceptions of the ideal mate. For example, Buss (1989) found that when choosing mates, men and women in China, India, Indonesia, Iran, Taiwan, and Israel (Palestinian Arabs) placed a higher value on chastity than did men and women in Sweden, Norway, Finland, the Netherlands, West Germany, or France, who placed little importance on prior sexual experience when selecting mates. Hatfield and Sprecher (1995) found that American college students valued expressiveness and openness more than Russians or Japanese college students when selecting mates.

Gender Roles and Expectations Culture may also influence the gender roles and expectations of individuals in intimate relationships. In many Asian cultures, Confucian tradition views women as subservient to men (especially to their husbands) and as the primary caretakers of their families (especially of their sons, fathers-in-law, and husbands) (Okazaki 1998; Park and Cho 1995). It must be noted that the extent to which cultural beliefs regarding the role of women translate into actual practices varies according to the specific group. For example, women in Hmong culture have less latitude in their behavior than Vietnamese women, who are allowed more dominant roles in the family (C. Ho 1990, as cited in Min et al. 1995). Traditional Confucian norms expect men to be the carrier of the family line and tradition, the "supreme authoritarian" of the household, and the primary breadwinner of the family (Uba 1994). These cultural conceptions of gender roles may influence what individuals seek in their mates as well as how they behave in intimate relationships. For example, cultural expectations that Asian American men will continue the family line may influence their selection of partners and explain why fewer Asian American men than women marry members of other racial groups. Lee and Fernandez (1998) propose that unlike other Asian American groups, rates of Asian Indian intermarriage are higher among males than females because Asian Indian culture expects women more than men to continue family traditions.

Cultural stereotypes   Culture may also influence intimate relationships via cultural stereotypes. As stated above, although there is increasing tolerance for interracial coupling, many still view such relationships as abnormal (Kibria 1997). Stereotypes that intercultural couples are dissatisfied in their relationships, suffer from higher rates of divorce, and have children with low self-esteem and confused identities abound, even though recent empirical research debunks these stereotypes (Cauce et al. 1992; Mass 1992). For instance, in our dating sample, interracial Chinese American–European American couples did not differ from Chinese American couples or European American couples in how satisfied they were with their relationships (mean = 5.69 [SD = 1.11], on a scale from 1 = very unhappy, 4 = neutral, 7 = perfectly happy).

As reported by the married couples in our study, Asian American interracial couples are often stereotyped as military men with their war brides or as one respondent put it, "White guys with their Oriental pearl, exotic wife." These stereotypes may influence how individuals perceive interracial couples and may result in prejudice and discrimination. For example, an Asian American female respondent from our married sample said, "It's not usually anything overt. But it's the way that the maitre d' in a four-star restaurant will look at us and then look around and then decide where to seat us, which is not always the best place."

In addition to stereotypes about interracial couples, individuals may be influenced by stereotypes about Asian American men and women (Jackson et al. 1997; Walsh 1990). Asian American women are often depicted as sexual and domestic (Louie 1993; Chan 1988; Kitano and Chai 1982; Okazaki 1998; Ranard and Gilzow 1989; Ratliff, Moon, and Bonacci 1978). These stereotypes are commonly found in films and periodicals. Mayall and Russell (1993) examined the content of pornographic materials and found that the Asian women were depicted either as "sweet young lotus blossoms" or objects of bondage; Louie (1993) found that images of Asian American women as sexual and domestic pervade popular novels. The influence of stereotypes of Asian American women on interracial marriage has been most widely discussed in the context of marriages between Asian women and American military men. Kim (1997) suggests that during the Korean War, American military men may have been influenced by stereotypes of the exotic nature of Korean women. Similarly, many Korean women may have perceived American servicemen as "superior" and "powerful," which may have increased their attractiveness as potential husbands.

Unlike Asian women, Asian men have long been stereotyped as asexual and/or effeminate. These stereotypes can be traced to early twentieth-century literature (Teng 1997). Other stereotypes of Asian American men include the "wise kung fu master" and the cold-hearted and shrewd businessman/gangster (Okazaki 1998). These images were conceived during World War II and have been perpetuated through films and television. Although these images convey a more masculine Asian man, paradoxically, he still remains relatively asexual, untrustworthy, and undesirable. Findings from empirical studies suggest that European American college students endorse these stereotypes: Asian males are perceived as overly studious, socially inept, weak, cunning, hostile, and unemotional. Asian American males are also rated lowest in physical and social attractiveness and are seen as more feminine than males of other minority groups (Jackson et al. 1997). Tucker and Mitchell-Kernan (1995) found that African American and Latina women excluded Asian American men as viable marriage partners. Significantly less research has examined stereotypes of European American men and women, who are often depicted as symbols of the dominant, privileged culture. More importantly, research has not determined whether stereotypes about specific cultural groups impede or promote interracial relationships.

Sources of Individual Variation

Culture may influence individuals and their intimate relationships through conceptions of love, ideal partners, gender-role expectations, and stereotypes. How individuals respond to these cultural influences, however, may depend on various factors, including their cultural identity, awareness of gender issues, exposure and experience with members of different cultural groups, and their personalities.

Cultural Identity Individuals vary in the extent to which they identify with their cultural heritages, which may influence the roles culture and race play in their intimate relationships. For example, individuals who do not have strong cultural identities may not consider cultural heritage an important criterion for mate selection, whereas individuals with

strong cultural identities may. Cultural identity may influence the meaning of interracial coupling. For example, Tsai, Ying, and Lee (2000)
found that overseas-born Chinese Americans had "unidimensional" cultural identities, whereas American-born Chinese Americans had "bidimensional" cultural identities. Individuals with unidimensional cultural
identities perceive their cultural identities as being inversely related to
each other (e.g., the more Chinese one is, the less American one is).
Individuals with bidimensional cultural identities perceive them as being
independent of each other (e.g., how Chinese one is does not relate to
how American one is). Thus, overseas-born Asian Americans may
equate intermarriage with the loss of their Asian heritage; as a result,
they may rarely engage in intermarriage. American-born Asian Americans, however, may not equate intermarriage with the loss of their Asian
heritage, and therefore, engage in intermarriage more frequently. This
may explain why intermarriage is higher among American-born than
overseas-born Asian Americans (Lee and Fernandez 1998).

The meaning of intercultural and interracial coupling may also depend on one's stage of cultural identity development. For example, for
some groups, ethnic identity may comprise three sequential developmental stages: (1) foreclosure, (2) immersion-emersion, and (3) internalization (Phinney 1990). Asian Americans who have been raised in
primarily European American communities (with little exposure to
Asian culture) may be at the foreclosed stage of ethnic identity development. That is, they may identify with European American culture
more than Asian American culture. This may influence how likely they
are to date other Asian Americans. Consistent with this hypothesis, Fujino (1997) found that the more Asian American males and females
endorsed mainstream European American standards of beauty and
power, the more they refused to date Asian Americans. Individuals who
are exploring their Asian American heritage (e.g., by taking courses on
Asian American history, joining Asian American community groups)
may be at the immersion-emersion stage of ethnic identity development
and may reject individuals of different cultural backgrounds as potential
mates. For example, in Walsh (1990), an interview respondent was
quoted as saying, "I don't see how Asian women can take Asian-
American Studies courses and learn about how American culture has
'feminized' Asian men [i.e., stereotyped Asian men as effeminate], and
then continue to date white men" (Walsh 1990).

On the other hand, individuals who base their cultural identities less
on external criteria (e.g., the cultural background of their friends and

partners) and more on their own internal standards (e.g., what *meaning* they attach to their cultural background) may be at the internalization stage of ethnic identity development. Therefore, they may not view interracial coupling as a threat to their cultural identity. So far, no studies have examined what role cultural identity has, if any, on non-Asians' decisions to date and marry individuals of Asian descent.

Awareness of Gender Inequalities   Another source of variation is how aware individuals are of traditional gender roles, expectations, and inequalities, and how acceptable they find them. For example, awareness of traditional gender inequalities may vary by cultural orientation. Individuals who are more traditionally Asian may accept traditional gender inequalities, whereas more Americanized individuals may not. Asian American women who desire more egalitarian relationships may choose to date individuals from cultural groups that endorse less traditional gender roles (Fujino 1997). As one of the married sample participants remarked, "From the very beginning I was aware that as a girl, I had less rights and privileges than my brother, so when people ask when did I become a feminist, I say when I realized my brother had privileges I didn't. And so from the very beginning I determined for myself that I wanted to be in an equal relationship. I've always said 'I will be your partner . . . not your subservient wife.' "

Not surprisingly, Fong and Yung (1996) found that Chinese and Japanese American women who were feminists had the most difficult time accepting traditional Asian values that placed women in positions subordinate to men. These women also reported being the most drawn to non-Asian men who were likely to have nonsexist attitudes. Interestingly, Fujino (1997) found that Americanized college-age Asian American men also sought dating partners who did not possess traits characteristic of traditional Asian women. The more they believed that Asian American women were obedient, deferential, and polite, the more they dated European American women.

Exposure to and Experiences with Members of Other Cultures   Although stereotypes about interracial couples and about members of particular cultural groups abound, individuals may vary in their responses to these stereotypes, depending on their exposure to and experience with members of the stereotyped group. Asian Americans and non-Asian Americans who have limited exposure to Asian Americans may be more susceptible to such stereotypes than those who have had extensive exposure to Asian Americans. Furthermore, depending on the previous experience one has had with members of specific groups, particular stereotypes may be more salient than others, which may influence mating preferences. For example, an Asian American woman who is influenced by negative stereotypes about Asian American female–European American male relationships may be less likely to couple with a European American male than an Asian American woman who is less influenced by these stereotypes.

Personality   Last, but not least, personality may be a source of variation in the roles that culture and race play in intimate relationships. Personality variables may influence the meanings and consequences of interracial and intercultural relationships. For example, Cottrell (1990) has proposed that individuals who date or marry across cultural lines are either marginal, rebellious, detached, emancipated, adventurous, or embracers of culture. Although no studies have examined whether these descriptors are accurate, they do suggest that the meaning of interracial and intercultural relationships might differ by personality type. Whereas "cultural embracers" may seek partners of different cultures in order to learn more about the world, "marginal" persons may be involved in intercultural relationships because no other partners are available.

THE DYNAMIC NATURE OF CULTURE AND RELATIONSHIPS

Feminist psychological perspectives also emphasize the importance of viewing individuals holistically (Hare-Mustin 1978). The bulk of the literature on interracial and intercultural dating examines relationships at a single moment in time. Few, if any, studies have examined how cultural differences that exist in the beginning of a relationship change over the course of the relationship. Research demonstrates that partners become more similar over time (Smith and Moen 1998; Gruber-Baldini, Schaie, and Willis 1995, as cited by Berscheid and Reis 1998). Thus, it is possible that initial cultural differences may become less pronounced, especially as the couple creates its own culture. Interestingly, Asian American wives and their European American husbands in our married sample reported no differences in how "American" or how "Asian" they felt. Although it is possible that these couples were similar in their cultural orientation when they began dating, it is also possible that over the course of their marriages, they have become more culturally similar than different. For example, one of the respondents from our married sample wrote on her questionnaire, "People have assumed that I have assumed Caucasian ways, when in reality my spouse has assumed more Asian ways."

Thus, the couple's "culture" may be a synthesis of the cultural customs and traditions that each partner brings to the relationship as well as their joint experiences as a couple. A respondent from the married sample provided this example: "We were not compatible in child-rearing practices and we really had to make that mesh. . . . We had some major differences in how you handle babies, how you handle discipline, how you handle cleanliness, and how you handle eating and just everything! I wouldn't say we were incompatible but we had a lot of things to work out so that we were both satisfied with how we were raising our kids."

The roles of race and culture in intimate relationships may change at different stages of the relationship. In the context of short-term relationships, both females and males report physical attractiveness as being the most important traits in their mates (Buss 1998; Regan and Berscheid 1997). In the context of long-term relationships, both males and females seek partners that are kind, understanding, and intelligent and that have other qualities that relate to being a good mate. Thus, the physical characteristics of individuals of different racial and cultural groups may be important for women and men in the context of dating and short-term relationships, but they may be less important in the long run. Our married couples reported such changes in their conceptions of their ideal mates.

Similarly, social pressures exerted on the couple based on their racial and cultural differences may change as the relationship develops. For example, negative family reactions to interracial relationships have been cited as a considerable source of stress for Asian American intermarried couples (Sung 1990). However, our married couples reported that their families' acceptance of their relationships significantly increased from the time they began dating to when they were married to the time they participated in our study ($F[1,16] = 4.30, p = .05$).

Of course, conflicts due to cultural and racial differences may also arise at different stages of the relationship. For example, although couples may resolve their cultural differences at one stage of their relationship, these cultural differences may resurface at later stages, for instance, during milestones for which they may hold different cultural traditions and expectations (child rearing, care of aging parents). Mackey and O'Brien (1998) found that ethnicity influences how couples resolve conflict associated with these different milestones. They compared the amount of conflict experienced by African American, Mexican American, and European American intraracial couples during the "early years," "child-rearing years," and "empty-nest years." Compared to the other two groups, African Americans reported more conflict in the early years. During the child-rearing years, however, African Americans reported no increases in conflict, whereas the other two groups did. Cultural differences in conflict associated with different milestones may cause even greater distress in interracial and intercultural relationships. Consistent with this hypothesis, our married couples reported cultural conflicts around child rearing and care of elder relatives.

Finally, cultural influences and cultural categories themselves may change over time. For example, American stereotypes of Asian women are becoming more masculine (Espiritu 1997). Taylor, Lee, and Stern (1995) and Taylor and Stern (1995) found that Asian American women are represented more in technical and business magazines than in women's and hobby magazines. Asian American female images occurred in work rather than in outdoor, social, or home settings. In these contexts, Asian American women are presented as individuals who are more focused on their careers than on their families, contradicting older stereotypes that portray Asian American women as domestic and submissive. How will these emerging stereotypes influence interracial intimate relationships? The emergence of a pan-Asian ethnicity also demonstrates the dynamic nature of culture. As described by Kibria (1997), the birth of a pan-Asian ethnicity may alter second-generation Asian Americans' conceptions of interracial and intercultural dating.

FUTURE RESEARCH DIRECTIONS

Feminist psychological methodology emphasizes the importance of understanding individual experience, allowing individuals to interpret their own experience, viewing people holistically, and integrating qualitative and quantitative methods. These recommendations are extremely relevant for research on interracial coupling. Future studies must explore how members of "interracial" and "intercultural" relationships define themselves. Studies that combine qualitative and quantitative research methods can explore the various meanings of involvement in interracial and intercultural relationships as well as the generalizability of such meanings. By including measures of both cultural variables (e.g., awareness of cultural stereotypes) and individual differences (e.g., cultural identity, gender-role expectations, personality), we can better understand how individuals respond to their cultures and how these interactions influence intimate relationships. With respect to gender, most studies of Asian American intermarriage focus primarily on Asian American female–European American male unions. More research that examines interracial unions formed by Asian American males is needed. In addition, most of the existing research focuses on heterosexual relationships. Asian American interracial unions also exist in gay and lesbian communities (Hoang 1991). Future studies should more explicitly examine the interaction of gender and culture in these relationships. Studies should also explore the extent to which the surrounding cultural milieu and acceptance of interracial coupling influences such relationships. Finally, longitudinal studies that follow couples over time can examine how culture and relationships mutually influence each other and how these influences change during various stages of intimate relationships.

A FINAL CAVEAT

Thus far, we have argued in this chapter that using a feminist perspective will greatly advance our understanding of Asian American intermarriage and interdating. While this is true, we have one caveat. It is possible that in some cases, the feminist perspective may require some modification in order to be applicable to groups of non-Western cultural descent. Feminist ideals place great emphasis on equal rights of all groups; this emphasis is based on American values of individualism and justice. For women and men of non-Western descent, however, gender equality and inequality may be less important, may have different meanings, and may even assume different forms. Thus, we must carefully assess the extent to which we are imposing our cultural norms, standards, values, and ideals on individuals with cultural traditions different from our own.

CONCLUSION

In this chapter, we have argued that existing research on Asian American interracial and intercultural dating and marriage is limited. We have suggested ways of studying Asian American interracial relationships by using feminist psychology research methodology and have illustrated these suggestions with findings from our preliminary work. Systematic empirical research will help us dispel inaccurate stereotypes about the individuals within these relationships and about the relationships themselves. Furthermore, such studies will advance our knowledge about an issue that is of particular concern to the Asian American community. Most importantly, future research will inform us about the ways in which race and culture influence relationships—knowledge that is critical as our society grows ever more multicultural and as our interracial and intercultural interactions become ever more intimate.

NOTES

The authors would like to thank Ellen Berscheid, David Lykken, Matt McGue, and Yu-Wen Ying for their comments on an earlier version of this chapter.

1. For more information about the Chinese American and European American intraethnic couples, see Tsai and Levenson (1997).

2. Our married sample comprised six native-born Japanese American women married to European American men; two Korean or Korean Chinese women married to European American men; one Korean American woman married to an African American male; and one Chinese American woman married to a European American male. When quoting individuals from this sample, we will refer to their ethnicity as "Asian American" in order to maintain confidentiality.

REFERENCES

Ahren, F. M., R. E. Cole, R. C. Johnson, and B. Wong. 1981. Personality attributes of males and females marrying within vs. across racial/ethnic groups. *Behavior Genetics* 11:181–94.

Berscheid, E. 1999. The greening of relationship science. *American Psychologist* 54(4):260–66.

Berscheid, E., and H. Reis. 1998. Attraction and close relationships. In *The handbook of social psychology*, edited by D. T. Gilbert and S. T. Fiske. 193–281. Vol. 2. 4th ed. Boston: McGraw-Hill.

Blau, P. M., T. C. Blum, and J. E. Schwartz. 1982. Heterogeneity and intermarriage. *American Sociological Review* 47:45–62.

Brayboy, T. L. 1966. Interracial sexuality as an expression of neurotic conflict. *Journal of Sex Research* 2:179–84.

Buss, D. M. 1989. Sex differences in human mate preferences: Evolutionary hypotheses tested in thirty-seven cultures. *Behavioral and Brain Sciences* 12: 1–49.

———. 1998. The psychology of human mate selection. In *Handbook of evolutionary psychology: Ideas, issues, and applications*, edited by C. B. Crawford et al. 405–29. Mahwah, N.J.: Lawrence Erlbaum.

Cauce, A. M., et al. 1992. Between a rock and a hard place: Social adjustment of biracial youth. In *Racially mixed people in America*, edited by M. P. P. Root. 207–22. Newbury Park, Calif.: Sage Publications.

Chan, C. 1988. Asian American women: Psychological responses to sexual exploitation and cultural stereotypes. *Women and Therapy* 6:33–38.

Chang, T. 1974. The self-concept of children of ethnically different marriages. *California Journal of Educational Research* 25:245–53.

Cottrell, A. B. 1990. Cross-national marriages: A review of the literature. *Journal of Comparative Family Studies* 21:151–69.

Crester, G. A., and J. J. Leon. 1982. Intermarriage in the U.S.: An overview of theory and research. *Marriage and the Family Review* 5:3–15.

Cross, W. E., and P. Phager-Smith. 1996. Nigrescence and ego identity developmental: Accounting for differential black identity patterns. In *Counseling across cultures,* edited by P. B. Pederson. 108–23. 4th ed. Thousand Oaks, Calif.: Sage Publications.

Espiritu, Y. L. 1992. *Asian American panethnicity: Bridging institutions and identities.* Philadelphia, Pa.: Temple University Press.

———. 1997. Race, gender, and class in the lives of Asian Americans. *Race, Gender, and Class* 4:12–19.

Fong, C., and J. Yung. 1995/1996. In search of the right spouse: Interracial marriage among Chinese and Japanese Americans. *Amerasia Journal* 21:77–98.

Fujino, D. C. 1997. The rates, patterns, and reasons for forming heterosexual interracial dating relationships among Asian Americans. *Journal of Social and Personal Relationships* 14:809–28.

Glick, P. C. 1970. Intermarriage among ethnic groups in the United States. *Social Biology* 17:292–98.

Hall, C. C. I. 1992. Please choose one: Ethnic identity choices for biracial individuals. In *Racially mixed people in America,* edited by M. P. P. Root, 250–64. Newbury Park, Calif.: Sage Publications.

Hare-Mustin, R. T. 1978. A feminist approach to family therapy. *Family Process* 17:181–93.

Hatfield, E., and S. Sprecher. 1995. Men's and women's preferences in marital partners in the United States, Russia and Japan. *Journal of Cross-Cultural Psychology* 26:728–50.

Haynes, V. D., and V. J. Schodolski. September 8, 1998. Interracial marriages increase: But Black-White unions still face most resistance. *Chicago Tribune,* A1.

Heer, D. M. 1970. The prevalence of black-white marriage in the United States, 1960 and 1970. *Journal of Marriage and the Family* 36:246–58.

Hoang, H. 1991. Beyond the China doll: The search for the *real* Asian woman.

Hwang, S. S., R. Saenz, and B. E. Aguirre. 1997. Structural and assimilationist explanations of Asian American intermarriage. *Journal of Marriage and the Family* 59:758–72.*Transpacific* 6:41–44, 64–65.

Jackson, L. A., D. A. Lewandowsk, J. M. Ingram, and C. N. Hodge. 1997. Group stereotypes: Content, gender specificity, and affect associated with typical group members. *Journal of Social Behavior and Personality* 12:381–96.

Johnson, R. C. 1984. Group income and group size as influences on marriage patterns in Hawaii. *Social Biology* 31:101–7.

Johnson, R. C., and C. T. Nagoshi. 1986. The adjustment of offspring of within-group and of interracial/intercultural marriages: A comparison of personality factor scores. *Journal of Marriage and the Family* 48:279–84.

Johnson, R. C., and G. M. Ogasawara. 1988. Within- and across-group dating in Hawaii. *Social Biology* 35:103–9.

Jones, E. E., and A. Thorne. 1987. Rediscovery of the subject: Intercultural approaches to clinical assessment. *Journal of Consulting and Clinical Psychology* 55(4):488–95.

Kibria, N. 1997. The construction of "Asian American": Reflections on intermarriage and ethnic identity among second-generation Chinese and Korean Americans. *Ethnic and Racial Studies* 20:523–44.

Kim, B. L. C. 1972. Casework with Japanese and Korean wives of Americans. *Social Casework* 53:273–79.

———. 1998. Marriages of Asian women and American military men: The impact of gender and culture. In *Re-envisioning family therapy: Race, culture, and gender,* edited by M. McGoldrick. 309–19. New York: The Guilford Press.

Kitano, H. H. L., and L. K. Chai. 1982. Korean interracial marriage. *Marriage and Family Review* 5:75–89.

Landrine, H., and E. A. Klonoff. 1992. Cultural diversity and methodology in feminist psychology. *Psychology of Women Quarterly* 16:145–63.

Lee, S. M., and M. Fernandez. 1998. Trends in Asian American racial/ethnic intermarriage: A comparison of 1980 and 1990 census data. *Sociological Perspectives* 41:323–42.

Lee, S. M., and K. Yamanaka. 1990. Patterns of Asian American intermarriage and marital assimilation. *Journal of Comparative Family Studies* 21:287–305.

Liu, E. June 11, 1998. Mingling bloodlines isn't enough to bridge the race gap. *USA Today,* A17.

Louie, A. 1993. Growing up Asian American: A look at some recent young adult novels. *Journal of Youth Services in Libraries* 6:115–27.

Mackey, R. A., and B. A. O'Brien. 1998. Marital conflict and management: Gender and ethnic differences. *Social Work* 43:128–41.

Mass, A. I. 1992. Interracial Japanese Americans: The best of both worlds or the end of the Japanese American community? In *Racially mixed people in America,* edited by M. P. P. Root. 265–79. Newbury Park, Calif.: Sage Publications.

Mayall, A., and D. Russell. 1993. Racism in pornography. *Feminism and Psychology* 3:275–81.

Merton, R. K. 1941. Intermarriage and social structure: Fact and theory. *Psychiatry* 4:361–71.

Min, P. G., et al., eds. 1995. *Asian Americans: Contemporary trends and issues.* Thousand Oaks, Calif.: Sage Publications.

Monahan, T. P. 1976. The occupational class of couples entering into interracial marriages. *Journal of Comparative Family Studies* 7:175–92.

Nagata, D. 1989. Japanese American children and adolescents. In *Children of color: Psychological interventions with minority youth,* edited by J. T. Gibbs et al. San Francisco: Jossey-Bass.

O'Conner, A. April 27, 1998. Mixed unions changing the face of marriage. *Los Angeles Times,* A1.

Okazaki, S. 1998. Teaching gender issues in Asian American psychology: A pedagogical framework. *Psychology of Women Quarterly* 22:33–52.

Park, I. H., and L. Cho. 1995. Confucianism and the Korean family. *Journal of Comparative Family Studies* 26:117–33.

Peterson, K. S. November 3, 1997. Interracial dating is no big deal for teens. *USA Today,* A10.

Phinney, J. S. 1990. Ethnic identity in adolescents and adults: Review of research. *Psychological Bulletin* 108:499–514.

Qian, Z. 1997. Breaking the racial barriers: Variations in interracial marriage between 1980 and 1990. *Demography* 34:263–76.

Ranard, D. A., and D. F. Gilzow. 1989. The Amerasians. *America: Perspectives on Refugee Resettlement* 4:1–21.

Ratliff, B. W., H. F. Moon, and G. A. Bonacci. 1978. Intercultural marriage: The Korean-American experience. *Social Casework* 59:221–26.

Regan, P., and E. Berscheid. 1997. Gender differences in characteristics desired in a potential sexual and marriage partner. *Journal of Psychology and Human Sexuality* 9(1):25–37.

Sandor, G. 1994. The other Americans. *American Demographics* 16:36–42.

Smith, D. B., and P. Moen. 1998. Spousal influence on retirement: His, her, and their perceptions. *Journal of Marriage and the Family* 60(3):734–44.

Spickard, P. R. 1989. *Mixed blood: Intermarriage and ethnic identity in twentieth-century America.* Madison: University of Wisconsin Press.

Sung, B. L. 1990. Chinese American intermarriage. *Journal of Comparative Family Studies* 21:337–52.

Takaki, R. 1989. *Strangers from a different shore: A history of Asian Americans.* Boston: Harcourt Brace Jovanovich.

Taylor, C. R., J. Y. Lee, and B. B. Stern. 1995. Portrayals of African, Hispanic, and Asian Americans in magazine advertising. *American Behavioral Scientist* 38:608–21.

Taylor, C. R., and B. B. Stern. 1995. Asian Americans: Television advertising and the model minority stereotype. *Journal of Advertising* 26:47–60.

Teicher, J. D. 1968. Some observations on identity problems in children of negro-white marriages. *Journal of Nervous and Mental Disease* 146:249–56.

Teng, J. E. 1997. Miscegenation and the critique of patriarchy in turn-of-the-century fiction. *Race, Gender, and Class* 4:69–87.

Ting-Toomey, S. 1994. Managing conflict in intimate intercultural relationships. In *Conflict in personal relationships,* edited by D. D. Cahn. 47–78. Hillsdale, N.J.: Lawrence Erlbaum.

Tinker, J. N. 1982. Intermarriage and assimilation in a plural society: Japanese-Americans in the United States. *Marriage and Family Review* 5:61–74.

Tsai, J. L., and R. W. Levenson. 1997. Cultural influences on emotional responding: Chinese American and European American dating couples during interpersonal conflict. *Journal of Cross-Cultural Psychology* 28:600–625.

Tsai, J. L., Y. Ying, and P. A. Lee. 2000. The meaning of being Chinese and being American: Variation among Chinese American young adults. *Journal of Cross-Cultural Psychology* 31(3):302–32.

Tseng, W. S. 1977. Adjustment in intercultural marriage. In *Adjustment in intercultural marriage,* edited by W. S. Tseng, J. K. McDermott, and T. Maretzki. 93–103. Honolulu: University Press in Hawaii.

Tucker, M. B., and C. Mitchell-Kernan. 1995. Social structural and psychological correlates of interethnic dating. *Journal of Social and Personal Relationships* 12:341–61.

Uba, L. 1994. *Asian Americans: Personality, patterns, identity and mental health.* New York: The Guilford Press.

U.S. Bureau of the Census. Current Population Reports. 1992. *Population projections of the United States by age, sex, race, and Hispanic origin: 1992 to 2050,* P(25)-1092. Washington, D.C.: U.S. Government Printing Office.

U.S. Bureau of the Census Reports. Population Subject Reports. 1960. *Marital Status,* PC(2)-4A. Washington, D.C.: U.S. Government Printing Office, 1963.

———. Census of Population: 1970a. *Detailed Characteristics,* PC(1)-D1. Washington, D.C.: U.S. Government Printing Office, 1973.

———. Population Subject Reports: 1970b. *Marital Status,* PC(2)-4C. Washington, D.C.: U.S. Government Printing Office, 1972.

———. Census of Population: 1990. *General Population Characteristics,* CP1-1. Washington, D.C.: U.S. Government Printing Office, 1993.

Walsh, J. December 2, 1990. Asian women, Caucasian men: The new demographics of love. *Image, San Francisco Examiner/Chronicle,* 11–16.

Weiss, M. S. 1970. Selective acculturation and the dating process: The patterning of Chinese-Caucasian interracial dating. *Journal of Marriage and the Family* 32:273–78.

Wilson, Y. July 27, 1998. The colorblind heart. *San Francisco Chronicle,* A1, A7.

CHAPTER 13

Arranged Marriages

What's Love Got to Do with It?

Monisha Pasupathi

In American culture, choice is related to happiness, independence, autonomy, and equality. We do what we choose longer, with more pleasure, and greater ambition (e.g., Cordova and Lepper 1996), and what we choose is to a great extent who we are. Or so it seems, looking both at the world in which we live and at the worlds of social and developmental psychology in which I work. What could be more self-evident, then, than the idea that arranged marriages, which deny the individual the power to make a very important life choice, are an anachronistic and oppressive practice?[1] Further, newspaper and magazine articles (e.g., Lamb 1999) attribute rising rates of female suicide in countries like China and Pakistan partly to arranged marriage practices in these cultures. But a quick count of my own relatives and friends suggests that those whose cultural backgrounds provide them with both alternatives—a marriage of choice and one that is parentally arranged—don't always take the route of choice. The fact that people who are well-acquainted with and open to Western marriage practices do not necessarily adopt those practices suggests that there may be more to arranged marriages than oppression, depression, and suicide.

ON A PERSONAL NOTE: WHAT HAVE I GOT TO DO WITH ARRANGED MARRIAGES?

I am the product of a love marriage between two cultures, that of southern India and that of the southern United States. My father, the son of

Brahman Hindus living in southern India, near Madras, was the only one of his siblings to select his own spouse. I was raised in the United States, with a European American mother and the assumption that I would choose my own spouse when I was an adult. However, many of my cousins in India and the United States (on my father's side of the family) have continued the family tradition of predominantly arranged marriages. So far, all my cousins remain married. Sadly, and perhaps ironically, some of my American friends have already divorced spouses they selected for themselves. My main goal in this chapter is to question the image of arranged marriages as necessarily oppressive and harmful for women. I do not want to imply that all arranged marriages are wonderful or to cast doubt on the real horror stories that have been told elsewhere (Haider 1995). My goal here is simply to show a more positive and less headline-worthy side of arranged marriage practices. Let me begin with a family story.

MY COUSIN'S STORY

My cousin told her parents she wanted to complete her MBA and work for one year prior to considering potential marriage partners. She wanted to enjoy some time as an independent woman without domestic pressures, although she always knew that she eventually wanted to get married. Her parents (my father's brother and his wife) were quite comfortable with this request. When the time came to search for a husband, my cousin contributed some criteria for the search process, stipulating educational level, asking for someone who would be flexible about whether she worked or not, someone easygoing with a sense of humor, who was vegetarian, and did not smoke. As is quickly evident, these kinds of criteria would not look out of place in an American personals advertisement, which supports the idea that most people seek someone nice as a spouse (Zeifman and Hazan 1997; Hazan and Diamond 2000). My cousin also met each candidate and spoke with him about her own preferences and expectations and about his. When the two prospective spouses found their views were incompatible, the matter of a potential match was immediately dropped. Eventually, one candidate was found, living quite far away (in the United States) but with a suitable horoscope. Due to the distance, my cousin spoke several times by phone with the prospective groom, and cousins living in the United States made an effort to speak to the groom by phone and to meet with him personally as well. In India, my cousin and her parents were able to meet the parents of the prospective bridegroom. When the match appeared potentially good, the prospective groom made a trip to India and after some meetings, he and my cousin decided to marry. My cousin reports being quite content with her decision, and her summary of her first months of marriage as requiring "adjust[ing] to each other's idiosyncrasies" also does not sound particularly different from any other new marriage in the United States.

Had my cousin met someone and fallen in love, her marriage choice would probably not have been opposed by her parents, according to both herself and her mother. When this did not happen, she chose to go with a modernized version of the traditional practice. Her situation is not unusual in India today and probably not particularly unusual in other cultures either.

My cousin's marriage is very new, less than two years old as this chapter goes to press. But her mother, whose marriage was also arranged, wrote me that "whether it is an arranged marriage or love marriage, when two individuals with . . . different backgrounds start living together, many situations will arise where each has to make compromises and adjustments. . . . The definition of a perfect marriage is: living together in good and bad times, providing children a good education, and raising children to be good citizens." Such a marriage, my aunt suggests, requires the husband and wife to understand and respect one another without being excessively selfish. My cousin similarly notes that "any marriage calls for lots of adjustments by both the husband and the wife." These abstract principles of compromise, respect, and understanding imply the kinds of communication advocated by American and Western European marital researchers, based on research and therapy with Western couples.

Clearly, arranged marriages in my family have been successful, at least if marital longevity and the apparent happiness of participants are any indication. Further, within my family, practices of finding spouses for children are largely similar for female and male children and in their modern form do not involve practices such as bride-viewing or child marriages (my paternal grandmother was probably betrothed prior to puberty, consistent with the practices of her generation, although exact knowledge of her age at the time of the betrothal is hard to obtain). The success and moderate nature of arranged marriages within my family must necessarily be seen as central to my own views of arranged marriage practices.

In this chapter, I review what psychological approaches have told us about arranged marriages. The distinction between arranged marriages and love marriages is not straightforward, but for simple convenience, I have adopted these terms throughout. By love marriages, I mean marriages based on romantic attraction, arranged by the bride and groom. By arranged marriages, I mean marriages in which people other than the bride and groom, typically parents or other family members, play important or decisive roles in determining who marries whom.

TOWARD A FEMINIST VIEW OF ARRANGED MARRIAGES

The overwhelming majority of people marry or participate in long-term, marriage-equivalent relationships (Zeifman and Hazan 1997; Hazan and Diamond 2000). Within these relationships, people bear and rear children, provide and are given emotional support, companionship, and instrumental support. Arranged marriages represent one class of procedures for forming such alliances, and by anthropological accounts, they are in widespread use. As many as 80 percent of cultures outside the Western sphere employ arranged marriage practices, although relatively few of these cultures rely exclusively on arranged marriages (Small 1993).

Because the procedures involved in arranging marriages lead to differences in the autonomy with which individual women can choose their spouses, those procedures bear some scrutiny from a feminist standpoint. Do arranged marriages give women an unfair share in their own self-determination? Arranged marriages could pose a particular problem if (1) they are arranged with less input from women than men; (2) they produce inequities of power between women and men; and (3) they are an integral part of a host of other practices reflecting and maintaining women's lower societal status, permitting treatment of women as commodities or property. If arranged marriages mean denying women choice and power and treating them as commodities, then arranged marriages are obviously a feminist nightmare. And if movement toward more choice in marriages would combat clear injustices of other types (less schooling for women, for example), then it is also clear that arranged marriage practices might be a target for feminist reform.

But the evidence, as I note below, suggests a more complex reality for several reasons. First, because of historical changes in arranging marriages and because of the variability of the practices in the modern world, it is difficult to generalize about arranged marriages in terms of their consequences for women's status. Certainly, not all arranged mar-

riages involve less self-determination on the part of the bride as compared to the groom. Even in extreme cases, arranged marriages may
simply result in different modes of self-determination and spouse selection than those Western women employ (e.g., Abu–Lughod 1993b). Arranged marriage practices are not monolithic rituals with no loopholes
that provide the possibility of subversion and resistance. Second, when
examined from a psychological perspective, differences between arranged marriages and other marriages are sometimes difficult to demonstrate, whether at the level of what sorts of people are chosen as mates
or at the level of what ingredients make up a good marriage. Different
procedures for forming alliances may not, in the end, produce different
alliances. This similarity makes it difficult to argue that arranged marriages present special difficulties for women. Third, the degree to which
arranged marriages produce inequity among men and women, or to
which they are an integral part of the oppression of women and control
of women's sexuality, is debatable; this is an issue to which I return at
the end of the chapter.

HISTORICAL CHANGES AND
CROSS-CULTURAL VARIABILITY

Although we think of arranged marriages as a feature of less-developed
nations and more traditional cultures, such marriages were not unheard
of in the Western world, particularly among the wealthy (Lasch 1997).
For example, Lasch discusses the controversy over the British Marriage
Act in the mid 1700s, which pitted a rather ideologically modern middle
class (i.e., one that supported choice in marriage) against an established
aristocracy. The aristocracy hoped to preserve control over marital alliances and, therefore, the distribution of wealth. The aristocracy lost. In
more recent times in the United States, members of the "Moonies" un-
derwent arranged marriages. The Reverend Sung Myung Moon
matched pairs and conducted a group wedding ceremony. Severe restrictions on interactions between partners were enforced, including a prescribed separation period and cohabitation contingent on meeting religious obligations (Galanter 1986). Groups as varied as Hasidic Jews and
immigrant Hindus in the United States also continue to arrange marriages, despite substantial exposure to Western norms and practices (Segall 1998). Looking at countries where the arranging of marriages is
practiced more broadly, there are still considerable variations in how the
procedure takes place and the role that the prospective spouses play. For

example, in China at least through the 1980s, children typically did not have a say in spouse selection, and the matching might be done by parents or by professional matchmakers. The couple traditionally did not meet until their wedding, both a bride-price and a dowry were paid, and following the marriage, the pair normally resided with the family of the groom (Engel 1984). Although the children are now exercising more choice, relatives and/or matchmakers still play a role in selecting prospective spouses and arranging meetings; further, accepting a date has the implication of likely commitment (Engel 1984). Korean marriages among the working class are likely to have been formed by a matchmaker, who might have been a friend, relative, or professional. A first meeting was followed by a period of dating and then marriage, with romantic love playing a relatively small role in comparison to other considerations, like a commitment to starting a family (Choi and Keith 1991).

Sharper changes due to international and colonial influence can be seen for the Igbo people living to the west of the Niger River. The traditional system of marriage-arranging by families, with the prospective spouses playing little role in the negotiations at any phase, is giving way to a romantic love-based self-selection of spouses (Okonjo 1992). Even where families still do the arranging, girls may have more power to select or reject than is apparent from studying "usual procedures." For example, Small (1993) relates the story of a Kung San teenager who did not like the first spouse her family chose for her. When she demonstrated her protest by refusing to share a sleeping space with the man, preferring instead to sleep in the bush, her family relented and found a second candidate, who was accepted.

Saudi Arabia, too, shows signs of shifting marriage practices. A sample of older Saudi women (ages fifty-five and over) were in predominantly prearranged marriages, often taking place at very young ages (twelve to thirteen), involving matches between cousins, and with absolutely no input from the prospective bride (Alsuwaigh 1989). In contrast, the marriages of their daughters (ages thirty-five and under) took place at later ages and were more likely to be only partially arranged or even to involve personal choice. A recent study in Turkey found approximately half of current marriages to involve some degree of family selection (Hortaçsu and Oral 1994). The degree of personal choice in such marriages, however, varied broadly, ranging from very little (family selection of the spouse) to almost total self-determination with the family simply supplying prospective dates.

Historical variability in practices is complemented by variations between what is stated to be the case and the actual ways in which marriages are contracted or resisted. Ethnographic work on Bedouin women highlights this very complex picture (Abu-Lughod 1993a, 1993b). In principle, men arrange marriages between daughters and sons, often between first cousins. However, there is ample evidence for women's resistance and exercising of choice, both in the older generations examined by Alsuwaigh and in the youngest generation studied by Abu-Lughod. Mothers may intervene in marriages they see as inappropriate or potentially harmful, and daughters can pose as temporarily insane to avoid alliances (Abu-Lughod 1993a, 1993b).

In India, details about the practice of marriage-arranging vary considerably across history, region, and subgroup. At present in northern India, among Hindu families with relatively high educational levels, parents often act as matchmakers by selecting appropriate possible spouses and conducting introductions for their children of marriageable age. Although this practice seems like a parentally facilitated version of dating in the United States, it is not. As in the case of China, multiple meetings carry strong implications of commitment. If multiple meetings occur and no commitment follows, the respective families may be very disappointed and relations between the offending child and his or her family can be quite strained. Among the tribal peoples of Kerala, things are slightly different (Kattakayam 1996). The maternal uncle may be appointed to find a suitable bride. He negotiates for consent from the bride's parents, following which the marriage can be arranged. Lack of consent from the bride, groom, or either set of parents means that the entire arrangement is dropped. Although not practiced historically, dowries have become relatively more common since the 1970s and signal an acknowledgment of the "worth" of women.

In India, early (e.g., preindependence era) matches tended to emphasize parental choice, with some input from the boy but little from the girl. Marriages were contracted relatively early, sometimes when the bride was prepubescent. The bride then moved to the house of the husband, sometimes playing a servantlike role. Marriage contracts also involved a practice called "bride-viewing." During this event, the bride was displayed to prospective suitors and their families so that they could view her attributes before making an offer. The occasion highlighted her abilities in cooking and fine arts and her ability to serve guests appropriately. She might have been asked to sing a classical song or play a musical instrument. Finally, the bride historically had no ability to veto a marriage. Although there was substantial pressure on sons to accept the parental choice, sons were somewhat more able to reject potential brides. All of these practices reinforced a system in which women were chosen like any other item that might be purchased or contracted for. This past practice, which may still go on in some parts of the world (e.g., rural Pakistan, Lamb 1999), leads to obvious inequities between the male and female children involved and treats women like property in a painfully obvious way. However, in many cases, the modern practice is substantially different.

The arranging of marriages today that is typical in traditional Hindu families like my own, a southern Brahman family, may first involve the selection of a suitable boy, followed by matching horoscopes (based on the birth date of the child) for both boy and girl. Selection of initial candidates may rely on matrimonial advertisements as well as word-of-mouth and personal recommendation. A meeting is then arranged between the two sets of parents, and often between the girl and boy. These meetings are quite brief but allow for a mutual assessment of one another by both parties. In many cases, and perhaps increasingly so, there may be phone conversations, email, or other communications between the prospective spouses, all with the aim of allowing the two to make a relatively informed decision about marrying one another. This was my cousin's experience. She was able to provide a list of qualifications that guided the search for a husband, she did not have to perform for prospective suitors in any way, and she retained at all times the power to veto any candidate.

As can be seen in this very sketchy overview, differences across countries and over time suggest considerable variability in practices for arranging marriages. Two conclusions can be made. First, movement within cultures is generally away from practices that treat women as property to be exchanged in the course of familial alliances and toward practices that endow both daughters and sons with more say in the matter. This has been empirically examined for Saudi Arabian women (Alsuwaigh 1989) and for African Igbo women (Okonjo 1992), and anecdotal evidence within my own family and among Indian friends suggests similar changes from the time of my grandmother's marriage to the marriages of my cousins in recent years. Second, variation within and across countries makes it very difficult to have a single perspective on arranged marriage; developing a feminist framework for viewing such marriages will require an adequate assessment of practices in their culturally contextualized form.

Thus far, I have concentrated on outlining basic practices in the arranging of marriages over time and across space. This broadly painted picture provides a sense of the breadth of practices in arranged marriages and the historical changes occurring in the past century. It does not, however, provide comparisons between love marriages and arranged marriages.

CHOICE IN LOVE VERSUS ARRANGED MARRIAGES: HOW DIFFERENT?

Are love and arranged marriages fundamentally different in terms of degree of choice and criteria employed? Friends and family often introduce us to the people we eventually marry out of personal choice, and those having an arranged marriage often exercise some choice in the selection of the future spouse. Such facts complicate this division between arranged and love marriages considerably. Perhaps the most accurate distinction is one between personal and collective choice as methods for selecting spouses.

As seen above, the relative degree of personal choice exercised by individuals in arranged marriages can, in fact, be substantial. But even when the bride and groom have had extensive contact prior to the marriage, they have not usually had the kind of acquaintanceship and dating that leads to romantic love. Given that this is a central criterion for marriage in the United States and other Western industrialized nations (Levine, Sato, Hashimoto, and Verma 1995), the logical conclusion is that arranged and love marriages are based on different criteria for selecting spouses (i.e., romantic love versus pragmatic or family concerns). As I demonstrate below, however, even this assumption proves too simplistic.

In fact, the psychological literature suggests that there may be fewer differences between arranged marriages and love marriages than is apparent on the surface. In the remainder of the chapter, I focus on two questions: (1) whether arranged marriage practices and love marriages employ different or similar *selection criteria;* and (2) whether arranged marriages and chosen marriages lead to *different outcomes* (e.g., marital satisfaction). The literature reviewed here is by no means exhaustive, and I have concentrated primarily on the relatively sparse psychological literature on arranged marriages rather than on the substantial anthropological literature.

CHOOSING A "SUITABLE BOY"

Social psychological views of finding a spouse, based predominantly on Western samples, have shown that the most central factor is proximity, which often comes about by chance (Hazan and Diamond 2000; Bandura 1982). We marry the people we encounter. Still, whether those looking for their own spouse are seeking the same qualities desired by those who select spouses for their children is a different issue. Arguments for cross-cultural variability in the qualities that make for a good mate, as well as arguments for cross-cultural universality, have been advanced. Below, I address these differing arguments in turn and then examine whether comparisons of arranged-marriage cultures and love-marriage cultures support universality or variability.

Different Cultures, Different Goals, Different Practices

It may seem obvious that different cultures will consider different criteria in mate selection, particularly when the cultures differ in marriage practices. Love-marriage selection criteria seem to reflect individuals' personal concerns, such as personal and interpersonal qualities of the prospective mate and compatibility issues, while arranged-marriage selection criteria, not surprisingly, reflect concerns of the total family unit (Blood 1972). These family concerns include socioeconomic status, health, strength, fertility, temperament, and emotional stability of the prospective spouse. This may be because arranged marriage practices are associated with residence patterns and are more likely in countries where a new couple lives in an extended family dwelling (Fox 1975; Lee and Stone 1980). All of the qualities important to the family not only contribute to collective well-being they may be particularly important when the new spouse moves in with the extended family.

One Species, Similar Criteria

Alternative perspectives suggest that mating practices may be more similar than different across cultures because of similarity in shared historical pasts or the pressures of evolution upon mating behavior (see, e.g., Hazan and Diamond 2000). In fact, some researchers argue that the formation of romantic pair bonds depends on attachment processes exapted[2] from the mother-infant relationship over the course of evolution (Hazan and Diamond 2000; Zeifman and Hazan 1997). Thus, people should report preferences for qualities that enhance or increase the likelihood of secure attachment. The available and relevant data come from two sources: people's preferences about hypothetical mates, and criteria that appear to govern actual mate selection.

Preferences

In a study of thirty-seven cultures, male and female college students reported the qualities of (1) dependability, (2) intelligence, (3) kindness-understanding, and (4) emotional stability as most important in a prospective mate (Buss et al. 1989). Mutual attraction and love were also considered quite important in all cultures sampled. Thus, data on preferences for hypothetical spouses showed few differences across cultures sampled, consistent with shared history or evolutionary arguments. However, in African, Asian, and Middle Eastern countries, where arranged marriage is still practiced, love was ranked somewhat lower than in Western industrialized nations. Similar findings about the importance of romantic love for establishing a marriage in the industrializing Eastern/Asian world were also demonstrated in another study of college students across eleven cultures (Levine et al. 1995). This study bears a closer look because it asked specifically about the role of love as a decision criterion. Respondents from Asian countries (particularly Pakistan, India, and Thailand) reported a willingness to marry a person they did not love, but who possessed all their desired qualities in a mate. They were also unwilling to consider divorce when love is not maintained, in contrast to Western and South American countries. Thus, Eastern/Asian respondents view love as somewhat less important at the beginning of a marriage and regard the absence of love as a less adequate criterion for divorce. One explanation for such findings could be that Eastern/Asian respondents believe that love develops during the course of a marriage, a view that would be consistent with existing evidence (Gupta and Singh 1982). But, as Hazan and Diamond (2000) point out, self-reported preferences are an inadequate source of information regarding actual selection criteria. For actual selection criteria, looking at the procedures for arranging marriages or the characteristics of mates that have been selected is more revealing.

Choosing a Spouse in India

In Kerala, India, the criteria for marriage partners are multidimensional and include (1) religion/horoscope matching, (2) character, (3) education, (4) dowry, (5) appearance (girls/women), (6) employment, (7) caste/subcaste, (8) geographic distance between families, (9) financial status, and (10) family status, tradition, and reputation. A minimum of five characteristics must be of a suitable nature (i.e., similar across both parties or acceptable given that family's expectations) for a match to be considered by the parents (Yelsma and Atthappilly 1988). My own relatives, from the state of Madras, report similar considerations: educational background, social background, and family qualities of the prospective bride and bridegroom are all at issue. These considerations are important in many countries other than India where parental or matchmaker-driven arrangement of marriage is practiced.

The result of these criteria is that arranged-marriage practices tend to pair spouses who are similar in terms of major background characteristics like class, economic status, and education. Arranged-marriage practices also take into consideration character and physical health, perhaps particularly so when the new couple will live with the entire family. On first glance, such criteria seem far removed from romantic love and mutual attraction. However, as discussed earlier, those from cultures where love marriage predominates also consider character when choosing marriage partners. The desirable character qualities such as kindness or a considerate nature tend to be similar across cultures. In addition, when probed, couples who do marry may give both romantic and pragmatic reasons for getting married, whether they enter into a love or an arranged marriage, as has been demonstrated in Turkey (Hortaçsu and Oral 1994). Further, as will become clearer below, the same factors considered important by families in selecting a spouse may be the factors that contribute to whether individuals fall in love and get married in cultures where individual choice predominates.

Love versus Demographics

Despite the prevalence of love as a self-reported reason for marrying, Americans tend to date and marry those who are similar to themselves across a wide range of qualities (see Berscheid and Reis 1998 for an extensive review). We fall in love with people who are like us in terms of socioeconomic status, education, and age (Houts, Robins, and Huston 1996; Waris 1997), as well as with people who are like us in terms of psychological qualities like personality characteristics, leisure interests, and the complexity with which we think about topics (Burleson, Kunkel, and Szolwinski 1997; Hahn and Blass 1997; Keller and Young

1996; Klohnen and Mendelsohn 1998; Thiessen, Young, and Delgado 1997). Some findings even suggest that we tend to date and marry those who are physically similar to us (Keller and Young 1996; Thiessen, Young, and Delgado 1997). Thus, we who choose our spouses think we choose them for love, but outside observers (who do not hear our professed internal feelings of love and adoration) might think we choose our spouses because they are like us. At this level of analysis, arranged marriages are not, in the end, all that different.

Proof for the idea that similarity functions to direct marriage choices, whether family or personally driven, would involve demonstrating that arranged marriages and love marriages lead to equivalent levels of similarity between spouses. In one study of more than seven hundred couples in Turkey, spouses in love marriages were as like one another as those in arranged marriages (Fox 1975). So similarity appears to be a powerful force in marriage making, whether selected by families or by the individuals themselves. If two different selection methods lead to relatively similar pairing outcomes, on average, then why should arranged or love marriages have different outcomes? The assumption of the importance of personal choice in determining happiness has frequently led researchers to question whether partners in arranged marriages will be as happy as those in love marriages.

IS HAPPILY EVER AFTER EQUALLY HAPPY IN ARRANGED MARRIAGES?

In this section, I focus on marital satisfaction because this has been the outcome variable used in most psychological studies comparing arranged and love marriages, as opposed to divorce rates or other potential indicators. Unlike divorce rates, which are affected by factors such as laws governing who may seek divorce and for what reasons, marital satisfaction indicates the subjective well-being of spouses. Are spouses who choose one another happier together than those who were selected for one another?

Consider some example findings. Israeli couples reported comparably high marital satisfaction regardless of whether their marriage was arranged or self-chosen (Shachar 1991). Perhaps even more surprisingly, the Moonies who entered into arranged marriages also report levels of marital satisfaction typical of community samples (Galanter 1986). Were the Moonies simply representing themselves and their unusual lifestyle positively without actually having similar levels of marital satisfaction? Because their general well-being was lower than that of community samples, a self-presentational bias seems unlikely to account for the findings. Galanter notes the importance of the religious community context in reinforcing and supporting these marriages. Given the right context, choice may not always be the paramount issue in marital satisfaction (see Sethi-Iyengar and Lepper 1999 for research making a similar point in a very different domain). In India, in fact, those in arranged marriages sometimes report higher marital satisfaction than their compatriots in love marriages and equivalent marital satisfaction to Western comparison samples (Kumar and Dhyani 1996; Yelsma and Atthappilly 1988).

There are many limitations in the types of studies that look at marital satisfaction in arranged versus love marriages. Perhaps one of the most difficult to resolve is the selection of appropriate comparison groups. Comparing love marriages and arranged marriages in India, for example, often means comparing marriages where partners have more disparate social backgrounds and less family support[3] to marriages between very similar spouses who receive enormous family and community support. This seems not a fair comparison, but the alternative of choosing an American or other Western European comparison group is no more optimal, as then a wealth of cultural differences comes into play. However, if we take the sparse available evidence seriously, then systematic relationships between marriage type and marital satisfaction cannot be found.

On the one hand, it may seem obvious that when different procedures result in similar pairings, the outcomes (e.g., marital satisfaction) will be similar. On the other hand, different processes might support marital satisfaction in different cultures.

Processes Underlying Marital Satisfaction

Western marital researchers emphasize the processes of communication about conflict areas as the critical factor in marital satisfaction and longevity (e.g., Clements et al. 1998; Gottman 1994; Gottman and Levenson 1988). In fact, they suggest that "the positive factors that draw people together—love, attraction, perceived and actual similarities, trust, and commitment—are indicative of marital choice, but not marital success" (Clements et al. 1998, 352). So what exactly does it mean to say that the way couples handle conflict is a critical factor in whether they maintain high marital satisfaction over time? For Gottman (1994) it means that couples maintain a relatively high level of positive emotional expression (as compared to negative emotional expression) when discussing conflicts. The *ratio* of positive to negative emotion must be high, regardless of the degree to which a couple is emotionally expressive. Clements and colleagues (1998) suggest that not escalating the conflict, not withdrawing or avoiding the conflict, and not attacking the partner personally when angry ("invalidation") are the keys to good conflict resolution. How does one avoid such behaviors? By engaging in conversational techniques that minimize distractions, ensuring that both partners are engaged, and ensuring that both partners respect one another's time to speak. In addition, employing time-outs that help prevent unfruitful escalation of the conflict or invalidation behaviors can be important. Put differently, this means a problem-focused, respectful, and compromise-oriented approach to negotiating issues where partners disagree. Although I was unable to find scientific work on the ingredients of success in arranged marriages, my own relatives' comments, presented earlier, are consonant with ideas about compromise, communication, and positive attitudes toward the spouse and imply that conflict-resolving processes will be important in all cultures, regardless of marriage type.

But, as noted, similar levels of marital satisfaction could also mask differences in marital processes that would be very interesting to examine. Even among American couples, there are multiple ways to achieve good (and bad) relationships (Gottman 1994). For example, spouses in instrumental marriages, with an emphasis on the separate roles of the individual partners, may be satisfied when the husband is a good wage-earner and the wife a competent homemaker (see, e.g., Kamo 1993; Rubin 1976). Spouses oriented toward the expressive socioemotional features of marriage may not be satisfied with the adequate fulfillment of role responsibilities but may require good communication and companionship as well.

There is, in fact, evidence that different processes might be important in other cultures. For example, in Japan, as in the United States, marital satisfaction is related to housework sharing and equality. However, for Japanese spouses, the income of the husband is also an important predictor of marital satisfaction, while in America this is not necessarily the case (Kamo 1993). In India, spouses in arranged marriages show different patterns of adjustment to marriage over time than those in love marriages, although sexual satisfaction contributes similarly to both partners' overall adjustment to marriage in both types of marriage (Kumar and Dhyani 1996).

Another type of difference includes verbal communication. Indian arranged marriages report the lowest level of communication, while Western love marriages report high levels, and Indian love marriages are between these two groups in terms of communication (Yelsma and Atthappilly 1988; see also Hortaçsu and Oral 1994 on Turkish marriages). Relationships of various types of communication (verbal, sexual, and nonverbal) to marital satisfaction were lower in Indian couples. The authors concluded that satisfaction among Indian couples may be better predicted by variables different from those traditionally assessed in the West, where communication about conflictual issues seems critical for marital outcomes (see, e.g., Gottman and Levenson 1992, 1988). These findings of different determinants of marital satisfaction contrast with findings suggesting cross-cultural similarity (e.g., Hooley and Hahlweg 1989; Rabin et al. 1986; Sharlin 1996). Much about the processes for attaining and maintaining marital satisfaction in different cultures and in different types of marriages remains poorly understood.

Who Is Responsible for Marital Satisfaction?

Gottman and Levenson (1988) have noted that the responsibility for managing the emotional climate of U.S. marriages falls largely on the shoulders of wives; it is wives who must initiate conflict-related discussion and wives who bear the health costs of unhappy marriages. My family members report similar pressure on women in Indian arranged marriages, noting that "the wife is expected to make more adjustments to make the marriage work" and that this pressure arises from family members and the culture as well. In Western love marriages, women maintain satisfaction by initiating discussion of conflicts toward resolution. In arranged marriages, women may do so by suppressing their own needs and desires in order to maintain a good emotional climate, but this remains largely unresearched.

Happily Ever After: Summing Up

Arranged and love marriages do show similar *levels* of marital satisfaction in the few studies available, and it seems that women in both types of marriage assume more responsibility for the emotional quality of the marriage than men. It is not clear whether similarity in levels of marital satisfaction is due to similar factors across cultures, like superior conflict-resolution skills, or to different factors, such as fulfilling culture-specific expectations for a good spouse, and this represents an area with rich potential and large pitfalls for psychological research.

CHOOSING BETWEEN IN THE "MODERNIZING" WORLD

In modern India, marriage for love is becoming more common. Many children of upper-middle-class Indians can choose either type of marriage. In the case of one friend, parental consent and approval for a love match were contingent upon the prospective spouse being Indian in ethnic background though not on caste or other more traditional considerations. Survey results also suggest that compromise between personal and parental choice in marriage is quite popular in India today (e.g., Umadevi, Venkataramaiah, and Srinivasulu 1992). In the United States, according to news reports, immigrant populations may also be moving toward more moderate forms of arranged marriage but without excluding parental involvement entirely (Segall 1998). My cousin reports that arranged marriages have shifted toward providing much choice for the prospective spouses, both in terms of who is selected and when the search for a spouse takes place. She also notes that love marriages in India are still met with some resistance, especially if the marriages are between people of different caste backgrounds. Not surprisingly, such resistance is particularly strong among religiously conservative families. Love marriages seem to have higher pressure to work well, while also receiving more disapproval from parents. The end result is that such couples may experience more difficulties, perhaps through no fault of their own. Still, the clear trend is for children to express more choice even as their parents arrange marriages.

ARRANGED MARRIAGES: WHAT CAN WE CONCLUDE?

As suggested above, both social science and personal experience suggest that (1) arranged marriages are heterogeneous across and within cultures in the degree of choice that spouses exert, (2) the factors in selecting spouses may be surprisingly similar regardless of whether marriages are arranged or self-chosen, (3) outcomes like marital satisfaction seem quite similar across marriage type, although it is not clear whether this is driven by underlying similarities (in choices and in the demands of married life) or by underlying differences (in expectations and interaction patterns). Further research may help us understand how the larger cultural context in which a couple lives may determine more everyday facets of their lives, in a relationship that seems to be a human universal in one form or another.

FEMINISM AND ARRANGED MARRIAGES

Having reviewed some of the empirical work on arranged marriages, it becomes clear that there are few simple perspectives on arranged marriages from a feminist standpoint.

Lack of Choice for Women

First, consider the matter of choice. Though historically, girls/women have had less say in their marriage arrangements than boys/men, that appears to be changing not only in India but also in many other places. In many of the cultures reviewed above, both men and women are denied freedom of personal choice in marriage partners, and the inequity observed revolves around power differentials between children and parents, not between men and women. In fact, Small (1993) found that in 106 societies that practice arranged marriage, only three give prospective grooms more choice than prospective brides. Brides very often (50 percent of the societies examined) had the power to reject a potential marriage. She points out that lack of choice in picking potential candidates doesn't necessarily mean coercion. Further, as suggested above, arranged marriages need not unfold very differently from Western ones once the marriage begins. From some evolutionary standpoints (e.g., Hazan and Diamond 2000), what is required for the formation of attachment bonds between two individuals is the kind of daily physical and psychological interchange that seems part of both types of marriages. Finally, Small problematizes the idea that Western women are totally free to select their own partners—after all, we want our families and friends to like and welcome our new spouses.

In fact, the power of self-determination that is lost for daughters may be the gain for mothers. The power accorded older women in some cultures in arranging marriages for their sons and daughters alike is not necessarily trivial as such alliances can be important determinants of wealth and property (Coles 1990). Derné (1994) notes the way that men and women together engage in strategic interactions to preserve existing inequities between spouses. Expanded to a generational view, this could well include the maintenance of arranged-marriage systems; frequently mothers-in-law achieve greater relative power, particularly in patrilocal cultures, when their sons marry. It is in their best interest to choose daughters-in-law who will support, rather than challenge, their authority. A daughter-in-law who is too well loved by the son might represent a potential problem for a mother. The son might not enforce traditional divisions of labor in which the daughter-in-law must care for or serve her mother-in-law. Further, the mother may be neglected in favor of her daughter-in-law—something considered appropriate in U.S. culture but not necessarily so elsewhere.

Finally, prioritizing choice in the domain of marriage partners may be undesirable in a country like India, where, as my cousin wrote, "parental approval is still considered quite important and children cannot easily walk away from that." In fact, the idea of personal choice is a relatively individualistic notion of what equality of self-determination means. Research on motivation suggests that culture plays a big role in how important and desirable autonomous choice may be (Sethi-Ingeyar and Lepper 1999).

Power Inequities in Marriage

There are obviously power inequities in arranged marriages. Are the power inequities observed in India necessarily greater than those in Western marriages? As noted above, wives have been pinpointed as bearing more of the burden of marriage management in the United States (e.g., Gottman and Levenson 1988); women do more housework, make greater career sacrifices, and ultimately have less negotiating power in the marital relationship (Mahony 1995). In fact, Mahony argues that the key factor influencing gender inequity in American marriages is gender-differential educational and career achievement. She suggests that American women who are less well educated and have lower paying jobs than their husbands (which may be true even given equal educational attainment) are at a clear disadvantage when it comes to negotiations about household responsibilities. Are women in arranged marriages likely to experience even larger educational inequity and therefore even less power? In my own family, educational inequities between women and men tend not to be larger than those in the marriages of my Western friends. But stereotypes of cultures that arrange marriages, with images of child brides and of vast numbers of women kept uneducated, suggest that arranged marriage and larger inequity between spouses, in terms of education, go together. Research findings also show that more-educated women appear more likely to have love, rather than arranged, marriages (e.g., Hortaçsu and Oral 1994), implying that arranged marriages disproportionately involve less-educated women, vulnerable to greater power inequity in their marriage.

There are several problems with such conclusions. First, it may be that arranged-marriage practices go hand in hand with less education for both spouses. Further, the assumption is that if women were liberated, they would choose their own partners, and thus women who accept an arranged marriage are not liberated women. This is not necessarily true. One of the most obvious confounds is that women who go on to higher education may have more opportunities to meet and fall in love with men of their own choosing. Further, there are many exceptions to the rule—many women are highly educated but still prefer to have some parental involvement in the selection of their spouse. Still, connections between educational attainment and marriage type raise a third issue, which is the role of arranged marriages in upholding sets of inequities within a culture.

Arranged Marriages Are Part of a Web of Inequities

Arranged marriages can be viewed as part of a system of inequities, with movement toward self-determination in marriage a route to improving other inequalities. Unfortunately, changes in marriage practices do not always result in improvements in other aspects of women's status. Alsuwaigh (1989) reports on changes in women's status in Saudi Arabia. One of her most striking findings, in a study of mothers and daughters from various economic classes, is a decline in prearranged marriages and the beginning of unarranged marriages (which must be carefully justified to avoid the implication that chastity was violated, something that is implicit in the presence of an emotional preference for a particular marital partner). She concludes: "Women's life in Saudi Arabia has been influenced by socio-economic changes, particularly in the structure of their marriages. . . . However, women are still locked into their traditional roles by the limitations of job opportunities on the one hand and considerations of traditional norms on the other" (77). Thus, increasing freedom in choosing a marriage partner may not be accompanied by improvements in women's status overall. As these other improvements in status may increase women's power within marriages (see Mahony 1995), it might be less important to take a stand against arranged marriage and more important to take a stand against inequitable educational and career opportunities.

Arranged Marriages Perpetuate a Notion of Women as Property

A final critique of arranged marriages is that they open the door for massive abuse of women by setting them up as property (Haider 1995). From the review above, it is clear that arranged-marriage practices do not necessarily treat women as property, although this can be the case. Some modern versions of marriage arranging, however, are better characterized as treating both sons and daughters as parts in a collective whole—that of the family. As parts of a family, sons and daughters should not select their spouses independently of the concerns of the family as a unit.

A second concern is that rates of spouse abuse are difficult to compare across cultures. Stories about battered women in arranged marriages may not be driven strictly by the way that marriages are arranged because spouse abuse occurs in love marriages in the United States and other Western countries, as well. In some cases, however, arranged marriages may make it easier for women to be abused or treated as property, in part because marriage practices reflect a general societal view of women as possessions. This may be especially true when religious systems and other ideologies within a culture reinforce the idea that women are of a lesser status.

Clearly, arranged marriages can be practiced in ways that demean, demoralize, and mistreat women. And women may be driven to extreme behaviors, such as suicide, to avoid arranged marriages. Whether these darker aspects of arranged-marriage practices are best handled by actively fighting the tradition of arranged marriages or by attempting to place safeguards against such behaviors within existing systems for arranging marriages is not an easy question to answer. Certainly permitting women (and men) to veto marriages seems a workable solution, and is one already implemented in many families. A more collective system of choosing mates may also imply more collective responsibility toward the welfare of the married. Such a perspective does not imply that either women or men are "property" but views the union between two people as collectively chosen and collectively maintained.

FINAL WORDS

One of the controversial conclusions of the present chapter is that the practices of arranging marriage do not necessarily lead to the oppression of women. In fact, arranged marriages are but one of many practices that require Western feminism to confront and resolve issues of cultural variability and heterogeneity in their striving for gender equality (see Abu-Lughod 1991). Without such confrontation, Western feminism will remain Western, at best ineffective in achieving its aims for benefiting women worldwide and at worst clumsily harmful. Unlike other culturally particularized rituals involving women (e.g., female circumcision), arranged marriages do not inherently require that women are injured or oppressed. Some of the existing gender inequities I discussed above are not, in the abstract, different from inequities that are part and parcel of modern American culture. The modernization of the arranged marriage occurring at present in India and elsewhere may maximize the benefits of personal and collective choice. Arranged marriages offer some unique benefits in comparison to love marriages; they are embedded in a strongly supportive context and tend not to be related to unrealistic expectations and demands. Combining these benefits while accommodating those who do meet a lifetime partner on their own may produce a very good alternative to the individual choice practiced in other cultures.

NOTES

Thanks are due to my aunt and cousin for their open and informative discussions about arranged marriages and love marriages and our own family; to my mother, Laura Carstensen; Lisa Diamond; Frank A. Drews; Marilyn Yalom; and Leigh Shaw for discussion, comments, and/or thoughtful criticisms on earlier drafts; and to Alexandra Freund for general encouragement. Finally, thanks are due to my colleagues at the Max Planck Institute and to the funding from the Max Planck Society that supported initial work on this chapter.

    1. In fact, recent research explicitly confronts the cultural bias of past work on choice and motivation and suggests that the role of choice in motivation may be quite dependent on the degree to which cultures emphasize individuality or group membership (Sethi-Iyengar and Lepper 1999).

    2. *Exapted* refers to an evolutionary process in which structures initially employed for one function are then appropriated for another, different function. In this case, Hazan and colleagues argue that attachment bonding evolved to ensure care and protection of dependent young but then was "appropriated"

over evolutionary history to ensure that both parents would be present for the child's early years because of their attachment to one another. The technical details of this argument are outside the scope of this chapter.

3. When partners' backgrounds are very similar, love matches are better accepted than when partners' backgrounds are not. For example, in my family, two male cousins who selected their own brides were treated somewhat differently; one chose a woman who fit all the religious and family background criteria that would have mattered, while the other selected a Christian woman, relatively problematic from the family's perspective. Although both marriages were accepted, initial reactions were more positive toward the more similar choice.

REFERENCES

Abu-Lughod, L. 1991. Writing against culture. In *Recapturing anthropology,* edited by R. G. Fox. Santa Fe, N.M.: School of American Research Press.

———. 1993a. *Writing women's worlds: Bedouin stories.* Berkeley and Los Angeles: University of California Press.

———. 1993b. Analyzing resistance: Bedouin women's stories. In *To speak or be silent,* edited by L. B. Ross, 25–38. Wilmette, Ill.: Chiron Publications.

Alsuwaigh, S. A. 1989. Women in transition: The case of Saudi Arabia. *Journal of Comparative Family Studies* 20:67–78.

Bandura, A. 1982. The psychology of chance encounters and life paths. *American Psychologist* 37:747–55.

Berscheid, E., and H. T. Reis. 1998. Attraction and close relationships. In *The handbook of social psychology,* edited by D. T. Gilbert, S. Fiske, and G. Lindzey, 193–281.Vol. 2. Boston: McGraw Hill.

Blood, R. O. 1972. *The family.* New York: The Free Press.

Burleson, B. R., A. W. Kunkel, and J. B. Szolwinski. 1997. Similarity in cognitive complexity and attraction to friends and lovers: Experimental and correlational studies. *Journal of Constructivist Psychology* 10:221–48.

Buss, D. M., et al. 1989. International preferences in selecting mates: A study of 37 cultures. *Journal of Cross-Cultural Psychology* 21:5–47.

Choi, S. H., and P. M. Keith. 1991. Are "worlds of pain" crosscultural? Korean working class marriages. *Journal of Comparative Family Studies* 22:293–312.

Clements, M. L., A. D. Cordova, H. J. Markman, and J. Laurenceau. 1998. The erosion of marital satisfaction over time and how to prevent it. In *Satisfaction in close relationships,* edited by R. J. Sternberg and M. Hojjat, 335–55. New York: Guilford Press.

Coles, C. 1990. The older woman in Hausa society: Power and authority in urban Nigeria. In *The cultural context of aging: Worldwide perspectives,* edited by J. Sokolovsky, 57–81. New York: Bergin and Garvey.

Cordova, D. I., and M. R. Lepper. 1996. Intrinsic motivation and the process of learning: Beneficial effects of contextualization, personalization, and choice. *Journal of Educational Psychology* 88:715–30.

De Munck, V. C. 1996. Love and marriage in a Sri Lankan Muslim community: Toward an evaluation of Dravidian marriage practices. *American Ethnologist* 23:698–716.

Derné, S. 1994. Hindu men talk about controlling women: Cultural ideas as a tool of the powerful. *Sociological Perspectives* 37:203–27.

Engel, J. W. 1984. Marriage in the People's Republic of China: Analysis of a new law. *Journal of Marriage and the Family* 46:955–61.

Fox, G. L. 1975. Love match and arranged marriage in a modernizing nation: Mate selection in Ankara, Turkey. *Journal of Marriage and the Family* 37: 180–93.

Galanter, M. 1986. "Moonies" get married: A psychiatric follow-up study of a charismatic religious sect. *American Journal of Psychiatry* 143:1245–49.

Gottman, J. M. 1994. *What predicts divorce? The relationship between marital processes and marital outcomes.* Hillsdale, N.J.: Lawrence Erlbaum.

Gottman, J. M., and R. W. Levenson. 1988. The social psychophysiology of marriage. In *Perspectives on marital interaction,* edited by P. Noller and M. A. Fitzpatrick, 182–200. Clevedon, England: Multilingual Matters.

———. 1992. Marital processes predictive of later dissolution: Behavior, physiology, and health. *Journal of Personality and Social Psychology* 63:221–33.

Gupta, U., and P. Singh. 1982. Exploratory study of love and liking and type of marriages. *Indian Journal of Applied Psychology* 19:92–97.

Hahn, J., and T. Blass. 1997. Dating partner preferences: A function of similarity of love styles. *Journal of Social Behavior and Personality* 12:595–610.

Haider, S. 1995. Lifting the veil of silence: Jamuna's narrative of pain. *Sociological Bulletin* 44:241–54.

Hazan, C., and L. M. Diamond. 2000. The limits of sexual strategies theory and the promise of attachment theory for explaining human mating. *Review of General Psychology: Special Issue on Attachment* 4:186–204.

Hooely, J., and K. Hahlweg. 1989. Marital satisfaction and marital communication in German and English couples. *Behavioral Assessment* 11:119–33.

Hortaçsu, N., and A. Oral. 1994. Comparison of couple- and family-initiated marriages in Turkey. *Journal of Social Psychology* 134:229–39.

Houts, R. M., E. Robins, and T. L. Huston. 1996. Compatibility and the development of premarital relationships. *Journal of Marriage and the Family* 58:7–20.

Kamo, Y. 1993. Determinants of marital satisfaction: A comparison of the United States and Japan. *Journal of Social and Personal Relationships* 10: 551–68.

Kattakayam, J. J. 1996. Marriage and family among the tribals of Kerala: A study of the Mannans of Idukky District. *Journal of Comparative Family Studies* 27:545–58.

Keller, M. C., and R. K. Young. 1996. Mate assortment in dating and married couples. *Personality and Individual Differences* 21:217–21.

Klohnen, E. C., and G. A. Mendelsohn. 1998. Partner selection for personality characteristics: A couple-centered approach. *Personality and Social Psychology Bulletin* 24:268–78.

Kumar, P., and J. Dhyani. 1996. Marital adjustment: A study of some related factors. *Indian Journal of Clinical Psychology* 23:112–16.

Lamb, L. October 1999. No exit here. *Utne Reader* 95:26–28.

Lasch, C. 1997. *Women and the common life.* New York: W. W. Norton.

Lee, G. R., and L. H. Stone. 1980. Mate-selection systems and criteria: Variation according to family structure. *Journal of Marriage and the Family* 42:319–26.

Levine, R., S. Sato, T. Hashimoto, and J. Verma. 1995. Love and marriage in eleven cultures. *Journal of Cross-Cultural Psychology* 26:554–71.

Mahony, R. 1995. *Kidding ourselves: Breadwinning, babies, and bargaining power.* New York: Basic Books.

Okonjo, K. 1992. Aspects of continuity and change in mate-selection among the Igbo west of the river Niger. *Journal of Comparative Family Studies* 23:339–60.

Rabin, C., et al. 1986. The areas of change questionnaire: A cross-cultural comparison of Israeli and American distressed and non-distressed couples. *American Journal of Family Therapy* 14:324–35.

Rubin, L. B. 1976. *Worlds of pain: Life in the working-class family.* New York: Basic Books.

Segall, R. 1998. Strangers at the wedding: Arranged marriages in America. *Village Voice* 43:46–53.

Sethi-Iyengar, S., and M. R. Lepper. 1999. Rethinking the value of choice: A cultural perspective on intrinsic motivation. *Journal of Personality and Social Psychology* 76:349–66.

Shachar, R. 1991. His and her marital satisfaction: The double standard. *Sex Roles* 25:451–67.

Sharlin, S. A. 1996. Long-term successful marriages in Israel. *Contemporary Family Therapy* 18:225–42.

Small, M. F. 1993. *Female choices: Sexual behavior of female primates.* Ithaca, N.Y.: Cornell University Press.

Thiessen, D., R. K. Young, and M. Delgado. 1997. Social pressures for associative mating. *Personality and Individual Differences* 22:157–64.

Umadevi, L., P. Venkataramaiah, and R. Srinivasulu. 1992. A comparative study on the concept of marriage by professional and non-professional degree students. *Indian Journal of Behaviour* 16:27–37.

Waris, R. G. 1997. Age and occupation in selection of human mates. *Psychological Reports* 80:1223–26.

Yelsma, P., and K. Athappilly. 1988. Marital satisfaction and communication practices: Comparisons among Indian and American couples. *Journal of Comparative Family Studies* 19:37–54.

Zeifman, D., and C. Hazan. 1997. Attachment: The bond in pair bonds. In *Evolutionary social psychology,* edited by J. A. Simpson and D. T. Kenrick, 237–63. Mahwah, N.J.: Lawrence Erlbaum.

CHAPTER 14

Marriage in Old Age

Susan Turk Charles and Laura L. Carstensen

Grow old along with me!
The best is yet to be.
The last of life,
for which the first was made.
>—Robert Browning
>"Rabbi Ben Ezra"

The common stereotype of old couples is that they are emotionally and romantically lifeless. Indeed, it is against this backdrop that young couples frequently speak of their commitment to keeping the "passion" in their relationships and avoiding the fate of "old married couples." What happens to marriages that have weathered the storms of early couple-dom, the rearing and launching of children, and the negotiations of household tasks and careers? What role does gender play in the lives of men and women who link their mutual fates, intertwine their dreams and aspirations, and pursue joint goals for more than half their lives?

Interestingly, marriage in old age, though understudied, appears to be quite different from the stereotypes noted above and more closely resembles the image conveyed in the Browning quotation that opens this chapter. On average, older couples are happier than younger couples. Even self-described unhappily married older couples state they are happier than they were when they were younger. Older married couples say that they argue less and have fewer marital conflicts than their younger counterparts. Older married couples also take more pleasure in many areas of married life, citing adult children, conversation, and recreational activities as distinct sources of happiness. Old married couples do report that erotic bonds are less central in their lives; friendship instead appears to be the cardinal feature of their lives. Gendered roles subside somewhat in old age, and perhaps relatedly, intimate relationships in old age are, by and large, harmonious and deeply satisfying. Mark Twain may have gotten it right when he wrote in his notebook in 1894, "Love seems the swiftest, but it is the slowest of all growths. No man or woman really knows what perfect love is until they have been married a quarter of a century."

Most of the research on couples published in the social-science literature focuses on the trials and tribulations of young married couples and, in recent history, mostly on the predictors of marital demise. In this chapter we overview the social-science literature on marriage in old age. We describe the nature of married life in old age and report the stated fears and joys of marriage at this final stage of life. We also address the end of marriage in old age which—due to differences in life expectancy combined with cultural traditions of women marrying older men—prototypically occurs when the husband dies. Finally, we critically examine the social structural conditions that place women who have dedicated themselves to these important relationships for most of their lives at risk for financial and social problems in very old age. Unfortunately, few studies have examined same-sex couples, and no comprehensive study has examined same-sex older couples. For this reason, our chapter discusses relationships between husbands and wives.

THE LIFE COURSE OF MARRIAGE

Researchers interested in the course of marital happiness long held that satisfaction with marriage declines after the initial "honeymoon stage" comes to a close (e.g., Pineo 1961). Although these early studies were restricted primarily to relatively new marriages, viz., the first fifteen years, the tendency was to reason by extrapolation that by very old age, marriages were likely to be marked by significant apathy and disenchantment (Pineo 1961).

However, as the longitudinal studies themselves aged, research revealed a distinctly different pattern (Field and Weishaus 1992). Overall satisfaction follows a curvilinear pattern, with satisfaction high in the early years of marriage, relatively low in the middle years, and returning to higher levels in old age (Rollins 1989). Other studies examining differences across age groups of married couples also find a curvilinear pattern. When both positive and negative aspects of marriage are assessed—that is, when spouses are asked separately about the good and the bad qualities of their marriage—young couples describe many positive aspects of their marriages but also report considerable conflict. In the middle years of a marriage, positive sentiment declines and conflict is heightened. By the later years, positive sentiment returns to levels nearly as high as the early years, and, importantly, conflict drops to very low levels. Thus, in some ways the best profile of marriage is in the later years (Gilford and Bengtson 1979).

Although research clearly does not support the "familiarity breeds contempt" hypothesis suggested by the early studies, we caution that the optimistic picture of marriage in old age should be tempered somewhat by potential alternative explanations. Older marriages inevitably represent those marriages that have survived the test of time. Studies based on comparisons of different age groups at one point in time may simply reflect the fact that the population of older couples has been distilled—so to speak—by divorce, leaving behind only the happily married older couples. In addition, relationship satisfaction is not impervious to outside influences. Couples who are happy may be happy due to circumstances unrelated to their marital functioning. Poverty, for example, is a risk factor for unhappiness, divorce, and mortality.

However, the finding that marriage grows better in old age is bolstered by findings from retrospective interview studies as well. When asked to reflect on their marriages, women who had been married for fifty years or more concurred that a curvilinear pattern of satisfaction best described these important relationships (Condie 1989). In fact, most older couples are quick to report that their marriages have not progressed along unvarying paths of marital bliss. When asked to give advice to young women concerning marriage, one widowed woman who had been married many years responded that one "shouldn't expect to always love your husband." In discussing her marriage, another woman we interviewed mentioned that younger couples often noticed how happy she and her husband acted when they were together and marveled at how lucky they were to have found each other and to have had such a successful marriage. Despite the intentions of these younger couples, this woman saw their remarks as misguided. She said that she was angry that they presumed her marriage was based on luck and a perfect compatibility. Her marriage had taken a lot of hard work, both from herself and her husband, and the happiness that they were experiencing was the result of years of working together, compromising, and surviving difficult ordeals. This is consistent with other studies where older adults have stressed that long-term marriage demands a commitment to the marriage (Condie 1989). Simply "being in love" or finding the "right person" is not enough to sustain a marriage for many years.

MARRIAGE GETS WORSE BEFORE IT GETS BETTER

To reiterate, although some caveats are necessary, the profile of research findings about marital satisfaction in old age is quite positive. It is not true that marriage involves a gradual and steady discontentment with a spouse, but there is a decided drop in marital happiness in the middle years before couples achieve this higher level of satisfaction. The most burning question that arises from the life-span literature on marriage is: What goes wrong in midlife? In a word, the answer appears to be "children." Especially among women, dissatisfaction with marriage increases after the birth of the first child (Cowan and Cowan 1992) and remains relatively high until grown children are launched from the home. Even fluctuations in marital satisfaction are associated with fluctuating demands of child rearing. Dissatisfaction peaks when children are very young and again when they reach adolescence. Essentially two changes occur. Time spent together in pleasurable activities declines (Gilford and Bengtson 1979) and conflicts over child rearing arise (Gable, Belsky, and Crnic 1992). The latter appears to be the more important of the two.

Philip and Carolyn Cowan, family researchers at the University of California at Berkeley, place gender differences at the core of marital problems related to parenting. They point out that at the same time marital satisfaction is plummeting after the birth of a child, both mothers and fathers are deriving great satisfaction from the child. The Cowans argue that a simple fatigue factor does not account for marital dissatisfaction. Rather, in studies that track the transition into parenthood, the birth of a first child brings about a striking division of labor that falls squarely along gender lines—even among couples who have managed highly egalitarian marriages to that point—and these strict gender roles lead to marital discontent (Cowan and Cowan 1988).

After the birth of a child, most women experience dramatic changes in their lives. They immediately fall in love with the baby and identify strongly as mothers. Among fathers, the change is often more gradual. It may take a year before a new father comes to feel comfortable and identified with his role. Day-to-day life typically changes in very different ways for new mothers and fathers. Mothers nearly always assume more

child-care responsibilities than fathers. Fathers often resume their jobs
full time several days (if not hours) after the birth of a child and often
do so with greater pressure than ever to be financially successful. Mothers often reduce work outside the home for weeks, months, or years.
Thus, for women, motherhood exerts a tremendous influence on daily
life and personal identity. These very gendered approaches to becoming
parents can alienate spouses from one another. Mothers can resent the
fact that they are assuming the lion's share of child rearing, and fathers
can feel alienated from rapidly bonding mother-child pairs. Perhaps especially because parenthood is such a significant developmental mile-
stone, new parents can feel that something must be very wrong with
them if they are feeling less close to one another.

Other research supports the Cowans' analysis. Findings from "natural experiments" reveal a similar pattern with the parents. Not only do
marital interactions improve when children leave home, they decline
again in cases where adult children return to live with their parents.
Given this strong relationship, we must be clear. Children are not the
direct source of personal distress. Mothers and fathers typically count
their children among their greatest sources of joy, but *couples* appear to
be happiest with their marriages when their children are grown and
living independently.

THE UPWARD TURN IN MARITAL HAPPINESS

It is unlikely that children leaving home is the only reason that relationship satisfaction improves over time. In fact, considering that children
could be used as a reason to stay together, one might predict a flurry of
divorces after children leave home. But this is not the case. Perhaps the
Nietzschean adage "What doesn't kill me, makes me stronger" applies.
Experience, no doubt, plays a role in spouses' growing satisfaction with
one another. Over the years, couples report that they have solved many
of their problems and learned to put aside most of the unsolvable ones.
It also may be that conflicts take on different meanings in the context
of very long-lived marriages. The closeness and predictability of long-
term relationships allow conflicts to be resolved with greater security
and comfort than can be found in relatively new relationships. Indeed,
it may be within such contexts that people master the art of regulating
their own emotional states while at the same time soothing and caring
for another.

Older couples do appear to be better able to resolve the conflicts they have. One study in which older and middle-aged couples were directly observed as they discussed conflictual aspects of their marriage found that older husbands and wives were more likely than middle-aged couples to interweave expressions of affection along with expressions of anger and discontent (Carstensen, Levenson, and Gottman 1995). Importantly, this study included both happily and unhappily married couples. Even so, older couples engaged in this pattern more so than their middle-aged counterparts.

Forced to choose one word that describes older couples' relationships, we would have to say "friendship." Older couples describe increasing closeness over the years (Atchley 1977; Field and Weishaus 1992). One study queried happily married older couples as to what they perceived was responsible for the success of their marriages (Lauer, Lauer, and Kerr 1990). The three top-ranked criteria were the same for men and women (although the order varied somewhat). They were commitment, liking their spouse, and having their best friend for a spouse. Older widows, reflecting on the reasons their marriages had survived for so many years, also talked about conditions that resonate with notions of friendship. In their view, compromise and being able to pursue individual as well as joint interests accounted for success in marriage (Malatesta 1989).

The term "friendship" can convey a lack of sexual passion. But here, too, an image of asexuality in old age does not reflect the true nature of older relationships. Sexual intercourse does decrease in frequency over the course of a long-term relationship. Sexual activity is most likely to cease, however, due to the illness of a partner rather than disinterest. And although there are couples who stop all sexual contact in old age, many other older people report that sexual activity improves with age. In part *because* intercourse and orgasm are less central, lovemaking can grow more relaxed and emotionally intimate. Thus, there are changes in sexual functioning over the course of a marriage, but "asexual" does not well characterize them.

Is there something about growing older that makes people better partners? One life-span developmental theory suggests that this may be so. According to socioemotional selectivity theory (Carstensen 1993; Carstensen, Isaacowitz, and Charles 1999) throughout life people monitor the passage of time, not just clock time or calendar time but lifetime. At conscious and subconscious levels people are aware of their place in the life cycle. Early in life, when the future is perceived as expansive, attention is focused on the long term. As people age, they become increasingly aware that time is, in some sense, running out. Under these conditions, people focus on the here and now. Goals change from expanding one's horizons to deepening emotional ties in existing relationships. One of the more fascinating social-science findings is that people approaching the end of life are not sullen and morbid (Taylor and Brown 1988). Rather, many say that it is the best time in life (Carstensen, Isaacowitz, and Charles 1999). People live their lives investing greater efforts in obtaining emotionally meaningful goals and pursuing important relationships.

Analogies can be made between the individual life course and the life course of a relationship (Carstensen et al. 1996). Early in a relationship, when the future is looming large, the resolution of conflicts is extremely important and adaptive. Even if negative emotions are experienced intensely during conflict discussions, the payoff may be considerable. Yet, as couples move through life, two things happen. For one, quite a number of conflicts are resolved. Second, the motivation to resolve certain other conflicts may subside. Socioemotional selectivity theory suggests that the motivation to regulate the immediate emotional climate of intimate relationships increases in later life. Especially if endings are primed, through the illness of a spouse or even the illness of age-mates, couples may attempt increasingly to maintain a positive emotional climate. It is not that conflicts do not exist; rather, their discussion is viewed as having little purpose during this penultimate phase of life. In a letter to Clara Spaulding dated August 20, 1886, Mark Twain wrote, "There isn't time—so brief is life—for bickerings, apologies, heartburnings, callings to account. There is only time for loving—and but an instant, so to speak, for that."

Emotionally close social relationships offer a number of benefits in old age. Intimate emotional relationships in later life appear to buffer individuals from mental and physical health problems. In addition, studies comparing married individuals to those who are not married indicate that married people are generally physically and mentally healthier, economically more advantaged, and embedded in a broader social support network over and above the addition of the spouse (Renne 1971; Ross and Mirowsky 1989). Having a spouse also decreases the chances of living alone and increases the availability of both instrumental and emotional support. For men and women, actual support from their spouses is related to well-being, although this relationship is far stronger for women than men (Acitelli and Antonucci 1994). In addition, perceived support is also an important predictor of well-being for women. Among men, marriage is also related to better physical health and even mortality (Renne 1971). One factor linking physical health and marriage is that married men are less likely to engage in high-risk behaviors that endanger health, such as excessive drinking and other drug use (Costello 1991).

Unfortunately, most of the research comparing married and unmarried people tacitly considers unmarried people a monolithic group. The few studies that have examined differences among subgroups of widowed, divorced, and ever-single individuals suggest that there are important differences. Moreover, gender differences are apparent in the advantages and disadvantages within subgroups.

The deleterious effects of being single fall most heavily upon the divorced and widowed. Ever-single people look similar to the long-term married (Huyck 1995; Verbrugge 1979), suggesting that it is not the lack of a spouse that causes problems, but the process of losing one (a point to which we return later). For never-married individuals, women also rank higher on measures of adjustment and satisfaction compared to men. Never-married men, in contrast, rate themselves as less satisfied than never-married women and more desirous of marriage (Frazier et al. 1996). In addition, never-married women report better health than never-married men as well as better health than men and women who had been divorced or widowed (Cramer 1993).

These findings at first seem counterintuitive given social mores that depict marriage as more desired for women and refer to unmarried women derogatively as "spinsters" and "old maids." (For men, no equivalent derogatory words exist.) Although widowed women report feeling sorry for women who do not have family, these negative connotations do not appear to be adopted by the never-married women themselves (Newtson and Keith 1997). In interviews with never-married women, many expressed having no regrets, and the ones who did express regrets mention not having children (Alexander et al. 1992). Few expressed regret over not being married (Newtson and Keith 1997). Single women tend to have larger social support networks with friends and are more likely to care for other family members compared to their male counterparts.

In addition, gender differences also emerge when examining divorced and widowed men and women. Men who have divorced are more likely to increase alcohol consumption and commit suicide than other men. This association does not exist for women (Rossow 1993). Moreover, widowerhood is associated with a greater mortality among men, but again no such association exists among women (Helsing, Szklo, and Comstock 1981). Women report better health and larger, more embedded social networks compared to men when faced with the dissolution of their marriage through death or divorce. The advantage men have over women in this situation is financial; a greater percentage of women face economic hardships as a function of dissolved marriages than men.

RETIREMENT AND GENDER ROLES

When social scientists began to study the effects of retirement on marriage, they primarily studied couples of which men were the primary wage-earners and women seldom held occupations outside their homes. The expectation of these researchers was that the entry of the husband into the home full time would result in a disequilibrium in the marriage and discontent, especially on the part of the wife. Women, it was felt, would resent their husbands' intrusion into the household domain. If husbands felt that wives were now available to them all of the time to prepare meals, run errands, and so on, retirement could translate to more work for wives. One woman we talked with mentioned that when her husband retired, he wanted her to participate in his new hobbies, which took her away from her usual social activities with her friends.

Although there certainly are cases of women citing problems associated with their husbands' retirement, the literature does not support the general view that retirement hails dissatisfaction with marriage. On the contrary, there is some reason to think that the retirement years are marked by a modest—only modest—softening of gender roles, a point to which we return below. Some studies find that retirement improves marriage (Atchley 1976), others conclude that it slightly reduces satisfaction (Lee and Shehan 1989), and still others conclude that there are not significant changes in either direction (Vinick and Ekerdt 1991).

Vinick and Ekerdt, for example, studied husbands and wives during the first year after retirement. They found that husbands and wives reported engaging in more leisure activities together. In addition, nearly 40 percent of the women in this study reported that they experienced a reduction in social activities with their friends but that this decrease was not related to their satisfaction. Upon closer examination, findings suggested that wives approached their husbands' retirements as opportunities to selectively prune their activities, keeping those that were more important and dropping less important engagements. Because these women reported that they enjoyed time with their husbands, spending more time with them had no deleterious effects on their overall satisfaction with life.

With retirement comes a potential reorganization of home life and the opportunity for gender roles to lessen. Care of the home, traditionally wives' concern, can be divided equally after husbands retire, resulting in a more equitable marital relationship. In addition, the power and authority associated with husbands' breadwinning status also may diminish after retirement, contributing further to a reduction in disparities in power. However, here too, research suggests that changes are not substantial. The availability of the husband to share in the household tasks does not appear to translate into less work for the wife. Men do report spending more time on household chores than ever before, but these chores largely comprise large-scale projects, such as remodeling, repairs, or yard work (Vinick and Ekerdt 1991). Husbands, even after retirement, contribute far less to the daily responsibilities of running a home.

Szinovacz and Harpster (1994) divided tasks into "female" chores, comprising mainly food preparation, laundry, and cleaning the house, and "male" chores, which included errands, outdoor tasks, and paying bills. They found that husbands of working wives did engage in more "female" and "male" household chores than husbands of homemaking or retired wives. However, regardless of the employment status of the wife or husband, wives invested more hours in household work than husbands. Not surprisingly, gender roles were maintained even after retirement. Husbands continued to engage in more male-typed chores than wives and wives to engage in more female-typed chores than husbands. The crossover was greater for women, however. Wives spent thirty-two hours a week on female-typed tasks and nine hours per week on male-typed tasks. Husbands spent seven hours per week on female-typed tasks and twelve hours per week on male-typed tasks. As during earlier life stages, wives spend many more hours per week working in the home than husbands (Szinovacz and Harpster 1994).

Although one could argue that this disparity reflects female interests, inequity in the division of household labor is related to dissatisfaction with the marriage, particularly when wives expect their husbands to participate more in household duties after retirement (Lee and Shehan 1989). One change associated with late life that does appear to shift gendered roles is physical decline. When one spouse is disabled, the other does assume responsibility for tasks previously assigned to the partner. That is, husbands do increase their contribution to household chores, such as washing dishes, if physical problems make the task difficult for wives (Szinovacz and Harpster 1994). Similarly, when husbands' frailties inhibit their ability to complete male-typed tasks, wives assume the responsibility. Cognitive decline in a husband, for example, often results in a wife's increased involvement in estate planning and other financial matters previously assigned to the husband.

Thus, gendered role assignments in the home do soften slightly after retirement, but substantial changes in the completion of household tasks do not occur unless and until spouses are physically disabled.

RISK FACTORS OF MARRIAGE

To this point, we have reviewed general findings about the late years of marriage, and on average, the picture is quite positive. However, not all long-term marriages are happy. This is especially true in current cohorts of older married couples. Because divorce was far less acceptable in older generations, many couples did stay together despite considerable dissatisfaction. What happens to unhappily married couples in old age?

Once again, the effects are gendered and disadvantages fall predominantly on wives. Unhappily married older women have more physical and mental health problems than happily married older women. However, among older husbands, the quality of the marriage is unrelated to physical and mental health status (Levenson, Carstensen, and Gottman 1993). Although clear answers to this question are unknown, one study of younger wives found that bad marriages were associated not only with loneliness and depression but immune systems were also affected to such an extent that resistance to infections was lowered as well (Kiecolt-Glaser et al. 1987). It may be that compromised immune systems related to enduring emotional dissatisfaction can have lasting physical effects (Davidson et al. 1999).

The general consensus among marriage researchers is that differential effects of bad marriages stem from differential meanings of marriage for women and men. Wives are the keepers of marriage, in some sense. Regardless of age, wives appear to feel responsible for the emotional quality of the marriage. When the emotional quality of a marriage is poor or when couples are simply not close, it influences how wives feel about themselves (Tower and Kasl 1996). When husbands grow disenchanted with a marriage, in contrast, it is less likely to be reflected in how they feel about themselves as individuals.

This gender difference may reflect more general differences in the ways in which men and women define themselves. In American society, women readily adopt a view of themselves as part of a social network (Cross and Madsen 1997). Asked to describe themselves they typically say that they are wives, mothers, and friends. Men, in contrast, describe themselves as workers or athletes or in dispositional terms such as efficient or strong. Interdependence in self-construals may make one more vulnerable to emotional distress. If a husband is depressed or a marriage discontented, a wife may incorporate these factors into her own sense of self. In contrast, men may be better able to separate themselves emotionally from an unhappy partner or unhappy marital union.

Even in close marriages, there is an emotional cost to caring deeply about another person. For example, depression in one spouse predicts depression in the other (Tower and Kasl 1996a), and this association increases as the level of intimacy increases (ibid. 1996b). This might be one factor of the co-occurrence of clinical depression in older couples (Eagles et al. 1987). Again, however, there is a gender difference. Men are less likely to become depressed if they have a depressed spouse than the reverse scenario (Hagnell and Kreitman 1974). In addition, when a husband reports marital distress, both he and his wife report more depressive symptoms and life stress; when the wife reports marital distress, only she reports more depression and life stress (Whiffen and Gotlib 1989).

ILLNESS AND CAREGIVING

In Ann Landers's December 13, 1995, column, she quoted an elderly couple, Rose and Bruce Bliven. In three poignant sentences, they had captured the essence of marriage in old age. They wrote, "When we are old, the young are kinder to us and we are kinder to each other. There is a sunset glow that radiates from our faces and is reflected on the faces of those about us. But still, it is sunset."

A near inevitability of long-term marriage is that one spouse falls ill before the other and comes to require assistance in basic activities of daily living. When the infirm spouse is the husband, the wife almost always assumes the caregiving role. And because of differences in life expectancy coupled with cultural tendencies for women to marry older men, wives are far more likely to nurse their husbands through serious illnesses at the end of life than the reverse. Thus much of the reason that women are more likely to be caregivers than men involves the statistical odds of which spouse will require care. Relatively older husbands with relatively shorter life expectancies are simply more likely to succumb to serious illness before their relatively younger wives with relatively longer life expectancies.

But odds, luck, or chance do not account for the entire story. Caregiving responsibilities fall along gender lines. The path of responsibility does not flow directly down bloodlines or generations and is not reciprocated evenly between husbands and wives. Wives nearly always care for husbands, but it is often daughters who care for elderly mothers. In families where there are only sons, daughters-in-law often provide care. And when daughters-in-law are not available, the burden is likely to fall on a granddaughter or a niece. Only rarely are caregiving responsibilities assumed by sons (Horowitz 1985). As during earlier stages of life, the vast majority of unpaid caregivers of the infirm elderly are women (England et al. 1991).

Not only is the likelihood of becoming a caregiver different for women and men, the experience of caregiving is different as well. Wives are more likely to be the sole providers of care. Husbands, in contrast, are more likely to share caregiving responsibilities with others. When a wife, as opposed to a husband, becomes ill, other family members are more likely to contribute to caregiving (Morris et al. 1991). Moreover, husbands are more likely to hire professional aides to assist with caregiving, and even friends and neighbors are more likely to help a husband care for a wife than vice versa (Zarit, Orr, and Zarit 1982).

Very likely this difference relates to the fact that caregiving is common among women. At all points in adulthood, women provide care. Most *older* women have considerable expertise in caring for other people. Over the years, they have cared for children, adult parents, and other relatives. In many cases, people rightly assume that women are less likely to need help providing care than men. Many wives actively refuse offers of help because they feel that their husbands would prefer to receive care directly from them. Thus, in some ways, it seems only natural that wives care for husbands when they become ill.

Natural or unnatural, a toll is clearly taken. Wives generally describe the caregiving experience as more stressful than do husbands (Barusch and Spaid 1989). Caregiving is related to a wide range of emotional distress including feelings of anger, hostility, and anxiety. Indeed, caregiving is the greatest known risk factor for clinical depression. Fully half of all caregivers become clinically depressed (Gallagher et al. 1989). In addition to threats to financial security and physical health that extended illness presents, caregiving responsibilities often place severe restrictions on engagement in other activities, ranging from work to social events. Otherwise pleasurable activities are forgone so that caregivers can care for their partners. Interestingly, activity restriction appears to mediate the association between caregiver burden and depressed affect even more than the direct physical demands of caregiving (Williamson, Shaffer, and Schulz 1998).

Not surprisingly, the quality of the marriage prior to the illness influences the caregiving experience (Williamson, Shaffer, and Schulz 1998). For example, the relationship between restriction of activities and psychological distress varies according to how caregivers describe their relationship when their spouse was healthy. People in reciprocally affectionate relationships stand to lose the affection and support they received from their spouse in addition to absorbing the new strains of caregiving. For those whose relationships were relatively independent of the other, the caregiving role is marked by fewer losses but also by greater resentment.

Even when a spouse is not the primary caretaker for his or her partner, the relationship can change drastically due to the illness of one partner. Arguably, the most significant assault to an otherwise happy marriage in the later years is dementia. Strokes, multi-infarct dementia, and Alzheimer's disease are several of the more common causes of cognitive impairment in later life. In such cases, caregiving involves yet another wicked twist. The infirm spouse—robbed of his or her memory—eventually does not recognize the caregiver as his or her spouse; in very advanced stages, dementias destroy the sense of self. In a series of interviews with spouses of institutionalized demented patients, Gladstone (1995) reported that almost half of the study participants described their marriages as distant memories. They spoke of their relationships in the past tense and, even in cases where spouses expressed considerable love for their partners, they described the "real" person as "gone."

Many caregivers, despite the perceptions that the marriage was over, however, emphasized the perceived responsibility of caring for their spouse. One person expressed a strong sense of duty to care for the "body" of the spouse lost. Still others described their marriages as illusions or as having drastically changed. Some wives described their spouses in childlike terms. For many people, the situation represents a permanent purgatory from which they cannot advance. One older man expressed great emotional turmoil because he was contemplating seeing another woman and "cheating" on his wife. This husband visited his wife every day in a nursing home even though she had ceased to recognize him almost a year earlier. Placing the spouse in an institution does not seem to lighten the caregiving stress as much as one might surmise. The level of emotional distress related to caregiving remains high among spouses after partners are placed in institutions (Stephens, Kinney, and Ogrocki 1991).

WIDOWHOOD: WHEN MARRIAGE ENDS

With the exception of those rare occasions when spouses die together, one spouse typically survives the other, and the survivor is usually the wife. In fact, most men live out their lives as part of a married couple. Most women do not. For women, the average length of widowhood is fifteen years. At the age of eighty-four years, 62 percent of men are still married, but only 20 percent of women are married. Thus, in some ways Western marital customs are well designed for husbands. At all stages of marriage, husbands report greater marital satisfaction than wives. Married men, but not married women, derive protective physical and mental health benefits from marriage. And at the end of life, when marriages appear to be more happy than ever before, women are more likely than men to spend their last years alone.

In widowhood, women face a cruel irony. Immediately following what is arguably the least gendered time in life for women and when heterosexual intimate relationships appear—by and large—to be close and deeply satisfying, older women face a time in life in which the cumulative effects of lifetimes of discrimination loom larger than ever before. In widowhood long-standing social and cultural practices come head-on with economic structures, perhaps more so than any other time in life.

Many women—even those who enjoyed reasonably high socioeconomic status earlier in their lives—live out the end of their lives alone and poor (Carstensen and Pasupathi 1993). And one of the principal contributors to the problems older women face is related to the process of becoming widowed. Importantly, the problem is not the psychological loss. The vast majority of widowed women adjust—psychologically—notably well (better than widowers, whose mortality risk increases). Rather, the problem involves the cultural and economic process of becoming widowed.

The disadvantages for married women come about for three reasons. First, because wives—throughout life—usually earn less than husbands, their own retirement income is less, and they are also the logical candidates for career compromises when the need presents itself. Second, because part-time work rarely involves retirement benefits, those compromises reduce the likelihood that women will accrue private pension benefits to supplement their already lower Social Security income.

Third, older women frequently retire from the workforce in order to care for ailing spouses, parents, or siblings. Consequently, women receive approximately 24 percent less than elderly men in Social Security benefits *and* have less private supplemental income. The Social Security system *penalizes* women for the very work patterns our society encourages because of the enormous benefits they yield for husbands and children. Health care costs and legal requirements for the spending down of assets before government assistance is provided for their sick and dying spouses are the last blows. Because women are typically the survivors of marriages, they are the ones to bear the brunt of these practices and often face the end of life poor and isolated.

In many ways, women and men grow similar in later life. Marriages appear to be happy and fulfilling. Yet due to the culmination of societal practices over a lifetime, in the end women and men face maximally different lives. And marriage is at the root of the disadvantages women face. Massive structural inequities experienced due to the culmination of societal practices over a lifetime come to the fore. Whatever a woman's marital status is in middle age, she will probably be single in old age and she will probably be less secure financially and socially than she was earlier in her life.

CONCLUSIONS

In our society, couples—typically freely chosen unions—assume tremendous importance. Symbolically, couples represent significant social "units." They lay the foundation for family building and serve as building blocks in friendship networks. Moreover, whether heterosexual or same sex, intimate relationships are invariably intertwined with gender, and invariably, they age.

Research on marriage suggests that those couples who survive together for forty, fifty, or sixty years are rewarded with richly satisfying relationships in later life. An often unnoted fact is that long-term marriages are historically new and may soon become a thing of the past. Until this century, the length of marriage was constrained by life expectancy. Contemporary older couples represent the first cohorts in human history where so many people have married and stayed together for life

(Belsky 1999). Current levels of divorce and the increasingly common practice of serial monogamy may mean that the numbers of long-term relationships will be smaller in future generations. Thus, older couples today represent an interesting phenomenon: unions of men and women that last a lifetime. They are testament to the need for relatedness and to the coupling about which this volume was written.

REFERENCES

Acitelli, L. K., and T. C. Antonucci. 1994. Gender differences in the link between marital support and satisfaction in older couples. *Journal of Personality and Social Psychology* 67:688–98.

Alexander, B. B., et al. 1992. A path not taken: A cultural analysis of regrets and childlessness in the lives of older women. *Gerontologist* 32:618–22.

Atchley, R. W. 1976. *The sociology of retirement.* Cambridge, Mass.: Schenkman.

———. 1977. *The social forces in later life.* 2d ed. Belmont, Calif.: Wadsworth.

Barusch, A. S., and W. M. Spaid. 1989. Gender differences in caregiving: Why do wives report greater burden? *Gerontologist* 29:667–75.

Belsky, J. K. 1999. *The psychology of aging: Theory, research and interventions.* 3d ed. Pacific Grove, Calif.: Brooks Cole.

Carstensen, L. L. 1993. Motivation for social contact across the life span: A theory of socioemotional selectivity. *Nebraska Symposium on Motivation* 40:209–54.

Carstensen, L. L., J. M. Gottman, and R. W. Levenson. 1995. Emotional behavior in long-term marriage. *Psychology and Aging* 10:140–49.

Carstensen, L. L., J. Graff, R. W. Levenson, and J. M. Gottman. 1996. Affect in intimate relationships: The developmental course of marriage. In *Handbook of emotion, adult development and aging,* edited by C. Magai and S. McFadden, 227–47. Orlando, Fla.: Academic Press.

Carstensen, L. L., D. M. Isaacowitz, and S. T. Charles. 1999. Taking time seriously: A theory of socioemotional selectivity. *American Psychologist* 54:165–81.

Carstensen, L. L., and M. Pasupathi. 1993. Women of a certain age. In *Critical issues facing women in the '90s,* edited by S. Matteo, 66–78. Boston: Northeastern University Press.

Condie, S. J. 1989. Older married couples. In *Aging and the family,* edited by S. J. Bahr and E. T. Peterson, 143–58. Lexington, Mass.: Lexington Books.

Costello, E. J. 1991. Married with children: Predictors of mental and physical health in middle-aged children. *Psychiatry* 54:292–305.

Cowan, C. P., and P. A. Cowan. 1988. Who does what when partners become parents: Implications for men, women, and marriage. *Marriage and Family Review* 12:105–31.

———. 1992. *When partners become parents: The big life change for couples.* New York: Basic Books.

Cramer, D. 1993. Living alone, marital status, gender and health. *Journal of Community and Applied Social Psychology* 3:1–15.

Cross S. E., and L. Madsen. 1997. Models of the self: Self-construals and gender. *Psychological Bulletin* 122:5–37.

Davidson, R. J., C. Coe, I. Dolski, and B. Donzella. 1999. Individual differences in prefrontal activation asymmetry predict natural killer cell activity at rest and in response to challenge. *Brain, Behavior, and Immunity* 13:93–108.

Eagles, J. M., et al. 1987. The mental health of elderly couples: II. Concordance for psychiatric morbidity in spouses. *British Journal of Psychiatry* 150:303–8.

Ekerdt, D. J., and B. H. Vinick. 1991. Marital complaints in husband-working and husband-retired couples. *Research on Aging* 13:364–82.

England, S. E., et al. 1991. Community care policies and gender justice. In *Critical perspectives on aging: The political and moral economy of growing old,* edited by M. Minkler and C. Estes, 227–44. Amityville, N.Y.: Baywood Publishing.

Field, D., and S. Weishaus. 1992. Marriage over half a century: A longitudinal study. In *Changing lives,* edited by M. Bloom, 269–73. Columbia: University of South Carolina Press.

Frazier, P., et al. 1996. Desire for marriage and life satisfaction among unmarried heterosexual adults. *Journal of Social and Personal Relationships* 13:225–39.

Gable, S., J. Belsky, and K. Crnic. 1992. Marriage, parenting and child development: Progress and prospects. *Journal of Family Psychology* 5:276–94.

Gallagher, D., et al. 1989. Prevalence of depression in family caregivers. *Gerontologist* 29:449–56.

Gilford, R., and V. Bengtson. 1979. Measuring marital satisfaction in three generations: Positive and negative dimensions. *Journal of Marriage and the Family* 39:387–98.

Gladstone, J. W. 1995. The marital perceptions of elderly persons living or having a spouse living in a long-term care institution in Canada. *Gerontologist* 35:52–60.

Hagnell, O., and N. Kreitman. 1974. Mental illness in married pairs in a total population. *British Journal of Psychiatry* 125:293–302.

Helsing, K. J., M. Szklo, and G. W. Comstock. 1981. Factors associated with mortality after widowhood. *American Journal of Public Health* 71:802–9.

Horowitz, A. 1985. Sons and daughters as caregivers to older parents: Differences in role performance and consequences. *Gerontologist* 25:612–17.

Huyck, M. H. 1995. Marriage and close relationship of the marital kind. In *Handbook of aging and the family,* edited by R. Blieszner and V. H. Bedford, 181–200. Westport, Conn.: Greenwood Press.

Kiecolt-Glaser, J. K., et al. 1987. Marital quality, marital disruption, and immune function. *Psychosomatic Medicine* 49:13–33.

Lauer, R. H., J. C. Lauer, and S. T. Kerr. 1990. The long-term marriage: Perceptions of stability and satisfaction. *International Journal of Aging and Human Development* 31:189–95.

Lee, G. S., and C. L. Shehan. 1989. Retirement and marital satisfaction. *Journal of Gerontology* 44:S226–30.

Levenson, R. W., L. L. Carstensen, and J. M. Gottman. 1993. Long-term marriage: Age, gender and satisfaction. *Psychology and Aging* 8:301–13.

Malatesta, V. 1989. On making love last a marriage: Reflections of 60 widows. *Clinical Gerontologist* 9:64–67.

Morris, R. G., et al. 1991. Gender differences in careers of dementia sufferers. *British Journal of Psychiatry* 158:69–74.

Newtson, R. L., and P. M. Keith. 1997. Single women in later life. In *Handbook on women and aging,* edited by J. M. Coyle, 385–99. Westport, Conn.: Greenwood Press.

Pineo, P. C. 1961. Disenchantment in the later years of marriage. *Marriage and Family Living* 23:3–11.

Renne, K. S. 1971. Health and marital experience in an urban population. *Journal of Marriage and the Family* 23:338–50.

Rollins, B. C. 1989. Marital quality at midlife. In *Midlife myths: Issues, findings and practical implications,* edited by S. Hunter and M. Sundel, 184–94. Newbury Park, Calif.: Sage Publications.

Ross, C. E., and J. Mirowsky. 1989. Explaining the social patterns of depression: Control and problem solving or support and talking. *Journal of Health and Social Behavior* 30:206–19.

Rossow, I. 1993. Suicide, alcohol, and divorce: Aspects of gender and family integration. *Addiction* 88:1659–65.

Stephens, M. P., J. M. Kinney, and P. K. Ogrocki. 1991. Stressors and well-being among caregivers to older adults with dementia: The in-home versus nursing home experience. *Gerontologist* 31:217–23.

Szinovacz, M., and P. Harpster. 1994. Couples' employment/retirement status and the division of household tasks. *Journal of Gerontology* 49:S125–36.

Taylor, S., and J. Brown. 1988. Illusion and well-being: A social psychological perspective on mental health. *Psychological Bulletin* 103:193–210.

Tower, R. B., and S. V. Kasl. 1996a. Depressive symptoms across older spouses: Longitudinal influences. *Psychology and Aging* 11:683–97.

———. 1996b. Gender, marital closeness, and depressive symptoms in elderly couples. *Journal of Gerontology: Psychological Sciences* 51:P115–19.

Verbrugge, L. 1979. Marital status and health. *Journal of Marriage and the Family* 41:267–85.

Vinick, B. H., and D. J. Ekerdt. 1991. Retirement: What happens to husband-wife relationships? *Journal of Geriatric Psychiatry* 24:23–40.

Whiffen, V. E., and I. H. Gotlib. 1989. Stress and coping in maritally distressed and nondistressed couples. *Journal of Social and Personal Relationships* 6:327–44.

Williamson, G. M., D. R. Shaffer, and R. Schulz. 1998. Activity restriction and prior relationship history as contributors to mental health outcomes among middle-aged and older spousal caregivers. *Health Psychology* 17:152–62.

Zarit, S. H., N. K. Orr, and J. M. Zarit. 1982. *The hidden victims of Alzheimer's disease: Families under stress.* New York: New York University Press.

Contributors

Jennifer L. Best is a graduate student in psychology at the University of Southern California.

Laura L. Carstensen, Ph.D., is professor of psychology and the Barbara D. Finberg Director of the Institute for Research on Women and Gender, Stanford University, 1997–2002.

Susan Turk Charles, Ph.D., is assistant professor of psychology at the University of California, Irvine.

Cynthia Fuchs Epstein, Ph.D., is distinguished professor of sociology, Graduate Center, City University of New York.

Mary Felstiner, Ph.D., is professor of history, San Francisco State University.

Edith B. Gelles, Ph.D., is senior scholar, Institute for Research on Women and Gender, Stanford University.

Ellen Lewin, Ph.D., is professor of women's studies and anthropology, University of Iowa.

Nel Noddings, Ph.D., is Lee Jacks Professor of Education Emerita, Stanford University.

Monisha Pasupathi, Ph.D., is assistant professor of psychology, University of Utah.

Diane E. Przymus teaches at the University of Minnesota.

Deborah L. Rhode, J.D., is Ernest W. McFarland Professor of Law, Stanford University Law School.

Esther D. Rothblum, Ph.D., is professor of psychology, University of Vermont.

Arlene Skolnick, Ph.D., is visiting professor of sociology, New York University.

Myra H. Strober, Ph.D., is professor of education, Stanford University.

Jeanne L. Tsai, Ph.D., is assistant professor of psychology, Stanford University.

Kate Washington, Ph.D., is an independent scholar and writer.

Marilyn Yalom, Ph.D., is senior scholar, Institute for Research on Women and
    Gender, Stanford University.

Index

Text: 10/13 Sabon
Display: Sabon
Indexer: Pat Deminna
Compositor: Binghamton Valley Composition, LLC
Printer/Binder: Thomson-Shore, Inc.